Empathetic Education:
An Ecological Perspective on Educational Knowledge

Ronald S. Laura and Matthew C. Cotton

FALMER PRESS
Taylor & Francis Group

UK	Falmer Press, 1 Gunpowder Square, London, EC4A 3DE
USA	Falmer Press, Taylor & Francis Inc., 325 Chestnut Street, 8th Floor, Philadelphia, PA 19106

First published in 1999

A catalogue record for this book is available from the British Library

ISBN 0 7507 0764 X   cased
ISBN 0 7507 0763 1   paper

Library of Congress Cataloging-in-Publication Data are available on request

Jacket design by Caroline Archer

Typeset in 10/12pt Times by
Graphicraft Limited, Hong Kong

Printed in Great Britain by Biddles Ltd., Guildford and King's Lynn on paper which has a specified pH value on final paper manufacture of not less than 7.5 and is therefore 'acid free'.

Contents

Contents

Introduction: Challenging the Contemporary Paradigm of Educational Knowledge

In recent years a vast literature has accumulated to debate just what society should and should not be doing when it engages in the institutional processes of educating its citizens. With due respect to the ongoing debate it is not part of our purpose here to join in the fray of post-mortem polemics which have arisen out of it. To do so would be to let ourselves be seduced into a framework of thinking which it is our intention to reject. Our aim in this book is indeed to say something of importance about what education means, but by focusing less on the debate itself than on the presuppositions which have served to misdirect it. Our central contention is that the dominant concept of knowledge which is systematically propagated in our schools is enshrined in a framework of values left largely unarticulated by educational thinkers.

However one ultimately defines education, there is no doubt that our present system of education involves at least the transmission of knowledge. While much has been written about the concept of knowledge in the vague hope of ensuring that what is taught in schools corresponds to what is actually known (that what is taught is truth), far too little attention has been paid to the question of whether what we know is *really worth knowing and thus truly worth transmitting*. In what follows we shall argue that much of what we know is not worth knowing and thus that much of what we teach is not worth teaching.

To establish this highly provocative thesis we shall endeavour to show first that much of what is known and accordingly taught in our schools is a *particular form of knowledge* which has led directly to an environmental crisis of monumental terms. We shall argue that the form of knowledge propagated in our schools encourages a philosophy of nature inimical to both the ecological integrity of our environment on the one hand and the integrity of our social and personal relations on the other. Although the argument is possessed of several conceptual facets, the main component upon which these facets turn is the idea that the epistemology embraced by our schools presupposes that knowledge can be obtained only if the knowing subject (the investigator) detaches and distances himself or herself from the objects of the investigation. This imposed separation between the observer and the observed 'things of nature' must be made, so the presumption goes, if the goal of *objectivity* is ever to be realized. In a sense then, the very act of knowing separates us all from nature and the things we come to know in nature. In the name of *objectivity* we thus systematically educate students at every institutional level to sever their relationship with the things of nature they seek to understand. Inasmuch as the study of all things, both inanimate and animate, presupposes the separation of the observer from what is observed, we end up severing our relationship in important ways not only with plants and animals but with each other. And the more we distance ourselves form the things of nature and each other, the less moral responsibility we feel in manipulating and exploiting the whole realm of living things which make up our world. Detachment in the service of objectivity is an epistemic value which diminishes the value of what is known. We shall in this book be concerned to show that the presupposition of detachment as a mode of methodological enquiry for educational epistemology has led and continues to lead to environmental intrusions which impact adversely on every living and non-living thing on this planet — and if the reports of earth-rubbish in space are to be believed, beyond this planet as well.

The second thread of the argument we shall weave into our conceptual knit of epistemic tapestry depends on making explicit what is only an implicit feature of educational epistemology, and it relates to the *value-ladenness* of the particular form of knowledge which dominates the curriculum of our schools. We shall in the chapters that follow be concerned to show that of the many possible forms of knowledge available to the human mind, the western world has selected a form of knowledge motivated and informed by the value which we, as a culture, *place on power and control*. The particular form of knowledge we have institutionalized, that is to say, is conceptually conditioned by our preoccupation to dominate and direct the living destiny of every living and non-living thing on this planet. This being so, the underlying rationale which motivates preferring one form of knowledge over another is the value we as a culture place on power and control. Our insatiable appetite for power drives us to a form of knowledge which covertly stipulates that the only knowledge worth having is that which allows us to re-order the world of nature in a way that suits our own ends and presumed interests. It will be argued in this book that the educational and social ramifications of the commitment of western culture to a form of knowledge driven by its obsession with power are staggering.

If the knowledge we transmit in our schools is structured and shaped by our obsession with power, both its form and application will reflect that obsession. If what we claim to know is covertly defined by the capacity of what is known to provide us with a power advantage over the things of nature, then the orthodox educational view that knowledge is neither good nor bad in itself can be exposed for the illusion it is. Far from being neutral, every piece of information which is accepted as knowledge is designed covertly to provide some control advantage over the world in which we live. In the light of the power presumption as a primary motivating factor in determining what we accept as knowledge, there is already a built-in or conceptually endogenous bias in favour of an epistemology of control and subjugation. This being so, the idea that what makes knowledge 'good' or 'bad' depends simply on how one uses it, betrays a conceptual distortion of a far subtler truth. Because we have as educators failed to recognize the extent to which the human drive for power and dominance has covertly delimited the forms of knowledge incorporated in the school curriculum, we have failed also to recognize that we have let our schools become the state-sanctioned vehicles for the cultural transportation of an ideology of power and control. Having institutionalized knowledge as a process of power, we have let education slip almost imperceptibly into a veritable industry for the development of technologies of increasing levels of power and progressive subjugation of the so-called 'forces of nature.'

Having organized our educational institutions in such a way that the development of such power-based technology stands as the ineluctable consequence of our unbridled commitment to an epistemology of power, western culture has lured generations of schoolchildren into the false belief that scientific knowledge and the technologies deriving from it are the ultimate tools of social and even personal salvation. The more we trust in the prelates of scientific knowledge, the more resources, both human and otherwise, we commit to the development of ever more powerful and controlling forms of technology. What we failed to see is that our progressive technological intrusions of control over nature serve not only to manipulate and transform the things of nature but to disrupt the established harmony of the natural order, including its capacity to reproduce itself and the contexts of social organization within which we have a genuine chance of living purposefully and well.

When all is said, the fundamental problem for education has little to do with developing more effective strategies for the transmission of knowledge. Nor does it have much to do with teaching children more effective strategies for the discovery of knowledge, if the knowledge we have taught them to discover is enshrined in a cultural mind-set of power, exploitation and control. In teaching them these things we bequeath them the power of giants, but their inheritance is the power of blinded giants without vision, blinded to the indiscretions of technologies they have themselves unwittingly programmed to destroy themselves and everything else around them. In the end our fanatical commitment to the educational technologization of our world results, we intend to argue, in the depersonalization of human activity, the dehumanization of human relations, and the desanctification of nature. What is needed is not more of the kind of power-based educational epistemologies we already have. What is needed is ultimately a reconceptualization of the very concept of knowledge which has become so entrenched and dear to our educational institutions that we think it is impossible to survive without it, when the truth is that we cannot survive with it. If there is a task of critical urgency confronting educators, it is to redefine our relationship to nature and to each other by redefining the fundamental concept of educational knowledge in a way which dignifies rather than diminishes our humanity by doing so. We need urgently to re-think also our willingness to re-order the world of nature through our technological transformations of it. When we are led in our search for knowledge to new and better ways of connecting with and participating in nature, we will be led also to technologies designed to preserve and reproduce the things of nature rather than transform them into artefacts whose value depends on their potential as commodities to be bought and sold. Appreciation of this very different paradigm of learning will help to build the educational framework within which we and our children can be educated in a form of knowledge that generates empathy and understanding rather than power and control. This is a book which professes a vision of a radically different educational epistemology — a vision of educational liberation capable of helping our children and ourselves to understand that education is about making people whole through finding new ways to live better in nature and with each other.

Chapter 1

The Price We Pay for Technology

The burden of this chapter is to draw together into a coherent perspective the challenge to education represented by the sundry facets of social and environmental degradation which characterize the modern age. Despite the remarkable technological achievements of our time, it is palpably clear that we are, on a global scale, in a state of overwhelming crisis. The world community now witnesses the destruction of approximately 100 acres of tropical rain forest every minute, the extinction of some 20,000 species of flora and fauna each year, the annual loss of billions of tons of agricultural top soil, and the accumulation of ever increasing quantities of toxic chemicals in the air we breathe, the water we drink and the foods we eat (Gordon and Suzuki, 1990, pp. 2–3). Along with the dessimation of the environment comes the disintegration of the very social fabric upon which society depends for its harmonious weave. Wars, violent crimes, unemployment, mind and soul-destroying drugs, depression, isolation, alienation and an exponential rise in the rate of suicide are just a few of the destructive tendencies which pervade the contemporary way of life. While it would be hopelessly naive to presume that this panoply of social ills has a single cause, we argue in what follows that the horrendous problems of our times betray a pattern of conceptual articulation which reflects those problems as the resultant application of a form of knowledge which has outlived its usefulness. Our central contention is that a society committed to the technological transformation of the natural environment into increasingly artificial environments is a society unwittingly contributing to its own dissolution. To establish this claim we shall in this chapter consider a litany of examples which illustrate that we are a culture on the brink of extinction. We have robbed, raped and ravaged the earth to braking point, without ever fully recognizing that we are ourselves a dispensable component in the earth system we are destroying. The environmental and social crisis we now face is monumental. It is thus futile to parade our optimism and arrogant supremacy over nature as if these attitudes might count as remedies for what is irremediable without reconceptualization. Let us now consider the magnitude of the crisis with an aim to making this argument clear.

The Impact of Vested Interests and the Lust for Power

That the world in which we live is a world whose environmental integrity has been and is continuing to be badly disrupted is a view now widely accepted. In respect of our mindless manipulations of the 'gene pool' and our destruction of the once wide varieties of flora and fauna, not to mention our ever increasing degradation of soils, water and air, there is good reason to believe that we have wounded the body of nature beyond repair.

Despite an abundance of convincing ecological data confirming that we are in a state of crisis, there is a strong temptation to turn a blind eye to the imminent danger of nature's demise. Gordon and Suzuki provide a sobering scenario to help those who might be lured to the nostalgia of happier ecological times to confront the frailty of ecological balance in no uncertain terms. Comparing the current ecological crisis to a biological phenomenon known as 'the boiled frog syndrome', they write:

> ... Put a frog in a pot of water and increase the temperature of the water gradually from 20 C to 30 C to 40 C ... to 90 C and the frog just sits there. But suddenly, at 100 C, something happens: the water boils and the frog dies ... [W]e have figuratively, and in some ways literally, been heating up the world around us without recognizing the danger ... We do not feel the acidity of the rain, see the ultraviolet radiation projected through the ozone hole, taste the toxins in our food and water, or feel the heat of global warming except, as the frog does, as gradual and therefore endurable. (Gordon and Suzuki, 1990, pp. 39–40)

Like Gordon and Suzuki's frog, we unwittingly live within an environmental time bomb, but unlike the frog, it is we who have created and continue to create the conditions which paradoxically threaten to destroy us.

Our obsession with power and control of nature encourages us to develop technologies capable of expropriating the resources of nature at ever increasing rates. To maintain our so called 'high standard' western lifestyle, one in which everyone has at their 'disposal an extraordinary array of consumer products and ingenious technological devices' (Goldsmith, 1977, p. 332) we feel compelled to assess society's success by its economic growth — the rate at which we consume the resources of nature. Thus industries and individuals consume exponential quantities of energy every day. Included in this bizarre consumption frenzy are: petroleum for motor vehicles and agricultural machinery; 'mono-crops' grown with petro-chemical fertilizers; energy for industrial maintenance and production; and energy — in the form of electricity — for domestic lighting, cooling, heating etc. Among the consequences of this unbridled energy transformation are the toxic by-products that continually threaten our fragile environment and become more conspicuous daily. The rationale — if one could call it that — behind increased growth, primarily for the extraction and transformation of increasingly limited stocks of energy, is self stultifying. It is this commitment to unlimited growth which encapsulates western society's preoccupation with unlimited growth, especially in regard to the 'throw away' ethic of western consumerist society.

In regard to the throw away society it is clear that one way of establishing the process of self-perpetuating economic turnover is best ensured by making things which are characterized by their built in obsolescence. From an economic perspective, the more quickly a commodity becomes jaded, outdated, or worn out, the better it is. Throw away items, which now include almost every conceivable thing, such as razors, gloves, hats, plates, utensils, serviettes, cameras, etc. encourage us to consume the resources of the earth at a monumental rate. We also produce waste at an equally monumental rate, thereby destroying the earth both by our obscene levels of expropriation and mindless contamination. Although it is clear that we are quite capable of maintaining a satisfactory standard of living by relying on a well-considered range of products which are designed to last, we are captive to the myth that low economic growth and, hence, low consumption, are tantamount to social disaster. As Boulding puts it:

> There is a kind of existential terror associated with the concept of 'limits to growth' for the Western person in the late twentieth century. The reason for the terror is evident enough. The type of growth associated with . . . economic productivity has somehow come to be synonymous with growth in personhood and growth in the body social. This produces the equation in people's minds: limits to growth equals death. (Boulding, 1977, p. 297)

As early as the 1970s some social theorists, such as Schumacher, had already expressed consternation at the realization that modern western economies had become obsessed with the economic goal of unlimited growth. The notion of a good society (its value) was even then being defined daily in terms of GNP and consequent levels of material consumption i.e., high consumption is good; low growth low consumption is bad. A society with a healthy GNP is a healthy society. Coupled with the growth of 'super technology' the whole process of growth preoccupation alienates people from each other as they become more isolated and competitive; just as it alienates them from their work by depriving them of any meaning their work might have beyond what they earn for the conformist objects of their production which are immediately taken away from them and sold in the market place. Schumacher, to his credit, was well aware that unlimited technological and economic expansion in a finite world is an impossibility. Ironically, the life expectancy of a materialist society he opines 'is the shorter the more successfully it pursues its expansionist objectives' (Schumacher, 1975, p. 143; see also Capra, 1988, p. 223).

Enshrined in the economic metaphysics of the industrialized world is the covert assumption that the planet contains an inexhaustible supply of energy which it is our right to exploit whatever the price. Any conceivable anxiety about the upper limits to 'material growth' is suppressed because the reservoir of nature's resources is to a large extent itself perceived as unlimited. By parity of reasoning, the gravity of the pollution problem has never been adequately appreciated, since it is covertly assumed that nature has an unlimited absorptive capacity (Meadows, 1977, pp. xvii–xxvii). Although governments have begun to acquiesce in the face of environmental concerns that our disruption to the established equilibrium of nature must be respected, there has been little sign that in the long run environmental issues will be given precedence over the economic ones. There is rather a persistent mind-set that there either is or will soon exist the technological ingenuity to deal with any problem that besets us. On this view it is only a matter of time before we find the technological solution to our environmental problems. We must continue, therefore, to grow and consume at the present rate, or at more rapid rates.

A Deeper Dimension of the Crisis

The multifarious ways in which technology disrupts the environment have been noted by many contemporary critics (see for example, previous references; particularly, Gordon and Suzuki, 1990). What we shall call the 'conventional critique' of technological obsessiveness depends primarily on the assumption first, that nature is an infinite sink which can continually swallow up our toxic by-products of industry and other contaminants, and second, that what is out of sight is out of mind. The idea is that as long as we cannot see our rubbish, rubbish is not a problem, so we become more concerned to ensure that our rubbish is out of sight than to ensure that we dispose less of it and that what we dispose is disposed of safely.

The Paradox of Progress

Appreciation of the foregoing philosophical considerations puts us in a better position to determine the extent to which western society's unbridled commitment to the technologization of nature is doomed to failure. We shall now turn our attention to what has elsewhere been called, 'The Paradox of Progress.' (See Ashton and Laura, 1998, pp. 1–40.)

By way of elaborating this paradox of progress we argue that much of what has passed for progress in our society is illusory. Motivated by an obsession with unlimited economic growth, the science of technology has been corrupted and shaped into a tool for the rape of the earth. Having confused the difference between an improved standard of living and an improved quality of life, we have unwittingly sacrificed the latter for the former. While the health and environmental risks associated with technological progress are slowly becoming recognized, the belief remains that new and improved technology will provide the way to resolve the massive ecological problems which technology has in the first place created.

Our aim in what follows here is to show by reference to a number of concrete examples that the driving force behind technology is the lust for control over the environment. By hoping to satisfy our insatiable appetite for dominance of the world in which we live, we have separated ourselves from nature and thus made it easier to exploit and degrade it without conscience. We have failed to see that the idea of rectifying the disastrous side-effects of scientific technology by developing more sophisticated forms of it is rather like trying to put out a fire by pouring kerosene on it. The problem is that preoccupied by the desire for dominance, technological intervention will continue to be fundamentally alienating and destructive. The paradox of progress is that our best efforts to make ourselves infinitely strong have in the end made us infinitely weak. Let us now see why.

Lust for Power: From Steam Engine to Nuclear Bomb

Before the development of the steam engine, all living things depended upon nature for their daily allocation of available energy. The rate at which solar energy was converted via plants into fuel energy for humankind and beasts of burden was determined predominantly by nature. Simple machines such as the water wheel, windmill and sail, eventually enabled our ancestors to harness the energy stored in water and wind, but again, it was nature which largely determined when, and how much of these resources were at any one time available. Innovation has always been the mother of invention however, and it was not long before our predecessors found new ways to loot and store the hidden treasures of nature for their own convenience.

The introduction of the mechanical steam engine in 1769 by James Watt, afforded the means by which solar energy from ages past, stored as coal, could be used to provide seemingly limitless power at the beck and call of anyone in the possession of the required technology. Man, not nature, would now determine how the resources of nature were to be used, and a new dimension to the goal of unlimited economic growth was uncovered. The power of the steam engine ensured that a single machine could do the work of virtually a hundred people. Created to exercise the power over nature we would ourselves have wished to exercise directly, the machine was created in the image of man on the one hand and in the image of a god on the other. In respect of the production of labour, the birth of the engine was in essence the birth of 'superman'. Bedazzled by our ingenuity, we were quickly deluded into thinking that the power we sought was finally in our hands; that we, rather than the machines we had created, were the true 'supermen' — but we were wrong. The technology of power is a power itself. In our desperate efforts to avoid being controlled by nature, the human species was being progressively controlled by machines. To get machines to do what we wanted them to do, we began to reorganize society in ways that made it more suited to what our machines could do rather than to people.

Factories were built to house these energy machines so that they could join systematically to transform the crude resources of nature into material goods at an unprecedented rate. The speed at which machines could do this in turn required that the resources of nature be harvested in increasing quantities, and then concentrated to provide the raw material needs of these energy-based industries. New machines would have to be invented to perform these tasks, and the tasks of humans would increasingly become focused upon interaction with machines, rather than with nature. Machines which could run all day and night, required people to work them all day and all night. Because of our devotion to the machine, we would come to have less and less contact with nature. To gain the power over nature desired, we unwittingly enslaved ourselves to the machines of our own creation. The needs and goals of technology had covertly influenced the very structure of society, along with our relationship to nature, and this influence would continue to grow.

The size of cotton and wheat fields, for example, soon came to reflect the capacity of the steam mill to process what was harvested. The more machines to fuel and the bigger their fuel needs, the deeper and more extensive the coal mine became. Similarly, forests were sacrificed to meet the capacity requirements of the steam-powered sawmill, and new technologies were required to cut the forests as fast as mills could process what was cut.

The concentration of energy in a particular location required a concentrating of resources, employment and housing in that location, and resulted in the growth of industrial cities and slums. Geographical concentration required transportation systems which could move increasing volumes of material from their place of origin to and from factories. Again the steam engine was harnessed and railways opened up vast tracts of land whose resources were soon transformed into more grist for the industrial mill.

Our obsession with controlling energy continued unabated. During the nineteenth century the efforts of S. Carnot, A.B. de Rochas, N.A. Otto, R. Diesel and others, enabled petroleum to be harnessed as a fuel, using the internal combustion engine which now dominates our sea, land and air transport systems. The power of the steam engine was thus supplanted by the power of the internal combustion engine. Society and nature would be similarly reorganized to meet its needs and capacity for devouring and transforming the earth's resources.

The nineteenth century also saw Michael Faraday discover the laws of magnetism and electricity, and in 1879 Thomas Edison successfully developed the electric light bulb. The development of electric power reached a transmission point when on 16 May 1888 Nikola Tesla read his famous lecture 'A new system of alternate current motors and transformer' before the American Institute of Electrical Engineers (Tesla, 1956, p. LI). His discovery of the use of a rotating magnetic field as a means of generating alternating current electricity made possible the practical, economic production and transmission of electrical power and is the basis of practically all the commercial power systems used in the world today.

Within half a century of Tesla's discovery, the energy initially provided by the steam engine became available in almost every factory and home of the developed world in the form of electrical energy along power lines. The availability of concentrated energy in our homes reinforced the assumption that technology had bequeathed a new inheritance of vast control over nature. With only the flick of a switch the darkness of night could instantly be transformed, almost magically, into the light of day. By simply pressing a button the cold of winter could be subdued and transformed into the warmth typical of a fine summer day. Or conversely, as the seasons would have it, the heat of summer could just as easily be displaced by cooling breezes from our air-conditioners. With the advent of electricity, a whole range of energy-consuming gadgets proliferated, from electric razors and hair dryers to electric can openers and heated water-beds.

Just five decades after Tesla's historic lecture, Leo Szilard filed a patent with the British Admiralty: 'a description of the release of energy in a chain reaction'. The culmination of the lust for power gave birth to the nuclear age (Berstein, 1985, pp. 37–42). Eight years later, on 2 December 1942 in the United States, the first sustained atomic reaction was unleashed. The goal of unlimited energy supplies to effect the total control of nature now seemed palpably within the reach of mankind, and scientific knowledge was elevated to a new position of eminence among human values. President Dwight Eisenhower, speaking on the Atomic Energy Commission's tests of hydrogen bombs in 1956, stated: 'The continuance of the present rate of H-bomb testing, by the most "sober and and responsible scientific judgement" . . . does not imperil the health of humanity' (Graham, 1970, p. 205).

Today, nuclear power stations provide energy in many developed countries, though the promise of a safe and healthy energy source has never been realized, Chernobyl and even the Three Mile Island disasters make plain.

Chemical Control of Nature: To Dope or Not to Dope

The industrial growth of the nineteenth century was spurred on, not only by the utilization of steam power, but also by the growth of chemical knowledge.

In 1774, Antoine Lavoisier demonstrated the difference between physical and chemical change and articulated the notion of a chemical reaction. Following this work, John Dalton put forward the theory that elements of matter are made up of small separate particles called atoms, and that all atoms of any one element are the same but differ from the atoms of all other elements. He suggested that chemical compounds are formed by the combination of atoms of different elements in simple ratios.

This atomic theory gave fresh impetus to the known chemistry of that time and the following one-and-a-half centuries saw thousands of researchers discover, analyse and synthesize millions of chemical reactions and compounds. One important example of chemical research was the work of Justus von Liebig. In 1835, Liebig discovered that ethylene dichloride ('oil of the Dutch chemists'), combined with alcoholic potash, produced a chlorine-containing gas, subsequently named vinyl chloride. This compound later became the basis of the now extensively used plastic, polyvinyl chloride or PVC.

In 1840, Liebig published his classical monograph on agricultural chemistry titled 'Chemistry in its applications to agriculture and physiology'. Liebig had found that phosphates mixed into the soil would promote the growth of plants. He also found that the ashes of plants gave useful information as to the requirements of crops and that a watery extract of humus gave little or no residue on evaporation. From this work the importance of nitrogen (N), phosphorus (P) and potash (K) in the soil was perceived, and the modern NPK mentality of chemical agriculture was born (Howard, 1943, pp. 181–2).

By the mid-twentieth century, the science of chemistry had enabled metals like aluminium and uranium to be won from the earth and utilized. From oil, via chemical processes, a vast array of plastics has been developed which could be moulded into an endless variety of 'things', or extruded into synthetic yarns. It was chemical technology that enabled forests to be converted to paper and cardboard. Pesticides, herbicides and fungicides have been produced in the vain and futile hope of changing the balance of nature to fight insects and check plant disease. Chemical knowledge has now become so specialized that drugs, chemicals and materials can be designed and synthesized to meet specific applications in medicine, industry, agriculture and the home.

Our technological power over nature has increased to such an extent that the best landscapes of nature can be cleared bare within hours, dug up and removed or diverted within days. To meet the insatiable demands of technological growth we have disrupted and decimated the very ecosystems upon which all economic growth ultimately depends. We have displaced nature with our cities, airports, freeways, farms and mines, and poisoned the air, streams, rivers and oceans either deliberately with pesticides or unthinkingly with our wastes.

In our technological efforts to gain ultimate control of nature we have transformed our society and ourselves along with nature. We have unwittingly become the servants of the technology we have created, and we have fashioned a throwaway society to sustain the goal of unlimited growth. Ultimate control and domination of nature is represented economically by our willingness not only to 'use nature up' but throw it away. The commercial viability of a product on this model is not that it lasts, but that 'it is disposable'. If you can convince people that the products of technology can with impunity be thrown away, then you have already convinced them that the products of technology can with impunity be bought again. The power comes in feeling that technology can produce all you need to buy, and dispose of all the garbage you need to eliminate. The truth is that it can do neither of these things. Nature is neither an infinite well nor an infinite drain. Let us see why.

Air Pollution: The Energy–Health Connection

By the end of the eighteenth century, the proliferation of steam power and associated industrial development, particularly in Great Britain, was such that it had already begun noticeably to reduce the quality of human health. As Rene Dubos observed:

> England had known first and on the largest scale the prosperity but also the terrific destruction of human values that accompanied the first phase of the Industrial Revolution. Laymen as well as physicians could not fail to recognise that disease and physical frailty were most common among the poor classes. In *Conditions of the Working Man in England* Engels spoke of the 'pale, lank, narrow-chested, hollowed-eyed ghosts riddled with scrofula and rickets, which haunted the streets of Manchester and other manufacturing towns. If ever men lived under conditions completely removed from the state of nature dreamed of by the philosophers of the Enlightenment, it was the English proletariat of the 1830s. (Dubos, 1959, p. 147)

These changes in public health had become so noticeable that in 1819 the British parliament appointed a Select Committee to enquire:

> how far it may be practicable to compel persons using steam engines and furnaces in their different works to erect them in a manner less prejudicial to public health and public comfort. (Bellini, 1987, p. 8)

Despite an active anti-smoke campaign from the 1840s to the 1890s, the obsession with steam power and industrial development prevailed, and the Industrial

Revolution gripped Europe and America in a cloud of pollution. The burning of coal not only put smoke into the air but also released gases such as carbon dioxide, water vapour and sulfur dioxide. In London, in particular, industrial emissions of smoke and gases were so high that harmful smogs became intolerable and extremely dangerous under certain weather conditions.

In December 1873, a week-long London smog is believed to have claimed at least 500 lives through respiratory failure alone. Scarcely six years later a three-week-long smog claimed about 2000 lives. Despite pronouncements that the problem was under control, the death rate from respiratory failure caused by polluted air continued to climb. As recently as December 1952, a smog engulfed London which, according to a subsequent Royal Commission, claimed about 4000 lives (Bellini, 1987, pp. 11–12).

The growth in air pollution produced a parallel increase in the incidence of rickets, particularly in children of the industrial cities. It turns out that smog absorbs the natural ultraviolet solar radiation which is essential for human vitamin D synthesis and calcium metabolism (Giese, 1976, p. 20). The advent of coal-fired steam electric power generation, while gradually replacing individual steam plants, enabled concentrated power in the form of electricity to be readily accessible to the community. The more readily available electricity became, the greater the electricity usage which in turn resulted in a steady increase in carbon dioxide and sulfur dioxide gas emissions. In 1860, about 2 million tonnes of sulfur dioxide were released into the atmosphere from the burning of coal and the smelting of ores. 125 years later, global sulfur dioxide emissions from burning coal and oil for energy and copper smelting had reached 90 million tonnes (Goudie, 1986, p. 253).

Within a few days of being in the atmosphere, sulfur dioxide gas is converted to sulfuric acid which is ultimately precipitated as acid rain. This rain has acidified extensive regions of North America and Europe, causing fish populations in freshwater lakes to dwindle, and toxic metals to be leached from the soil. Around the work, efforts have been made to reduce the effects of acid rain by liming lakes. However, it is now realized that liming does untold damage to freshwater biosystems and is not the simple panacea it was once thought to be (Woodin and Skiba, 1990, pp. 30–4). This is just one of many examples which demonstrate that further technological intervention is not the way to solve the problems created by technological intervention.

Instead, placing limits on the release of pollutants into our environment is becoming increasingly recognized as the only way we can save our environment. For example, many countries in Europe and North America have now signed a treaty to curb emissions of gases which cause acid rain as part of a Convention on Longrange Transboundary Air Pollution. It is planned that over the next 13 years up to 2010, acid rain-producing pollution from factories and power stations in Europe and North America should drop by up to 87 per cent from 1980 levels.

However, in 1996 Jan Thompson, chairman of the Convention's executive body, pointed out that the contribution of shipping to world-wide sulfur emissions could more than double by the year 2010 as ships burn cheap dirty oils with a high sulfur content. Shipping is already responsible for 7 per cent of global sulfur emissions (Bond, 1996, p. 4). While the average sulfur content of ship's fuel is about 2.8 per cent, marine fuel oil may contain in excess of 5 per cent sulfur. In this case each tonne of oil burnt, in combination with atmospheric moisture produces an equivalent of more than one tonne of 5-normal sulfuric acid (the concentration of acid commonly used in laboratories). Friends of the Earth International claims that the sulfur content of ships' fuel should be limited to 1 per cent or less, if environmentally sensitive areas are to be protected from acid rain (Bond, ibid.).

Air pollution from modern power stations is usually reduced by devices called electrostatic precipitators which can remove up to around 99.97 per cent of the particulate matter called fly ash. However these may not always be maintained to peak efficiency and can breakdown releasing large quantities of pollutants into the air.

One such incident occurred in October 1996 when two of the fire precipitator units at the 324 megawatt Indra Prastha power station in the heart of the city of Delhi in India broke down. The power station's chimneys were spewing an estimated 1500 tonnes of fly ash into the atmosphere of the city every day (Patel, 1996b, p. 8). A recent World Bank study shows that the air pollution level in 36 Indian cities is responsible for 40,000 deaths and 20 million hospital admission each year (Patel, ibid.). In addition to the contribution to Delhi's air pollution from power stations, about 70 per cent of the smog comes from vehicles powered by internal combustion engines.

The development of the internal combustion engine as a source of concentrated power for transport added an extra dimension to air pollution. For the past eight decades, vehicles on land, sea and in the air, have pumped ever-increasing quantities of combustion gases into the atmosphere. These gases include water vapour, carbon dioxide, carbon monoxide, unburnt hydrocarbons and oxides of nitrogen. In the presence of sunlight, some of these gases, namely hydrocarbons and nitric oxide are photo-oxidized in the air to form ozone, peracylnitrates (PANs), nitric acid and aerosol. This resulting mixture of chemicals in known as photochemical smog (Heicklen, 1987, p. 145).

This form of air pollution is now believed to be one of the main environmental factors causing dieback throughout the forests of Europe which has now reached epidemic proportions (Heicklen, 1987, p. 145). In 1989, West Germany reported that 53 per cent of its forests showed signs of dieback damage (The Conservation Foundation, 1987; see also Bellini, 1987, op. cit., pp. 64–65).

As we have seen, trees are not the only life form affected by smog. In 1994, French researchers reported that a higher percentage of people die from heart and lung diseases on smoggy days. Increases of 100 micrograms per cubic metre in the black smoke (from diesel engines) content of city air can lead to a 6 per cent increase in hospital admission for heart attack and a 30 per cent increase in asthma attacks. An equivalent increase in nitric oxide levels was found to lead to a 63 per cent rise in asthma attacks. A 100 micrograms per cubic metre increase in sulfur dioxide levels was linked to a 10 per cent rise in heart attacks. When a similar increase in the level of ozone in city air occurred, the admissions of elderly people with chronic breathing problems rose by 20 per cent and lower respiratory tract infections in children rose by 24 per cent (Patel, 1994b, p. 8). The French Public Health Society have estimated that between 1987 and 1990 as many as 350 people in Paris died prematurely each year from heart problems triggered by air pollution (Patel, 1994a, p. 7).

The Internal Combustion Engine and Ozone

Ozone is needed in the upper atmosphere to protect the earth's environment from harmful ultraviolet radiation, but in the air layer it is a poison to both plants and animals. Ozone is formed in the lower atmosphere when unburnt hydrocarbons from vehicle and industrial emissions react with nitrogen oxides (also produced by cars and power stations) in the presence of sunlight. While it has been known that ozone impairs breathing and irritates the eyes, nose and throat, recent studies throw new light on its toxicity. Human subjects exposed to ozone levels below the United States Environmental Protection Agency (EPA) recommended maximum exposure level of 120 parts per billion were found to have increased levels of chemicals in the lungs, which produce inflammation. Macrophages in the lungs were found to be less capable of consuming and destroying bacteria than normal. Furthermore, the ozone exposure increased the levels of the hormone-like substance prostaglandin E2 in the lung, producing a suppression of the immune response in this organ (Read, 1989, p. 14; see also Folinsbee, 1992, pp. 45–56). In the meantime, other studies have shown that ozone is a pulmonary carcinogen even at relatively low levels (Mustafa and Hassett, 1988, pp. 714–21; see also Edwards, 1995a, p. 4). Findings of the Office of Technology Assessment reported in 1989, show that more than half the population of the United States are now exposed to levels of ozone higher than the concentrations recommended by the EPA (see *New Scientist*, 22 July 1989, p. 5; see also Vaughan, 1990, pp. 42–5). In 1995 a study for the United States Department of Health's National Toxicology Program found that mice exposed to 2000 micrograms per cubic metre of ozone developed lung tumor at twice the rate of unexposed mice, and some scientists are now recommending that ozone be reclassified as a suspected carcinogen (Edwards, 1995a, p. 4).

A poisonous gas produced directly by internal combustion engines is carbon monoxide. This gas interferes with the blood's capacity to carry and circulate oxygen. Studies in Washington DC in 1983, showed that almost 20 per cent of city commuters who travelled 6–10 hours per week were exposed to levels of carbon monoxide exceeding the National Air Quality Standard (The Conservation Foundation, 1987, p. 7). In the 1920s, Thomas Midgley, a chemist working for General Motors, discovered that tetraethyl lead could raise the octane rating of fuel and prevent engine 'knock'. Lead has been added to petrol since that time. However, in the 1940s, more efficient high compression petrol engines were developed. This necessitated the addition of higher levels of 'anti-knock' agent to the fuel to prevent preignition. For over three decades, increasing quantities of lead were dispersed as fine dust into the air around the world. Analysis of a Greenland glacier at dated levels showed an exponential increase in lead concentration after 1950 (Lippmann and Schlesinger, 1979, p. 187). In 1980, approximately 1000 tonnes of poisonous lead dust from vehicle exhausts were deposited annually over cities such as Sydney,

Australia, (see *Choice*, 1980, p. 267) with about 250,000 tonnes of lead dust being released into the air of the cities of North America each year (Motluk, 1996, p. 6).

This anthropogenic or human-made atmospheric lead has now found its way into water, food and human lungs. Lead causes injury to bone marrow where red blood cells are produced, to the kidneys and to the nervous system including the brain. Intelligence quotient (IQ) deficits in children have been associated with blood lead levels as low as 100–150 micrograms per litre, (Bellinger, Leviton and Waternaux, 1987, pp. 1037–43) and there appears to be no evidence of a threshold for the effect (Davis, 1990, pp. 285–92). Hearing is also adversely affected by increased lead exposure, again with no evidence for a threshold (Schwartz and Otto, 1987, pp. 153–60). Elevated levels of blood leads are also associated with human developmental abnormalities including foetal neurologic damage, reduced birth weight, reduced stature and slower attainment of developmental milestones (Goyer, 1993, pp. 177–87). Several epidemiological investigations have noted an association between elevated blood lead levels and pressure (ibid.).

In 1996, the National Institute of Environmental Health Sciences, near Washington DC, released details of a study which suggests that women who once lived in an environment polluted with lead may pass on the poison to their unborn offspring. It appears that lead stored in a women's bones may be released into the bloodstream during pregnancy (Day, 1996, p. 4). Children are particularly susceptible to lead poisoning (Joyce, 1990, p. 4; see also Ember, 1980, pp. 28–34) and Jerome Nriagu at the University of Michigan points out that when childhood lead poisoning was widespread in the United States in the early 1980s, unleaded fuel was introduced 'not to protect public health, but to protect catalytic converters' (Motluk, 1996). Between the late 1970s and the end of the 1980s, the average blood lead levels in American children aged between 1 and 5 years declined by 77 per cent. However, even with stringent limits on industrial and vehicle emissions, 20,000 tonnes of lead are still exhausted into the air over North America annually (*ibid.*).

In 1996, an estimated 70,000 tonnes of lead was being added to petrol world-wide, with Russia, Nigeria, South Africa and Saudi Arabia among the leading users (Pearce, 1996a, pp. 12–13). Lead is now banned from petrol in the United States, Japan, Canada, Austria, Sweden, Brazil, Colombia and South Korea. In Australia and most European Union countries roughly half the cars run on unleaded petrol. However in more than 50 countries 20 in Africa, petrol containing 0.8 grams of lead per litre (more than five times the European Union limit) is still sold. Children in many of the cities of these countries will continue to suffer permanent mental retardation given that most research studies show an average IQ deficit of two to four points for every 100–150 micrograms per litre increase in blood leads (ibid.).

In Sydney, Australia, where leaded petrol is still sold alongside unleaded, children living within 10 kilometres of the Central Business District between 1992 and 1994 still had an average blood lead level of 81 micrograms per litre with 7 per cent of children having blood lead levels above 150 micrograms per litre (Donovan, 1996, p. 390). In 1996 in the United States, 15 years after unleaded petrol was introduced, the mean blood level in children had dropped to 29 micrograms per litre

(Pirkle, Brody and Gunter, 1994, pp. 284–91). Another side to the petrol saga is now emerging as leaded petrol is being phased out. Unleaded petrol can contain up to 2 per cent of the chemical benzene which is both carcinogenic and neurotoxic (Paustenbach, Bass and Price, 1993, pp. 177–200; see also Raabe, 1993, pp. 35–8). The change to unleaded fuels is clearly helping to reduce the lead problem, however, it should also be mandatory that refineries fractionate out benzene and use non-aromatic additives to raise octane levels such as methyl tertiary butyl ether (MTBE).

A new side to the combustion engine saga has emerged since the early 1990s. Fine particulates less than 10 micrometres (um) across are emitted by exhausts of cars, trucks and buses. In 1991, Joel Schwartz at the United States government's Environment Protection Agency (EPA) studied the concentration of these particles (referred to as PM10 levels) in the air of cities, and death rates, and found there was a strong correlation. After further data was collected, Schwartz estimated in 1994, that each year 60,000 people die in the United States and 10,000 people die in England and Wales as a result of these vehicle emissions. The American studies suggest that there are no safe levels of PM10 and that when the concentration in the air of a city increases by 10 micrograms per cubic meter, the death rate rises by 1 per cent (Brown, 1994, pp. 12–13). In the United States, the safety level for PM10 has been set at 150 micrograms per cubic metre, but in 1995 the United Kingdom government's Expert Panel on Air Quality Standards recommended a maximum standard of 50 micrograms per cubic metre averaged over 24 hours (Hamer, 1996, p. 12). In London between 1992 and 1994, this limit was exceeded on 139 days. In December 1991, London experienced a particularly bad episode of air pollution and the levels of PM10, the most worrying of the cocktail of pollutants emitted by road traffic, were estimated to be as high as 800–1000 micrograms per cubic metre (Brown, 1994).

Diesel engines emit up to 80 per cent more particulate matter than petrol engines. Some of these particles, produced by incomplete burning of fuel in diesel engines, are less than 2.5 micrometres across and can penetrate deep into the lungs. These particulates can also carry carcinogens such as benzopyrene, naphthalene and phenanthrene absorbed on the surface, and the International Agency for Research on Cancer is now warning that the exhaust from diesel engines probably causes cancer (Patel, 1995b, p. 10).

Not surprisingly, a 1996 Danish study found that diesel bus drivers in Copenhagen had a 60 per cent higher incidence of lung cancer than average. Copenhagen bus drivers operating in the city centre were also found to have significantly more chromosomal aberrations and more DNA damage than bus drivers in the suburbs. Approximately 60 per cent of the vehicles in Copenhagen are powered by diesel engines (Edwards, 1996a, p. 8).

The enormous problems of air pollution in the cities around the world and the serious health consequences are becoming increasingly apparent. Reducing the number of vehicles in our cities and the distance that they travel is a fundamental requirement of saving our environment and reducing the toll of human disease. The trend of increased commuting by car which took place in the 1980s must be reversed by imposing limits on our use of internal combustion engine powered vehicles in city and urban areas (Hamer, 1996, p. 5).

The greatest pollution produced by our power stations and vehicles is the emission of carbon dioxide into the atmosphere. It is interesting to note that this by-product of fossil fuel combustion was once considered innocuous. In 1860, about 100 million tonnes of carbon dioxide were released into the atmosphere from fossil fuel combustion. Since that time our use of fossil fuels to produce power has increased rapidly. In the 1990s, only 130 or so years later, the quantity of carbon dioxide being discharged into the atmosphere from vehicle and power generation has reached a rate of around 20 billion tonnes per year (Gribbin and Gribbin, 1996, pp. 1–4).

The Greenhouse Effect

Much of the carbon dioxide accumulated in the atmosphere, eventually alters its heat insulation properties and produces what is now commonly known as the greenhouse effect. As the concentration of carbon dioxide and other greenhouse-type gases in the atmosphere increase, less heat from the sun is radiated back into space, with the result that the Earth's temperature slowly rises. Since the early 1900s, there have been alarming increases in temperature.

In 1994, the atmospheric concentration of carbon dioxide (CO_2) was calculated to have reached 358 parts per million (ppm) (corresponding to around 760 billion tonnes of carbon dioxide), compared with carbon dioxide concentrations of around 280 ppm (equivalent to approximately 590 billion tonnes of carbon dioxide) before industrial activity (Jackson, Guest and Woodward, 1996, pp. 597–8). This change has increased the total solar energy absorbed by the Earth by 1 per cent (Pearce, 1995c, pp. 4–5).

Recognition of the greenhouse effect by bodies such as the World Meteorological Organization and the United Nations Environment Programme has led to the formation of the Intergovernmental Panel on Climate Change (IPCC). The IPPCs research led to the Climate Change Convention which was signed by a number of nations at the earth summit in Rio in 1992 and ratified in 1993. The Convention's aim is to stabilize greenhouse gases — which are now known to include chloroflurocarbons (CFCs), methane and nitrous oxide — in the atmosphere at 1990 levels by the year 2000 (Gribbin and Gribbin, 1996).

One of the direct effects of this temperature rise has been the expansion of the oceans and the melting of polar ice. Since the beginning of this century, sea levels have risen by about 15 centimetres (ibid.). Over the next century, the Intergovernmental Panel on Climate Change (IPCC) estimates that sea levels could rise by a further 31–110 centimetres (Pearce, 1995a, pp. 14–15). Rises of this magnitude could have drastic consequences around the world, especially in areas such as the Pacific Islands, the Netherlands and Bangladesh. There is also evidence that atmospheric warming has contributed to the relatively large 2.5 degrees Celsius increase in the average temperature of the Antarctic region over the past 50 years (Mackenzie,

1995c, p. 4). Recent satellite data has also shown that the rate of melting of Arctic Sea ice has increased from 2.5–4.3 per cent per decade (ibid.).

Global warming is likely to have both direct and indirect effects on human health. The First International Conference on Human Health and Global Climate Change was held in Washington DC in September 1995. Dr Anthony McMichael from the London School of Hygiene and Tropical Medicine told the Conference that severe heat waves could increase mortality rates similar to the 500 or so deaths seen during a heat wave in Chicago earlier that year (Hileman, 1995, pp. 19–20). He also pointed out that because the rate of development of parasites accelerates as temperature rises, diseases such as dengue fever are likely to invade the United States. The range of malaria, which now affects 45 per cent of the world's population, is likely to increase its potential range to affect 60 per cent of the population by the middle of the next century (ibid.).

Dr Paul R. Epstein, a Professor of Tropical Medicine at Harvard University, reported to the Conference that many climate models indicate global warming also makes the cyclical warming of the tropical Pacific Ocean and associated weather disturbances around the world (known as El Niño phenomenon) both more intense and more frequent. Definite connections between cholera and malaria outbreaks have been established and this could mean serious consequences for human health if El Niño becomes an almost constant feature of global warming (ibid.).

Insect attack on crops may also be increased by global warming. For example, the peach potato aphid, *Myzus persicae*, is a major agricultural pest in the United Kingdom, attacking potatoes, oilseed rape and sugar beet as well as spreading plant viruses. Aphid clones have now emerged which are resistant to major pesticides, though interestingly, these clones suffered far greater losses than non-resistant aphids during winter. It appears that the biggest factor in the aphid's demise was the amount of time they spent below 2 degrees Celsius. As global temperatures rise, the number of frosty nights per year will decrease which, in turn, reduces this natural insect control (Aldhous, 1995, p. 17).

While the greenhouse effect has been recognized by many governments, political promises and actions can, however, be quite different, especially under the continual pressure to increase economic growth. For example, between 1990 and 1994 carbon emissions from fossil fuels rose 5 per cent in North America, and in 1995 the United States government's Climate Action Plan was not on track to meet the year 2000 goal (Burton, 1995, p. 5). In July 1996, F. Pearce reported that stonewalling by the United States, Australian and other governments could sink negotiations aimed at halting global warming (Pearce, 1996b, p. 9). Australia and New Zealand have been the only Organization for Economic Cooperation and Development (OECD) countries not to support calls for legally binding targets and timetables to reduce greenhouse gas emissions at the United Nations Convention on Climate Change (Jackson, Guest and Woodward, 1996). The greenhouse effect is a clear example of where we must limit our use of technology in the name of conserving human health and the environment of our planet. John Burton has suggested that a steep carbon tax would effectively lower carbon dioxide emissions (Burton, 1995). Such a measure would also be a step towards counting the true economic cost of our modern lifestyles. Such actions may not be 'too soon'. In November 1996, a new climate model proposed by J. Sarmiento and C. Le Quere of Princeton University, suggests that global warming may be happening much faster than climate researchers had feared. They found that over the next 350 years the amount of carbon dioxide absorbed by the oceans could be 28–49 per cent less than assumed in current models, because rising temperatures could reduce the ocean's ability to absorb the gas. As a result of this 'positive feedback' effect, global warming would increase much faster than the IPCC predictions (Sarmiento *et al.*, 1996, p. 1346).

The bold assumption that we can continue to dump our technological waste into the atmosphere and the oceans without adverse environmental changes needs urgently to be challenged.

The Nuclear Energy Problem

Since the 1950s a steadily increasing proportion of the world's electricity demand has been met by nuclear power stations. In 1986, the year of the Chernobyl Nuclear Power Station disaster, the United States had 98 operable nuclear reactors generating about 16 per cent of total electricity production, with another 32 plants in some stage of planning or construction (The Conservation Foundation, 1987, pp. 247–8). Worldwide in 1985, some 528 nuclear power generating plants were either in existence or under construction (Bellini, 1987, p. 61).

Originally proposed as a 'clean' and safe form of power generation, the major health risks associated with nuclear energy can no longer be denied or covered up. Over the four decades of nuclear power up to 1986, there have been numerous incidents where radioactive material has been released into the environment (ibid., pp. 59–97). On 26 April 1986, the world's most disastrous nuclear accident occurred at Chernobyl in the Ukraine. An experiment in using residual kinetic energy to generate emergency power at the Chernobyl Nuclear Power Station went tragically wrong. The resulting explosion and fire released a cloud of radioactive material which was carried by prevailing winds to contaminate much of northern Europe.

The blasts destroyed one of the four reactors in the power station and extensively damaged the building that housed it. Pieces of hot, radioactive debris rained down on the roofs of neighbouring buildings and fires broke out. The graphite core of the reactor became a raging inferno and spewed radioactive gas and particles into the atmosphere for 10 days. During the aftermath, 31 people, most of them firefighters, died of acute radiation sickness (Mullins, 1996, pp. 41–3).

The World Health Organization (WHO) estimates that Chernobyl released 200 times as much radioactivity as the uranium-based bomb dropped over Hiroshima on 6 August 1945 and the plutonium bomb dropped over Nagasaki on 9 August 1945, put together (Edwards, 1995c, pp. 14–15).

Air, food and milk around Chernobyl were heavily contaminated with isotopes of iodine for weeks after the accident, and countries as far away as Greece were heavily contaminated by radioactive fallout. Years after the incident, the frightening extent of the harm to human health caused by the accident is still be revealed.

At an International Seminar on Humanitarian Medicine and Human Rights held in April 1990, for example, researchers reported that up to 250,000 people may be living in areas still too polluted from radioactive fallout for normal life and are therefore in need of urgent evacuation. In Byelorussi, which received 70 per cent of the radiation fallout, common illnesses have suddenly become 70 per cent prevalent amongst the population. Research efforts to explain the radical increase in common illnesses have come to the conclusion that the immune systems of the inhabitants were badly weakened by radiation exposure. It is estimated that one-fifth of the children in this region have received ratiation exposure of 10 gray (Gy; or 1000 rad) or more since the accident. This level of exposure is 10 times the figure associated with radiation illness and about 100,000 times the level from normal background radiation. In one region, Palessie, 50–70 per cent of the children now have health problems, with about 8 per cent having thyroid complications in forms that had not been observed before the Chernobyl accident. In another region, Minsk, the incidence of tuberculosis has risen by 14 per cent (Rich, 1990, p. 7; see also Borman, 1995, pp. 53–63). Nor is the problem confined to political boundaries. In West Germany, investigations have revealed that the number of infants dying within seven days of birth in the south of that country was significantly higher in the months following the disaster (Luning and Scheer, 1989, pp. 1081–3).

More health problems are emerging. At a WHO conference on Chernobyl held in Geneva in November 1995, the world's leading experts on thyroid cancer reached a consensus that the epidemic of thyroid cancer among children in the three states closest to Chernobyl (Belarus, Ukraine and Russia) has been caused by radiation from Chernobyl. At Gomel in southern Belarus, more than 200 kilometres north of the Chernobyl reactor, rain is believed to have deposited heavy iodine contamination. Here the number of children who have contracted the disease every year has increased from less than one per million before 1986 to more than 200 per million in 1994. At the time of the conference, 680 thyroid cancers had been diagnosed in children, 10 of whom had died (Edwards, 1995c). Six months later in April 1996, the number of confirmed thyroid cancer cases in children had reached 800 (Patel, 1996a, p. 7).

D. Williams, Professor of Histopathology at the University of Cambridge, believes that as many as 40 per cent of the children exposed to the highest levels of radiation fallout from Chernobyl when they were infants, could develop thyroid cancer as adults (Edwards, 1995b). Given these stark warnings, the French health ministry announced in April 1996 on the eve of the tenth anniversary of the Chernobyl disaster, that it planned as a preventative measure, to distribute iodine tablets to thousands of homes within a five kilometre radius of the country's 19 nuclear reactor sites. However such a plan has limited merit, as fallout from Chernobyl reached homes more than 2000 kilometres away (Patel, 1996a). There are also cancers other than thyroid cancer which are associated with exposure to radioactive fallout, such as breast cancer, all of which have been reported to have risen in the regions around Chernobyl since the explosion (Edwards, 1995c). The first evidence that radioactivity from the Chernobyl accident may have caused leukemia in young children as far away as Greece, has been reported recently by Professor

D. Trichopoulos of the Harvard Centre for Cancer Prevention in Boston. Babies exposed to radiation in the womb after the 1986 explosion were on average 2.6 times more likely to develop leukemia than children who were not exposed to radiation from the accident (Trichopoulos, 1996). Children exposed to radiation in the womb may also suffer brain damage. Preliminary findings from a WHO-sponsored study comparing 2189 children born in contaminated areas of Belarus, Ukraine and Russia, with 2021 children from nearby uncontaminated areas were released in November 1995. The findings suggest that children from the contaminated areas were suffering more mental retardation, more emotional disorders and more behavioural disorders, with approximately 50 per cent of children having experienced some kind of mental disorder (Edwards, 1995c). These findings reinforce the results of a study of 1100 Hiroshima children who were exposed to radiation in the womb and also suffered a higher than average rate of mental retardation (ibid.). The joint United States–Japanese Radiation Effects Research Foundation in Hiroshima has also found evidence which links radiation exposure to strokes, heart disease and cirrhosis of the liver (ibid.).

Joint British–Russian–Belarussian research has recently found evidence that exposure to radiation may damage sperm and ova and cause permanent genetic damage. The researchers found that children whose parents were exposed to radioactive fallout in Belarus after the Chernobyl disaster have twice as many mutations in their DNA as British children (Dubrova, Nesterov and Krouchinsky, 1996, pp. 683–6).

The environment has also been extensively contaminated by the Chernobyl nuclear accident. Pine forests in Belarus contain high levels of radioactivity which could take centuries to decay naturally to acceptable levels. Plans are now underway to burn the pine trees in specially designed power stations. It is hoped that 99.9 per cent of the radionuclides will be trapped in the ash and that in this way the contaminated forests may be removed within 40 years (Edwards, 1996b, p. 9).

Radioactivity from the Chernobyl area is contaminating large areas of Europe as a result of rain runoff and floods. Radioactive waste dumped around the reactor after it exploded over a decade ago has been washed down the Pripyat River to Europe's third-longest river the Dnieper, which flows 800 kilometres to the Black Sea. More than 30 million people are now considered at risk. Reservoirs downstream from the damaged reactor provide drinking water for 9 million people in Ukraine, as well as irrigation and fish for another 23 million people. There is also concern that radioactivity from these dumps could reach into groundwater and further contaminate waterways in 10–15 years time (Edwards, 1996d, p. 4).

One report has estimated that the Chernobyl explosion deposited 3890 terabecquerels (TBq) of strontium and plutonium on the flood plain around the reactor. Given that a terabecquerel represents 1012 radioactive disintegrations each second, an enormous amount of radioactivity was deposited into the environment. In Lake Kojanovskoe, 250 kilometres away, the level of radioactivity is 60 times higher than the European Union (EU) safety limit, and perch and pike from the lake contained radioactivity as high as 40,000 becquerels per kilogram of caesium-137 in 1994. (The EU safety limit is 500 becquerels per kilogram (ibid.).)

Workers in nuclear power stations and their children are also exposed to increased risks of cancer, even when these stations are functioning properly. In 1995, the maximum radiation dose generally considered safe for workers was still 50 millisieverts (mSv) in any one year (Patel, 1995a, p. 10). However, research by M. Gardner and co-workers, has revealed that where British workers received doses of radiation as low as 10 mSv in the six months prior to conception, their children faced a six- to eight-fold increase in the risk of developing leukemia (Beral, 1990, pp. 411–12).

Much of the technology used in nuclear power generation has been derived from nuclear weapons research and testing. This too has taken its toll on human health. The Chukot Peninsula in the former USSR is located in the vicinity where atmospheric tests were carried out in the 1950s and 1960s. It is not accidental that the population of this peninsula has the highest death rate from oesophageal cancer in the world. An investigation in 1989 by a commission of Soviet deputies and scientists found that more than 90 per cent of the population had chronic lung disease. In one village visited by the investigating team, every adult suffered from cancer and members of the commission calculated the life expectancy in the region to be around 45 years. The infant mortality was estimated to be 70–100 per 1000 live births, which was four times the official government figure (*New Scientist*, 2 Sept, 1989, p. 5). Workers at nuclear weapons sites in the United States have received similar radiation exposures. In Nevada, of 218 workers present at early bomb tests, 200 have since died of cancer (*New Scientist*, 6 Jan, 1990, p. 8). As early as the mid-1960s the hidden costs of progress in nuclear technology was being revealed. Less than eight years after President Eisenhower's assurance of the safety of atomic testing, President Lyndon B. Johnson, speaking of the new Nuclear Test Ban Treaty on 12 October 1964, announced:

> This treaty has halted the steady, menacing increase of radioactive fall-out. The deadly products of atomic explosions were poisoning our soil and our food and the milk our children drank and the air we all breath. Radioactive deposits were being formed in increasing quantity in the teeth and bones of young Americans. Radioactive poisons were beginning to threaten the safety of people throughout the world. They were a growing menace to the health of every unborn child. (Graham, 1970, p. 205)

Poisoned Air, Water and Soil: A Legacy of Chemical Progress

Emissions into the air from our industries of chemical technology over the past 150 years have now reached frightening proportions. M. Lippmann and R. Schlesinger list over 50 major air contaminants produced by industry during the extraction of raw materials and the manufacture of modern commodities (Lippmann and Schlesinger, 1979, p. 205). Industrial hygienists are now concerned over the increasing levels of more than 1000 hazardous compounds which are released daily into the air of the workplace and nearby environment (Board, 1996, pp. 1–4). A hundred years ago, the poisoned vegetation around copper smelters and related industries aroused little cause for concern. In recent times, environmental tragedies have forcefully borne witness to the price paid in terms of human health from the production of the chemical wares of progress. One such incident occurred at Bhopal in India. Around midnight on 2 December 1984, poisonous methyl isocyanate leaked from a nearby giant chemical plant and engulfed the town. Over 32,000 people died and an estimated 250,000 people suffered detrimental health effects (Keynes, 1996, pp. 265–6).

Much of our modern technology is dependent on the production of chemicals which now return a massive financial income to the global economy. In 1994, total chemical sales by the world's top 50 chemical companies exceeded US$330 billion dollars (Layman, 1995, pp. 23–4). However, the cost to the environment of this massive profit is also high. For example, in the United States, manufacturing industries generated 27 million tonnes of waste. Only about 12 million tonnes of this waste was recycled, treated or burned for energy recovery on site (Hanson, 1995, pp. 4–5). The majority are highly volatile and toxic. In 1993, United States industries released nearly 1.3 million tonnes of these chemicals into air, land or water.

While we have come to accept chemical pollution as an inevitable consequence of cities, we may also tend to reassure ourselves that there are still many parts of the world which are largely unaffected by toxic wastes. One such example might be New Zealand, which has relatively few smokestack industries. The apparently pristine forests and lakes give the country its reputation as a part of the world still relatively untouched by the ravages of industrial pollution and attracts tourists from all over the world. However in 1993, the New Zealand Ministry for the Environment released two reports which showed that more than 10,000 sites, including New Zealand's tourist jewel, Lake Rotorua, are contaminated with a legacy of toxic wastes from agriculture, forestry and industry (ibid.).

Lake Rotorua was found to contain levels of the highly toxic organochlorine chemical dioxin, which were 50 per cent higher than the levels in the lower Rhine in Europe, and twice as high as the levels in the heavily polluted Lake Ontario. Sewage, industrial waste and polluted water were found being discharged into Wellington Harbour, and pentachlorophenol, other organochlorines and industrial effluent were being washed into Manuka Harbour near Auckland. At the southernmost part of the beautiful South Island there were accumulations of hazardous waste and air pollution from an aluminium smelter. One of the main toxic chemicals found to be contaminating more that 420 timber-producing sites was the organochlorine chemical pentachlorophenol which is used extensively as a wood preservative.

Chlorine Compounds

Chlorine is widely used in industry to make paper, to treat water and in the manufacture of organochlorine chemicals. These have been used as solvents and as raw materials in a wide variety of industrial process and products, including the manufacture of plastics. Examples include chloroform, carbon tetrachloride,

dichloromethane, chloroflurocarbons, polychlorinated byphenols, pentachlorophenol and vinyl chloride, just to name a few. In times past, chloroform was used as
an anaesthetic while carbon tetrachloride was extensively used in fire extinguishers.
What is little realized is that large quantities of these compounds, many of which
are now suspected or known carcinogens, are evaporated into the atmosphere.
Dichloromethane, also known as methylene chloride, is a case in point.

Methylene chloride is widely used in industrial processes, food preparation
and agriculture. It is used as a solvent in paint removers, degreasing agents and
aerosol propellants; as a blowing agent in flexible urethane foams; and as a process
solvent in the manufacture of steroids, antibiotics, vitamins and tablet coatings.
Methylene chloride is used as an extraction solvent for spice oleoresins, hops, and
caffeine from coffee. Historically, it has been used as an inhalation anaesthetic and
as a fumigant for grain and strawberries. In 1980, the world production of this
chemical was reported as 517,000 tonnes and it has been estimated that 80 per cent
of this production was released into the atmosphere (Mennear and McConnell, 1988,
p. 343). At levels as low as 500 parts per million, this commonly used solvent has
been found to produce mammary gland tumours in rats (ibid., p. 348) while higher
exposure levels produced various cancers in mice (ibid., pp. 349–50).

The organochlorine compounds of industry are produced from the raw material chlorine which, in turn, is manufactured by the electrolysis of sea salt. An estimated 41 million tonnes of chlorine are produced worldwide each year, with North
American producing 12 million tonnes, western Europe producing 9 million tonnes
and Australia 140,000 tonnes each year. Australia also imports 80,000 tonnes of
chlorine in the form of vinyl chloride monomer each year, for the manufacture of
PVC plastics. Approximately 60 per cent of the chemical manufacturing industry in
Australia is dependent on chlorine and chlorine products (Clews, 1996, pp. 45–6).

There is growing evidence that the use of chlorine by industry can harm
vertebrates, including humans. In February 1994, the United States–Canada Joint
International Commission on the Great Lakes published evidence which showed
that environmental exposure to chlorinated compounds harms humans. The Commission found that women living around the lakes who ate large amounts of lake
fish, had acquired high levels of dioxins and related chlorinated compounds. The
children of these women, had low birth weights and were less intelligent and less
healthy than the children of women who had not been exposed to such high levels
of chlorinated compounds (Mackenzie, 1994, p. 10). These findings support the call
by the Commission, two years earlier in 1992, for a ban on the use of chlorine
around the Great Lakes because of the high concentrations of chlorinated compounds in lake water (ibid.).

Chlorinated compounds containing two-ring structures, such as dioxins and
polychlorinated biphenyls, can bind to a receptor on the nucleus of vertebrate cells,
where they mimic or block oestrogen and other steroid hormones. These findings
together with those of the Commission have prompted proposals to ban or limit
chlorine (ibid.). The industry federation has responded by arguing that many
organochlorine compounds occur naturally in the environment (Euro Chlor, 1995).
GW Gribble from Dartmouth College in Hanover, New Hampshire, has also

published a detailed study of the production of chlorinated compounds in nature (Gribble, 1995, pp. 310A–19A). Gribble suggests, for example, that dioxins are produced naturally by forest fires and that other chlorinated compounds are formed by the enzymatic reactions between chloride ion and phenolic humic acids (Gribble, 1995, pp. 4–5). However, B. Commoner from the City University of New York, points out that Gribble's study actually supports the view that these compounds are dangerous because none of the natural organochlorine compounds occur in vertebrates. Many are intermediates in chemical reactions within cells, and are secreted specifically as toxins by moulds, plants, algae and marine invertebrates. Vertebrates cannot have natural polycyclic chlorinated compounds because they would interfere with the animal's use of steroid hormones (Mackenzie, 1994). T.G. Spiro and V.M. Thomas from Princeton University, point out that modern human liver tissue contains much higher levels of dioxins than that of 400-year-old frozen Eskimo bodies or 2800-year-old Chilean mummies. The former are known to have been high consumers of fish and animal fat which concentrate organochlorine compounds, and the latter are known to have been frequently exposed to wood smoke (a reported natural source of dioxins) from interior fires (Spiro and Thomas, 1995, p. 5).

Sediment cores from lakes also provide a historical record of dioxin deposition. For example, in Siskiwit Lake, dioxin levels were low before 1940, increased rapidly during the industrial expansion of the 1950s and 1960s, and declined since the 1970s in parallel with the decreased production of chlorinated phenols. Spiro and Thomas suggest that:

> It is hard to see how these trends can be reconciled with predominantly natural sources. (ibid.)

In May 1995, the United States Environmental Protection Agency (EPA) circulated a draft report which found that low doses of dioxin, similar to the background levels now found in most United States citizens, can cause cancer, infertility and interfere with foetal development (Kleiner, 1995, p. 10).

Chloroflurocarbons

The magnitude of the impact of anthropogenic chemicals is illustrated by the production of chloroflurocarbons (CFCs). These chemicals were originally developed by chemists to replace ammonia in refrigeration plants. CFCs subsequently found extensive use as propellants in aerosol cans, and as the bubbling agent in the manufacture of certain plastic foams used to make such items as furniture, and so-called 'disposable' polystyrene cups and food trays. Originally, these compounds were believed to be inert but, as E. Longstaff points out, CFCs are not biologically inert. Some CFC compounds have been shown to be bacterial mutagens, cell-transforming agents and rodent carcinogens (Longstaff, 1988, p. 297).

The emissions of CFCs into the atmosphere worldwide in recent decades have been enormous, with possibly one million tonnes being released annually during peak production in the mid-1980s. Like carbon dioxide, these gases are greenhouse gases, changing the heat insulating properties of the atmosphere. However, *one molecule of CFC produces the same greenhouse warming effect as 10,000 molecules of carbon dioxide* (Mackenzie, 1995b, pp. 14–15). We also know that CFCs may remain in the atmosphere for long periods of time. The most abundantly produced classes of these compounds, known as CFC-11 and CFC-12, are estimated to remain in the atmosphere for approximately 75 and 110 years respectively. CFC pollution is a long term phenomenon ensuring that we will be reminded of the folly of our throw-away cups for decades to come.

There is also another side to the CFC story. In 1974, F. Rowland and M. Molina propounded their well-known hypothesis of ozone depletion by CFCs (Rowland and Molina, 1975, p. 1). Further elucidation of the mechanisms of the destruction of the ozone layer by chlorine atoms released by CFCs in the upper atmosphere have since been presented (Plumb, 1989, pp. 3–13). It is well known that the ozone layer shelters all life on this planet from harmful ultraviolet solar radiation. Diminishing this protective mantle threatens the health balance of all living plants and animals exposed to sunlight (Kripke, 1989, pp. 15–20; see also Kelly, 1989, pp. 187–90). Indirect and synergistic consequences may also impact on biological and physical processes such as the role of the oceans as a carbon dioxide sink or the formation of cloud condensation nuclei.

Phytoplankton in the oceans, for example, fix more than half the carbon dioxide produced globally each year. However, these marine organisms are highly sensitive to increased levels of ultraviolet radiation because they lack the protective outer layers enjoyed by higher plant and animal species. If the populations of phytoplankton decreased as a result of increased levels of ultraviolet radiation, the decreased carbon dioxide uptake by the ocean would result in much higher levels of carbon dioxide remaining in the atmosphere. This, in turn, would accelerate the greenhouse effect and result in rises in sea levels (Wood, 1989, pp. 179–85).

Similarly, the increase in ultraviolet (UV) radiation and resulting reduction in phytoplankton populations may, in turn, significantly alter the balance of solar radiation reaching the earth. The synergistic effect involved here is complicated, but it can be simplified as follows. Phytoplankton have been identified as the source dimethyl sulfide (DMS) which they release into the atmosphere. The flux of DMS from the ocean to the atmosphere is climatically important because the particles of sulfur released become the nuclei or droplets upon which clouds form. By altering the phytoplankton population, we are thus inadvertently modifying the density of clouds. This is important because as marine clouds become thinner, they become less effective at regulating the amount of solar radiation which hits the earth. The more ultraviolet radiation which gets through to the ocean's surface, the greater the degree of destruction to the phytoplankton — thus reinforcing a negative feedback loop with disastrous consequences for the ecosystem.

It is worth noting also that marine cloud formations figure as an integral factor in the generation of ocean turbulence associated with sea storms. Turbulence is itself crucial to the survival of phytoplankton, inasmuch as storms churn up the ocean, drawing food for phytoplankton from the cooler lower layers of ocean to the warmer surface areas where phytoplankton feed. Thus, the decrease in cloud formation — which, in turn, leads to a reduction in sea storms and ocean turbulence — reduces the available food for phytoplankton and diminishes the phytoplankton population in consequence, further reinforcing the vicious cycle referred to above (ibid.). Appreciation of this point about the synergistic connections amount ecosystems makes it easier to see that the destruction of the ozone layer by CFCs is, in turn, disrupting one of the most important systems of climatic regulation on the Earth.

The growing scientific consensus of the dangers of CFCs and also halons (bromoflurocarbons) in the environment, led to an agreement between 49 countries, meeting in Vienna in 1985, to protect the ozone layer. In 1987, 24 nations signed an agreement to reduce the production and use of CFCs, which has become known as the Montreal Protocol on Substances that Deplete the Ozone Layer. As scientific understanding of the processes and chemicals that destroy the ozone layer has grown, the number of countries signing the Protocol had increased to 96 by 1996 (Duncan and Simpson, 1996, pp. 41–2). In the meantime, several amendments have been made. The so-called London Amendments were agreed to in 1990. These required more stringent controls on the production and use of other ozone-depleting chemicals, such as carbon tetrachloride and methyl chloroform. The 1992 Copenhagen Amendments were added following the National Aeronautics and Space Administration's (NASA) finding that ozone depletion was occurring at a faster rate than was previously estimated (Hinwood, 1996). These amendments included restrictions on the use of hydrochlorofluorocarbons (HCFCs) which are now being substituted for CFCs, hydrobromoflurocarbons, and the pesticide methyl bromide. The CFCs phase-out has been affected in most countries, however, world production of CFCs in 1995 was estimated to still be about 360,000 tonnes (Mackenzie, 1994). Meanwhile the ozone layer is now believed to be thinning twice as fast as originally predicted (Mackenzie, 1995a, p. 5) and satellite data have confirmed that manufactured chlorofluorocarbons are the predominant source of the chlorine that is eroding the Earth's protective ozone layer (Zurer, 1995, p. 9).

The Unhealthy Food Chain

In January 1940, Sir Albert Howard wrote in the preface of his seminal work *An Agricultural Testament:*

> Since the Industrial Revolution the processes of growth have been speeded up to produce the food and raw materials needed by the population and the factory. Nothing effective has been done to replace the loss of fertility involved in this vast increase in crop and animal production. The consequences have been disastrous. Agriculture has become unbalanced: the land is in revolt; diseases of all kinds are on the increase; in many parts of the world Nature is removing the worn out soil by means of erosion. (Howard, 1943, p. IX)

Howard goes on to argue in his book that the use of inorganic fertilizers together with excessive irrigation and over-cultivation is destroying the fertility of the soil, and that as a consequence there is increased disease in plants, animals and man.

The over-cultivation and over-irrigation of the soil gradually occurred as agricultural progress came to be defined in terms of increased yield per hectare. The development of machines to convert concentrated energy to mechanical power gave a whole new sense to the concept of efficiency. Efficiency, the watchword of the mechanical paradigm and the Industrial Revolution, was carried into the realm of agriculture. Machines were increasingly used to divert and pump water in vast quantities and to cultivate the soil on a scale never before possible.

Liebig's observations of the increased growth of plants which occurred when phosphates were mixed with the soil, let to a proliferation of patent chemicals whose specific purpose was to increase the soil crop yield per hectare. One such example was the use of sulfuric acid to increase the solubility of phosphates, patented by J.B. Lawes in 1842 (Riegel, 1937, p. 147). This form of phosphate later became known as superphosphate. Within a few years, increasing quantities of potassium salts, from deposits at Stassfurt in Germany, and nitrate salts, from Chile, were being transported to various parts of the world.

Given this worldwide dissemination of superphosphates the composition of soil was rapidly altered on a worldwide basis. Fertilizers containing a mixture of nitrogen, phosphorus and potassium compounds became known as 'complete' fertilizers (ibid., p. 149), reinforcing and entrenching in the minds of farmers the misleading NPK mentality discussed earlier.

As research on the chemical control of plants continued, agricultural scientists discovered that individual types of crops were found to respond to particular ratios of NPK fertilizer mixes. For example, the ratio for potatoes was 4:8:10, for wheat 2:12:6, clover 0:12:15 and strawberries 5:8:7. These differing fertilizer requirements, together with the development of particular cultivation configurations of farm machinery for different crops, led to the practice of cultivating ever-larger areas of land for a single type of crop. Monoculturing was thus incorporated as part of the all-pervasive western perspective devoted to growth and efficiency. F. Graham comments:

> By the end of World War II, farming had evolved from a way of life to an industry. The farmer acquired the approach and the philosophy of the manufacturer. The small family farm, which once had produced a variety of fruits, vegetables, and dairy foods, now merged with a dozen of its fellows to form a single vast 'factory farm' producing a single crop. In the interests of economy, every move was directed, every machine was adapted, to plant, nourish, and harvest that crop — whether it was celery, apples, corn, or soy beans. A new word — monoculture — found a place in the dictionary. (Graham, 1970, p. 223)

Biodiversity is a life-supporting characteristic of nature (Will, 1996, pp. 38–42). Since the introduction of modern farming the genetic diversity of our agricultural plants has been rapidly vanishing. This century, the United States has lost more than 90 per cent of its 20,000 varieties of agricultural plants. Since 1930, 80 per cent of the varieties of maize in Mexico have been lost and China now only grows 1000 strains of wheat, compared with 10,000 or so strains it grew before 1949. This decline in agricultural biodiversity is leaving our crops prone to pest and plague (Edwards, 1996c, p. 14).

Monoculture is a distortion of nature which, in a sense, produces a 'plague' of plants. What was missed in the equation was that this extreme ecology inevitably results in a plague of insects. Given the commitment to technology as the panacea of all ills, chemical controls or pesticides were quickly enlisted in the battle against the armies of invading insects. It is revealing that the rapid growth of monoculture after World War II, which was paralleled by an inordinate expansion in farm machinery and fertilizer sales, was also accompanied by an expanding use of pesticides (see for example, *Alternative Agriculture*, 1989, pp. 40–8). What is even more apocalyptic is the evidence which establishes that concomitant with the growth of technological farming, the percentage of crops lost to pests and disease increased accordingly.

Giving evidence in 1951 before the Delaney Committee inquiry into pesticide use in the United States, R.L. Webster described how, in 1909, only single sprayings of arsenate were used each year. By 1926, pests had become so much more troublesome, that five or six additional sprayings were required during the season. He went on to say:

> Worm control in the Pacific North-west was becoming more difficult, year by year. We now know that the codling moth was acquiring a degree of resistance . . . More and more lead arsenate was used every year and at one time Washington State was using 25 per cent of the entire production in the United States. The peak came in 1943, when more than 17,000,000 pounds (lbs) were sold in the state. (Wickenden, 1961, p. 36)

Webster's observations contrast revealingly with those of Howard. Howard had reported that crops grown in humus-rich soils around 500,000 villages in India, suffered remarkably little from pests (Howard, 1943, p. 30). He also had argued that the replacement of animal manure and compost by artificial NPK fertilizers was directly linked to the increased susceptibility of plants to disease and insect attack.

With the spread of articificials and the exhaustion of the original supplies of humus, carried by every fertile soil, there has been a corresponding increase in the diseases of crops and of the animals which feed on them. If the spread of foot-and-mouth disease in Europe and its comparative insignificance among well-fed animals in the East are compared, or if the comparison is made between certain areas in Europe, the conclusion is inevitable that there must be an intimate connection between faulty methods of agriculture and animal disease. In crops like potatoes and fruit, the use of the poison spray has closely followed the reduction in the supplies of farmyard manure and the diminution of fertility (ibid., p. 19).

As nature revolted against the mechanical and chemical transformation of the environment, an extensive arsenal of poisons was developed to subdue the revolt. In 1939, P. Muller discovered the insecticide properties of ddt, a chlorinated organic compound first synthesized 65 years earlier. Since that time there has been an exponential increase in the number of synthetic insecticides, herbicides and fungicides available (Nicholson, 1984, pp. 214–15). In 1986, some 1500 active pesticide ingredients were registered in the United States (The Conservation Foundation, 1987, p. 351), with about 360,000,000 kilograms of these chemicals being applied annually in the agricultural sector alone (ibid., p. 146).

The link between monoculture, fertilizer requirements and pesticide use is well illustrated by the farming of corn in the United States. This single crop consumed 44 per cent of the total United States fertilizer use, with the application rate being as high as 340 kilograms per hectare (ibid., p. 350). At the same time, to control insect attack, a massive 43 per cent of the total pesticides used in the United States were applied to this same crop (ibid., p. 352). Despite this huge application of poisonous pesticides in the name of technological progress, R. Nader points out that the percentage of pre-harvest crops lost to insect damage has increased from 9 per cent in 1945 to 12 per cent in 1989 (Reisner, 1989, p. 30). This is due, in part, to the increasing resistance of many pests to pesticides (Carson, 1963, pp. 218–22) and also possibly to a decreased immunity of plants to pests, which Howard suggests is a consequence of the use of chemical fertilizers.

There is a mordant irony in the fact that in India, where in the 1930s crops grown on fertile soils suffered remarkably little from pests, the emphasis on economic growth and chemical technology has led to a tenfold increase in pesticide consumption during the past two decades. Motivated by the technological imperative, India in 1990–1, consumed an estimated one million tonnes of pesticides (Nigam and Karnik, 1988, p. 694).

Howard also noted that plants grown for food on fertile soil, free of chemical fertilizers but rich in humus, confer upon the animals and humans which eat them the health benefit of increased immunity to disease (Howard, 1943, pp. 171–80). Among the many examples of communities whose immune functions have been improved, Howard cites the Hunzas in Pakistan. The health, beauty, fitness and longevity of these people has provided discussion topics in numerous articles in the popular media (See for example, Taylor and Nobbs, 1962). It was not until 1964, however, that medical research began to confirm certain of the claims which figured in these popular reports (Toomey and White, 1964, pp. 841–2).

Recent finding have added further support to Howard's claims for compost-grown foods. D. Pitt and co-workers at Exeter University have found that garden compost can suppress economically significant plant diseases by between 60 and 80 per cent, and can sometimes eliminate them altogether. It was found, for instance, that an 80 per cent reduction in the disease 'take all' in wheat, could be achieved using compost, while red core in strawberries was reduced by 90 per cent. Club root in cabbage was eliminated completely. It appears that organisms in the compost suppress the growth of disease-causing bacteria and fungi (Hedges, 1996, p. 25).

The adverse effects of the worldwide use of chemical fertilizers for the health of the world's inhabitants are still only being recognized. For instance, the high-yield rice, wheat and maize varieties of the 'Green Revolution' which depend on the liberal use of inorganic fertilizers, are usually low in minerals and vitamins. Because these new 'technology' crops have displaced local foods, the diet of many people in the developing world is now dangerously low in iron, zinc and vitamin A, and other micronutrients (Seymour, 1996, pp. 32–7).

The extent to which artificial fertilizers undermine the microbial fungal eco-systems of the soil is still not adequately appreciated, though research in the area has established a connection between chemical fertilizers and soil erosion (Pimentel and Edwards, 1982, pp. 595–600). In 1950, J. Russell Smith, Emeritus Professor of Economic Geography at Columbia University, warned that modern crop-based agri-culture, such as that used in the production of corn, cotton and tobacco, was not only destroying soil fertility but was, in addition, contributing substantially to soil erosion. He argued urgently for the need to develop a sustainable 'permanent agri-culture' to reduce these problems. He made some startling comparisons. The aver-age annual yield of corn in the Appalachian Mountains was 500 kilograms per acre. The yield of chestnut orchards in the mountains of Europe is approximately the same. The chestnuts, however, yield year in and year out for centuries. Corn 'burns out' the solid rapidly. Yet the food value and palatability of the chestnut to live-stock are comparable to that of corn (Smith, 1977). Hundreds of other tree crops could be employed by American farmers for producing food for livestock and humans. Unfortunately, little attention has been paid to Smith's suggestions. In the meantime, the rapid depletion of natural soil conditioners such as humus fungi, bacteria, earthworms and insects — all of which have in recent years been dis-placed largely by chemical fertilizers and poisonous sprays — has, according to the technological view, necessitated additional mechanical tilling to achieve soil fertility. However, this additional technological intervention has, in turn, modified the physical structure of the soil, as well as its surface profile and has resulted in increased erosion by wind and rain (Taylor, 1996/1997, pp. 25–6). Soil erosion is now a major threat to crop production around the world, with a loss of some 80 billion tonnes of topsoil every year. This is the total amount of topsoil which underlies the whole of the Australia's wheatlands (Anderson, 1995, pp. 12–13).

The CSIRO report *State of the Environment Australia 1996* which reviewed current farming methods, found that many current practices are not sustainable, and biodiversity-based industries such as agriculture, pastoralism, forestry, fisheries and tourism often erode the very resources upon which they depend (State of the Environment Advisory Council, 1996, pp. 6–26).

Farm chemicals have also become a major source of environmental pollution (The Conservation Foundation, 1987, pp. 99–109). The application of nitrate fertilizers is a case in point. In the early 1900s, F. Haber and C. Bosch developed a process by which nitrogen from the atmosphere could be synthesized with hydrogen (produced by reacting steam with red hot coke) to form ammonia. Since ammonia could be easily oxidized to nitric acid for fertilizer production, the Haber operation conveniently enabled the commercial industry to tap the huge reservoir of nitrogen in the atmosphere. Clever as this sounds, the problem is that the process bypasses nature's own bacteria-moderated nitrogen-fixation processes in the soil itself, which protect the soil from nitrogen saturation.

Huge quantities of nitrogen fertilizers are now applied to the soil around the world each year to promote plant growth. In the United States in 1985, for example, 11 million tonnes of nitrogen were applied to the soil in the form of fertilizers (ibid., p. 351). Once again, this massive manipulation of the natural environment has not been without adverse effects. Nitrate pollution of groundwater and drinking water, for instance, is now a major problem in many countries (Strebel, Duynisveld and Bottcher, 1989, pp. 189–214).

Excessive nitrate levels in vegetables and plants have also become a problem. Attempts have been made to develop varieties of plants with low nitrate accumulation rates in the hope of reducing the health risk of nitrogen poisoning (Junge and Handke, 1987, pp. 346–8). Nitrates are converted by bacteria in the body to nitrites, which then bind to haemoglobin, impairing the capacity of blood to transport oxygen. Excessive nitrogen intake can thus result in a condition of the blood known as methaemoglobinaemia (Conway and Pretty, 1988, pp. 207–8).

Another possible health aspect of the application of nitrate fertilizers to our soils involves an indirect contribution to the greenhouse effect. P.A. Steudler and co-workers have reported that the application of nitrogen fertilizers may reduce the capacity of the soil to act as a sink or absorption table for methane gas (Steudler and Bowden, 1989, pp. 314–15). This being so, nitrate fertilizers may actually inhibit the subtle mechanisms in the soil which assist in regulating the atmospheric levels of this naturally produced greehouse gas.

Since highly soluble chemical fertilizers such as nitrates leach from the soil, they enter the waterways and seas producing a new and inharmonious ecological mix. In some areas, particularly in the North Sea, this new mix has encouraged the phenomenal growth of algae. When the algae die, the biomass is often so large that the bacteria breaking down the dead algae consume all the oxygen in the water, thereby causing fish and other species to suffocate.

Other research has shown that algae give off a sulfur-containing chemical, dimethyl sulfide, which oxidizes in air to form sulfur dioxide, the principal cause of acid rain. It has been estimated that in summer, 25 per cent of the acid rain falling over Europe now comes from huge algae masses in the North Sea (Pain, 1989, p. 6). This observation illustrates the difficulty in anticipating the extent of environmental disruption and degradation caused by technological intervention. Given the inter-connectivity and delicate interrelationships which we now know characterize nature, the more intensive the technology, the more it is bound to impact synergistically across the network of these relationships.

Disease: The Price of Progress

Over the past two centuries, we have used our increasing scientific knowledge to unlock the concentrated stores of energy in the earth's crust. This energy has been tapped and distributed for conversion into power, which has, in turn, enabled us to exploit to the fullest the resources of nature. With this empowerment we have altered in subtle but radical ways, the structure of our environment. We have changed not only the constitution of our air, water, soil, food and even our electromagnetic environment, but we have also affected the existence and distribution patterns of plant, animal and microbial species on this planet.

The desire for mastery over the environment has led to the evolution of a union between knowledge and technology which seeks to maximize our expropriation of the earth's resources, while minimizing the time and effort devoted to the task. Rather than seeking to dominate and control the environment, we need to seek to connect and empathize with it.

Although we shall in subsequent chapters address more thoroughly the whole range of health issues raised by technological development, there is a philosophical principle implicit in this chapter which should be made explicit. Characteristic of the human race and its patterns of 'progress' has been what might be called an attitude of 'species arrogance'. We see ourselves as separate from nature and superior to the extraordinary and vast array of creatures which it sustains. Because we see ourselves as a group apart, we have construed our survival as a species on the metaphor of a battle against nature. The security of our species, we have come to believe, is established through the domination and control of nature.

The truth of the matter is quite different. In general, we have as our species tried to control nature, either by transforming it to suit our needs (for example, the addition of chemical fertilizers to enrich soil), or by insulating ourselves from it, as in the construction of homes and offices which stand as fortresses against nature. The attitude of species arrogance notwithstanding, the problem is that we are in truth a part of nature, and thus contact with nature is as crucial to our health as is our contact with each other. Trying to make life easier, we have attempted to make nature adjust to it. The world we have therefore created for ourselves, either by way of our chemical interventions in nature or by the creation of antiseptic internal environments away from it is, in essence, an *artificial world*. What we did not foresee is that while we may have succeeded in minimizing the necessity of adjusting to the natural world, we have unwittingly maximized the necessity of having to adjust to the artificial world we have created for ourselves. The clean, crisp air which once refreshed the places in which we lived and worked has now been replaced by an atmosphere of chemical pollutants. Although we are physiologically adapted to meet most of the demands of our interface with nature, we have little provision to adapt to the chemical environments within which we are now held capture. The problem is that we are not made for the world we have made for ourselves.

To free ourselves, we need first to acknowledge the errors of our ways. The domination of nature and the economic goal of unlimited growth are two sides of the same coin. The time has come to institute a new form of currency and to reconceptualize our relationship with nature. The changes required doubtless challenge the many vested interests which depend upon pursuing the course of environmental exploitation already begun. In the chapters that follow, however, we shall see that what is at stake in the argument is not just the vested interests of a chemical company here or an electricity company there. What is at stake are the vested interests of the general public in their own personal health and in the health of their children. If our commitment to technological progress is systematically undermining the health of the community, then we need to re-think our commitment to the symbols of progress which define the world in which we presently live.

Despite the fact that modern technology has undoubtedly improved the standard of living for many people in the western world, the cost both to the natural environment and to human health has been prohibitive. The cost of our technological indiscretions now constitutes a massive debt to nature which, if we are to survive on this planet, will have to be paid with interest. While some may argue that it is impossible to halt progress, our reply is that given the current state of environmental degradation, it is imperative that the value of progress, and thus what we do in the name of progress, be defined in accord with its environmental sustainability. It is only by placing these limits on ourselves that we will provide the incentives to research and develop alternative processes which are in harmony with nature and thereby reinvent the future of our planet in ways that make living on it worthwhile.

References

(1989) 'Americans overdose on ozone', *New Scientist*, 22 July. **123**.

(1989) 'Cancers abound near Soviet Union's nuclear test site', *New Scientist*, 2 September. **123**.

(1990) 'Nuclear weapons industries "swept health risks under the carpet"', *New Scientist*, 6 January. **125**.

(1980) 'Time to get the lead out?' *Choice*, Sydney, September.

ALDHOUS, P. (1995) 'Global heat breeds superaphids', *New Scientist*, 23/30 December **148**, 2009.

ANDERSON, I. (1995) 'Australia's growing disaster', *New Scientist*, 29 July **147**, 1988.

ASHTON, J. and LAURA, R. (1998) *Perils of Progress: The health and environment hazards of modern technology and what you can do about them*, Sydney, Australia: UNSW Press.

BELLINGER, D., LEVITON, A. and WATERNAUX, C. (1987) 'Longitudinal analysis of prenatal and postnatal lead exposure and early cognitive development', *New England Journal of Medicine*, **316**.

BELLINI, J. (1987) *High Tech Holocaust*, Richmond, Victoria: Greenhouse Publications.

BERAL, V. (1990) 'Leukaemia and nuclear installations', *British Medical Journal*, **300**, 17 February.

BERSTEIN, B. (1985) 'The unsung father of the A-Bomb', *Discover*, August, pp. 37–42.

BOARD, P. (1996) 'Contaminated lands', *New Scientist* (inside science), 12 October.

BOND, M. (1996) 'Dirty ships evade acid rain control', *New Scientist*, 22 June.

BORMAN, S. (1995) 'Chemists reminisce on 50th anniversary of the atomic bomb', *Chemical and Engineering News*, 17 July.

BOULDING, E. (1977) 'Education for inventing the future', in MEADOWS, L. (ed.) *Alternatives to Growth 1: A Search for Sustainable Futures*, Cambridge, Massachusetts: Ballinger Publishing Co.

BROWN, W. (1994) 'Dying from too much dust', *New Scientist*, 18 May.

BURTON, J. (1995) 'Global warming', *Chemical and Engineering News*, 4 December.

CAPRA, F. (1988) *The Toa of Physics: An exploration of the parallels between modern physics and Eastern Mysticism*, London: Collins Publishing Group.

CARSON, R. (1963) *Silent Spring*, London: Hamish Hamilton.

CLEWS, G. (1996) 'Chlorine in perspective', *Chemistry in Australia*, January.

THE CONSERVATION FOUNDATION (1987) *State of Environment: A View Towards the Nineties*, Washington DC: The Conservation Foundation.

CONWAY, G.R. and PRETTY, J.N. (1988) 'Fertiliser risks in the developing countries', *Nature*, 21 July.

DAVIS, J.M. (1990) 'Risk assesment of the development neurotoxicity of lead', *Neurotoxicology*, **11**.

DAY, M. (1996) 'Past lead pollution poisons unborn child', *New Scientist*, 22 June.

DONOVAN, J. (1996) 'No lead is good lead', *Medical Journal of Australia*, **164**.

DUBOS, R. (1959) *Mirage of Health*, New York: Harper and Row.

DUBROVA, Y.E., NESTEROV, V.N. and KROUCHINSKY, N.G. (1996) 'Human minisatellite mutation rate after Chernobyl accident', *Nature*, 25 April.

DUNCAN, A. and SIMPSON, G. (1996) 'Compounds containing chlorine: How do we decide what is good for us?', *Chemistry in Australia*, January.

EDWARDS, R. (1995a) 'Ozone alert follows cancer warning', *New Scientist*, 27 May.

EDWARDS, R. (1995b) 'Terrifying outlook for Chernobyl's babies', *New Scientist*, 2 December.

EDWARDS, R. (1995c) 'Will it get any worse', *New Scientist*, 9 December.

EDWARDS, R. (1996a) 'Drivers risk cancer in the cab', *New Scientist*, 26 October.

EDWARDS, R. (1996b) 'Radioactive forests will bring power to the people', *New Scientist*, 26 October.

EDWARDS, R. (1996c) 'Tomorrow's bitter harvest', *New Scientist*, 17 August.

EDWARDS, R. (1996d) 'Chernobyl floods put millions at risk', *New Scientist*, 23 March.

EURO CHLOR (1995) 'The natural chemistry of chlorine in the environment', *Euro Chlor*, Brussels.

FOLINSBEE, L.J. (1992) 'Human health effects of air pollution', *Environmental Health Perspectives*, **100**.

GIESE, A.C. (1976) *Living With Our Sun's Ultraviolet Rays*, New York: Plenum Press.

GOLDSMITH, E. (1977) 'Settlements and social stability', in MEADOWS, L. (1977) (ed.) *Alternatives to Growth 1: A Search for Sustainable Futures*, Cambridge, Massachusetts: Ballinger Publishing Co., pp. 331–49.

GORDON, A. and SUZUKI, D. (1990) *It's a Matter of Survival*, Allen and Unwin.

GOUDIE, A. (1986) *The Human Impact on the Natural Environment*, Oxford: Basil Blackwell.

GOYER, R.A. (1993) 'Lead toxicity: Current concern', *Environmental Health Perspectives*, **100**.

GRAHAM, F. (1970) *Since Silent Spring*, London: Hamish Hamilton.

GRIBBIN, J. and GRIBBIN, M. (1996) 'The greenhouse effect', *New Scientist* (Inside Science), 13 July.

GRIBBLE, G.W. (1995) 'Organochlorine compounds', *Chemical and Engineering News*, 13 February.

HAMER, M. (1996) 'Cars must go to meet clean air target', *New Scientist*, 18 May.

HANSON, D. (1995) 'Toxic release inventory: Chemical industry again cuts emissions', *Chemical Engineering News*, 3 April.

HEDGES, S. (1996) 'Compost is a natural-born killer', *New Scientist*, 21 September.

HEICKLEN, J. (1987) 'The formation and inhibition of photochemical smog', *Annals of the New York Academy of Sciences*, **502**.

HILEMAN, B. (1995) 'Scientists warn that disease threats increase as earth warms up', *Chemical Engineering News*, 2 October.

HINWOOD, A. (1996) 'The role of scientist in the Montreal protocol', *Chlorine in Perspective*, Melbourne: CSIRO Division of Chemical and Polmers.

HOWARD, A. (1943) *An Agricultural Testament*, New York: Oxford University Press.

JACKSON, E.K., GUEST, C.S. and WOODWARD, A.J. (1996) 'Climate, health and medicine in a changing world', *Medical Journal of Australia*, **165**.

JUNGE, H.D. and HANDKE, S. (1987) 'Nitrate in vegetables — unavoidable risk?: Cultivation of new varieties offers some assistance', *Industrielle Obstund Gemuseverwertung*, **71**.

KELLY, G.J. (1989) 'Effects of W-B radiation on terrestrial planets', *Transactions of the Menzies Foundation*, 15.

KEYNES, M. (1996) 'Chemical industry and the environment': A view from history', *Chemistry in Australia*, June.

KLEINER, K. (1995) 'Dioxin authors stand firm against critics', *New Scientist*, 23/30 December.

KRIPKE, M.L. (1989) 'Overview: health consequences of stratopheric ozone depletion', *Transactions of the Menzies Foundation*, 15.

LAURA, R.S. and ASHTON, J.F. (1989) *The Perils of Progress*, Sydney, Australia: UNSW Press.

LAYMAN, P.L. (1995) 'Global top 50 chemical producers show rise in profit and sales', *Chemical and Engineering News*, 24 July.

LIEBIG, J. (1840) *Organic Chemistry in its Applications to Agriculture and Physiology*, CLAYFAIRE, L. (ed.) London: Taylor and Walton.

LIPPMANN, M. and SCHLESINGER, R.B. (1979) *Chemical Contamination in the Human Environment*, New York: Oxford University Press.

LONGSTAFF, E. (1988) 'Carcinogenic and mutagenic potential of several flurocarbons', *Annals of the New York Academy of Sciences*, **534**.

LUNING, G. and SCHEER, J. (1989) 'Early infant mortality in West Germany before and after Chernobyl', *The Lancet*, **2**, 1081–3.

MACKENZIE, D. (1994) 'Clinton backs call to ban chlorine', *New Scientist*, 12 February.

MACKENZIE, D. (1995a) 'Rich and poor split over ozone', *New Scientist*, 9 December.

MACKENZIE, D. (1995b) 'Ozone's future is up in the Air', *New Scientist*, 16 December.

MACKENZIE, D. (1995c) 'Polar meltdown fulfils worst predictions', *New Scientist*, 12 August.

MEADOWS, L. (1977) (ed.) *Alternatives to Growth 1: A Search for Sustainable Futures*, Cambridge, Massachusetts: Ballinger Publishing Co.

MENNEAR, J.J. and McCONNELL, E.E. (1988) 'Inhalation toxicology and carcinogenesis studies of methylene chloride (dichlormethane) in F 344/N rats and B6C3F mice', *Annals of the New York Academy of Sciences*, **534**.

MOTLUK, A. (1996) 'Lead blights the future of Africa's children', *New Scientist*, 23 March.

MULLINS, J. (1996) 'The case of the missing core', *New Scientist*, 20 April.

MUSTAFA, M.G. and HASSETT, C.M. (1988) 'Pulmonary carcinogenic effects of ozone', *Annals of the New York Academy of Sciences*, **534**.

NATIONAL RESEARCH COUNCIL (1989) *Alternative Agriculture*, Washington DC: Academy Press.

NICHOLSON, B.C. (1984) *Australian Water Quality Criteria for Organic Commpounds*, Australian Water Resources Council Technical Paper 82.

NIGAM, S.K. and KARNIK, A.B. (1988) 'Experimental and human surveillance on BHC and DDT insecticides commonly used in India', *Annals of the New York Academy of Sciences*, **534**.

PAIN, S. (1989) 'Pollutants collect on continental side of North Sea, study finds', *New Scientist*, 11 November.

PATEL, T. (1994a) 'French smog smothers hundreds', *New Scientist*, 17 February.

PATEL, T. (1994b) 'Killer smog stalks the boulevards', *New Scientist*, 15 October.

PATEL, T. (1995a) 'Clash over radiation saftey limits', *New Scientist*, 2 December.

PATEL, T. (1995b) 'France counts the costs of cheap diesel', *New Scientist*, 26 October.

PATEL, T. (1996a) 'Iodine first aid is not enough', *New Scientist*, 27 April.

PATEL, T. (1996b) 'Power station failure adds to Delih's woes', *New Scientist*, 12 October.

PAUSTENBACH, D.J., BASS, R.D. and PRICE, P. (1993) 'Benzene toxicity and risk assessment, 1972–92: Implications for future regulation', *Environmental Health Perspective Supplements*, **101**.

PEARCE, F. (1995a) 'Fiddling while earth warms', *New Scientist*, 25 March.

PEARCE, F. (1995b) 'World lays offs on global catastrophe', *New Scientist*, 8 April.

PEARCE, F. (1996a) 'A heavy responsibility', *New Scientist*, 27 July.

PEARCE, F. (1996b) 'Carbon targets up in the air', *New Scientist*, 6 July.

PIMENTEL, D. and EDWARDS, C.A. (1982) 'Pesticides and ecosystems', *Bio Science*, **32**.

PIRKLE, J.L., BRODY, D.J. and GUNTER, E.W. (1994) 'The decline in blood lead levels in the United States: The National Health and Nutrition Examination Surveys (NHANES)', *Journal of the American Medical Association*, **272**.

PLUMB, R.A. (1989) 'Atmospheric ozone — physics and chemistry', *Transactions of the Menzies Foundation*, 15.

RAABE, G.K. (1993) 'Review of the carcinogenic potential of gasoline', *Environmental Health Perspectives Supplements*, 101.

READ, C. (1989) 'Even low levels of ozone in smog harm the lungs', *New Scientist*, 9 September.

REISNER, J. (1989) 'Nader's new beef', *Food Business*, 5 June.

RICH, V. (1990) 'Concern over health of "Chernobyl children"', *New Scientist*, 21 April.

RIEGEL, E.R. (1937) *Industrial Chemistry*, New York: Reinhold.

ROWLAND, F.S. and MOLINA, M.J. (1975) 'Chlofluoromethanes in the environment', *Reviews of Geophysics and Space Physics*, **1**.

SARMIENTO, J. and LEQUERE, C. (1996) *Science*, **274**, 30 November.

SCHWARTZ, J. and OTTO, D. (1987) 'Blood lead, hearing thresholds and neurobehavioural development in children and youth', *Archives of Environmental Health*, **42**.

SCHUMACHER, E.F. (1975) *Small is Beautiful*, New York: Harper and Row.

SEYMOUR, J. (1996) 'Hungry for a new revolution', *New Scientist*, 30 March.

SMITH, J.R. (1977) *Tree Crops: A Permanent Agriculture*, Old Greenwich: Devin-Adair Co.

SPIRO, T.G. and THOMAS, V.M. (1995) 'Organochlorine compounds', *Chemical and Engineering News*, 13 February.

STATE OF THE ENVIRONMENT ADVISORY COUNCIL (1996) *Australia State of the Environment*, Collingwood, Australia: CSIRO Publishing, pp. 6–26.

STEUDLER, P.A. and BOWDEN, R.D. (1989) 'Influence of nitrogen fertilisation on methane uptake in temperate forest soils', *Nature*, September.

STREBEL, O., DUYNISVELD, W.H.M. and BOTTCHER, J. (1989) 'Nitrate pollution of groundwater in western Europe', *Agricultural Ecosystems and Environment*, **26**, 3/4.

TAYLOR, R. (1996/1997) 'What's causing sugar yields to fall', *Rural Research*, **173**.

TAYLOR, R. and NOBBS, M.J. (1962) *Hunza the Himalayan Shangri-La*, El Monte, California: Whitehorn Publishing Co.

TESLA, N. (1956) Lectures, Patents, Articles, Nikola Tesla Museum, Beograd.

TOOMEY, E.G. and WHITE, P.D. (1964) 'A brief survey of the health of aged Hunzas', *American Heart Journal*, **68**, 6.

TRICHOPOULOS, D. (1996) (on leukaemia in Greek children), *Nature*, 27 July.

VAUGHAN, C. (1990) 'Streetwise to the dangers of ozone', *New Scientist*, 26 May.

WICKENDEN, L. (1961) *Our Daily Poison*, New York: Hillman Books.

WILL, C. (1996) 'Safety in diversity', *New Scientist*, 23 March.

WILSON, E.O. (1989) 'Threats to biodiversity', *Scientific America*, September.

WOOD, W.F. (1989) 'The effects of ultraviolet radiation on the marine biota', *Transactions of the Menzies Foundation*, 15.

WOODIN, S. and SKIBA, U. (1990) 'Liming fails the acid test', *New Scientist*, 10 March.

ZURER, P. (1995) 'Satellite data confirm CFC link to ozone hole', *Chemical and Engineering News*, 2 January.

Chapter 2

Why Educational Knowledge Is Neither Theory Free Nor Value Free

In the previous chapter considerable evidence was provided to show that western society's obsession with technological growth has led to an environmental crisis of monumental proportions, the continual acceleration of which is very likely to take us to the brink of extinction. In this chapter our aim is to show that despite persistent protestations to the contrary, the dominant form of knowledge which gives rise to this technology and upon which our educative system rests is far from being value free. The argument of the chapter is intended to show that not only is knowledge theory-laden, but it is also value-laden, and that the values it enshrines are inimical to the ostensible goals of living harmoniously with the environment. Our argument is that we have institutionalized a form of knowledge the prime motivation of which is the quest for power, domination and control. Because western society is committed to a controlling form of knowledge, the technological reconstructions of nature which it generates are themselves social representations of power, control and expropriation. The source of the environment crisis to which we have alluded in the previous chapter is not — contrary to the conventional wisdom — a matter simply of misusing technology. Our point is that by virtue of the values which knowledge and in turn technology enshrine, they are by their very nature intrinsically divisive of the ecological integrity of the earth. The established system of education serves as the social vehicle by way of which society perpetuates its insatiable appetite for power and expropriation of the earth's resources. This being so, the dominant application of educational knowledge is tantamount to a systematic technological assault upon the regenerative capacities and interdependencies which define the patterns and rhythms of nature's renewal.

Knowledge as Theory-Laden

It is clear that the concept of knowledge embraced by western society is formalized within the tradition of science which defines the mode both of its discovery and its expression. Having distinguished itself by its departure from the theological concept of knowledge as revelation, western science affirms its faith in observation as the most secure foundation upon which the edifice of knowledge can be built. This predilection for observation as the fundamental source of knowledge of the world was quickly exalted and the dominant image of science as the sole arbiter of truth

40

was crystallized. That the character of science was observational exploited the common sense belief that 'seeing is believing' and secured the view that an isomorphic relation between the hypotheses of science and the facts they depicted could be realized. For natural science to be possible — it was supposed — the world must have a certain character. Natural science is possible because it is actual; therefore the world can be ascribed the logical character which natural science presupposes as the condition of its possibility.

But what sort of character would constitute nature as an object of natural science? One of the most influential answers was contained in Ludwig Wittgenstein's Tractatus, and it was the Logical Positivists who found it there. The world, Wittgenstein said, was the totality of facts. A simple suggestion, one might think, but its simplicity was supplemented by a sophisticated logical apparatus by reference to which it was elaborated and amplified. The result was a highly complicated account of language and the world which presumed a strict isomorphism between specific linguistic items and the atomic objects to which they corresponded. A philosophical thesis thus provided the formalization of a metaphysical presumption about the possibility of science. If one grants that the world is constituted of facts, somehow 'out there' awaiting discovery and collection by any normally sighted observer with an impartial mind, science can be regarded as a neutral mechanism for cataloguing facts. Knowledge derives from experience, and it is the task of science to systematize the observational procedures which do no more than record the undiluted observational or sensory data which serve to identity the facts. Science comes to be regarded as the edifice of knowledge built upon an experiential foundation, the elements of which are the facts of the world.

It is evident, however, that fruitful science must be something more than a systematized observational technique for fact-monitoring. For there is still the logical hiatus between this observational procedure and the experimental framework that underpinned its invention. To bring this out let us examine the role allegedly played by experimentation in the dominant image of science. Experimentation refers to the mechanisms in virtue of which we test our observations to assert the appropriate correspondence between the language in which they are recorded and the facts they purport to record.

One important philosophical impetus for the formalization of the experimental component derived from the correspondence theory of truth unpacked in truth-conditional terms. The position can be set out roughly as follows: A sentence is true if whatever it asserts to be case, is the case; moreover, we determine both what it asserts and whether what it asserts is the case by determining the conditions under which it would be true. On the truth-conditional account, the instantiation of a relevant condition necessitates the exclusion of a correlative possibility. So the conditions under which it would be true to assert 'the cat is on the mat' are conditions whose exclusion world render it false. Every assertion is tantamount to a denial. The possibilities it shuts out are by the possibilities it shuts in, and these in turn mark the conditions under which it would be true. The absence of the truth-conditions necessary for the affirmation serve as a sufficient condition for its denial. This being so, the general predilection for experimentation can be viewed as a general predilection for truth. Experiment shows the degree to which a given hypothesis or theory agrees with the undiluted observational data, and the experimental procedure becomes a verificatory procedure.

We are now in a position to delineate the components which feature in the dominant image of science. There is, first, the notion that the world is constituted of facts, our sensory faculties simply monitoring the basic observational data which the world provides. There is, second, that from the generalization of particular facts emerge general theories or laws in virtue of which prediction and explanation derive. The truth of specific explanations and predictions depends not only the undiluted observational data from which they derive, but also upon the verificatory procedures in terms of which they are substantiated. This is of course an epistemic, not an ontic judgment. It is not much that verification or the falsification makes an hypothesis true, as that if an hypothesis is true, it must admit either of verification or failure of falsification. Although the actual mechanisms of confirmation procedure are considerably more complex than this, the caricature preserves what is basic to the sophisticated framework of confirmation. It is the verificatory procedures of science and the observational foundation which has guided their construction that conjointly assist in establishing science in its position of epistemic priority. We believe that the judgments of science are reliable because they have been tested. That scientific claims have been corroborated guarantees, so the story goes, the supremacy of science over its unscientific competitors.

The time has now come to assess this view. Let us first consider what many would still regard as the uncontroversial conception of 'fact'. If it were not for those who proceed as if there are, one would have supposed that sufficient work has already been done in a number of disciplines to show that there are no such things as bare facts. We do not intend to spend much time rehearsing what are by now familiar points, but as our argument here is a cumulative one there is point in ensuring that our starting position is clear. Any attempt to characterize reality, or to specify the 'facts', requires a language or symbolic system of which the unit of significance is the 'concept'. Concepts, however, are not dictated unequivocally by the reality which stimulates and shapes them. Reality's contribution to our interpretation of it is flexible; the world does not present itself as a datum of apprehension fixed once and for all. This is why recalcitrant items of translation between language schemes reflect the extent to which different natural languages are really different ways of conceptualizing the world. This means that there are limits to what can be said in a particular language, so that the range of possible concepts conditions and delimits the range of possible facts. A scientific theory is thus not given to us ready-made by the data of observation. What we regard as a fact is itself determined by the language in which it is expressed as a fact. There is no undiluted observation independent of the language; there are only observations reported in observation languages. The very language in which our observations are reported is in turn conditioned by prior theories. In this respect there are no raw or uninterpreted data. Even mensuration and the numerical values it licenses depend upon theoretical assumptions more comprehensive than the procedure of measurement incorporated in them. A useful elaboration of this is given by Kevin Harris in his book,

Education and Knowledge (1979, pp. 10–20). Harris' example invites us to count the number of people on the university oval at a given particular time. Given that the observers beset with the task were all of normal vision and possessed of an ability to count, the presumption of theory-free observation is that the investigators simply front up at the oval, take their own count of the people on the oval and return to find their totals corroborated by the other investigators. While a concensus could no doubt be possibly reached, it may well be that the initial numbers reported could differ markedly. Harris' point is that because not even the activity of counting is theory free, different theories may influence what 'counts' as a person, as well as what counts as *being on the oval at a particular time*. Although we do have a general view about what a person is for purposes of counting persons, the nature of the personhood is mediated by theories of disparate assumptions. Some contemporary philosophers such as Michael Tooley, for example, would not count as persons tiny babies, small children and some mentally defective individuals. Depending upon whether the investigators come to the oval with the assumption that a foetus is a person, they are likely, if they are consistent with their views expressed on abortion, to count more people on the oval than the investigator who believes a foetus is not a person.

Another example of the theory-ladenness of observation relates to the concept of mass. That mass is an intrinsic and invariable property of a body, is a 'factual assumption' borne out of Newtonian mechanics. Within the universe of relativity theory the ascription of properties to mass is relativized in such a way that the whole notion of property invariance becomes empirically unattached. The point is that what we count as a fact will depend in part upon the universe of discourse in which the enumeration of fact obtains. Epistemology has taught us that there is no neutral observation language which transcends the theoretical framework within which a particular observation or set of observations admits of analysis.

There is an informal counterpart to the formality of the theory-ladenness thesis and its treatment will be apposite here. The idea that the world is the totality of facts gives rise to the commonplace view that 'seeing is believing'. A more cautious statement of the position is that we believe nothing of what we hear and only half of what we see. What we are not told, however, is how we know which half to believe. The difficulty is that the history of science is rife with examples which show that seeing is as much a matter of believing as believing is a matter of seeing. Consider, for instance, the difficulties surrounding the confirmation of the existence of the planet Neptune. In the early nineteenth century astronomers were worried by the anomalous orbit of the planet Uranus the orbital coordinates of which were clearly inconsistent with those predictions sustained by the mathematics of Newtonian gravitational theory. Rather than relinquish Newton's theory of gravitation in the face of conflicting evidence, the astronomers Leverier and Adams postulated the existence of the then unknown and unseen planet Neptune. In turn the Neptune hypothesis provided a putatively heuristic way of accommodating the discrepant data. But before the planet was actually first sighted by Galle, a number of astronomers reported having seen the planet, though their descriptions make plain that it could not have been Neptune or for that matter any other planet. In 1846 James

Challis set himself the task of confirming the Neptune hypothesis, though he did not consider it true. Believing the hypothesis to be false, he at first failed repeatedly to 'see' what was, as he later admitted, constantly before his eyes. Challis had organized his perceptual experience in accordance with his perceptual expectations. He had not expected to confirm the Neptune hypothesis and, for a considerable period, he was thus unable to do so (Abel, 1976, pp. 30–40). The example is perhaps better assimilated to the 'not-believing is not seeing' category, but this only strengthens rather than weakens the case against undiluted observation and bare fact.

It is clear that there is more to seeing than meets the eyeball; to see is to interpret (Hanson, 1958). Seeing is not passive reception; it is an active exercise in problem-solving. What we regard as 'the facts' depends upon the way in which our language, belief commitments, expectations and sensory apparatus contribute to our conceptual patterns of organization. There is no innocent eye; to believe in the virgin eye is, as Nietzsche put it, to commit the fallacy of immaculate perception.

We are in a position to consider the second component in the chain of reasoning that supports science as the dominant methodology. Science has proved itself, so the claim goes, inasmuch as its procedure of testability ensures the reliability of its hypotheses that survive the test. That an hypothesis has withstood our attempts to falsify it seems a strong ground for preferring it to an hypothesis which has not been tested or to one which has, but proved unsuccessful.

While the theory-free concept of knowledge relies upon the testability criterion as a guide to credibility, no acceptable statement of the criterion has yet been articulated. If one opts for a verifiability criterion, the conditions of testability would, as is well-known, disallow universal generalizations of exhaustive scope such as scientific laws and certain hypotheses. As the quantifier ranges over an infinite domain, no finite regimentation will suffice. That all observed swans are white does not, as is well known, preclude the possibility that the swan to be observed next will not be white.

If you are loyal Popperian you will doubtless object that the difficulty to which we have alluded can easily be overcome by adopting a falsifiability criterion. It is evident, for example, that universal generalizations are susceptible to falsification. While we believe this is not as evident as one might think, our immediate reply is that the falsifiability criterion is no logical panacea. The well-known difficulty is that while falsifiability may serve to test universal generalizations, it disallows all existential statements. The falsity of 'There exists at least one unicorn' cannot be derived from any finite class of observation statements. Our failure thus far to discover any unicorns does not entail that there are none to be found, nor indeed that we will not find one. Popperians have argued that the exclusion is innocuous, for the only statements science needs to preserve are the class of scientific laws and hypotheses which feature as the basic of explanation and prediction. Although it is difficult to fathom how science could do without testing its purely existential statements, we have no wish to contest this point here. Notwithstanding this concession, however, we submit that the falsifiability criterion is self-stultifying. The conditions of its consistent application undermine the conditions of its reliability. Falsifiability flouts the logical principle of what we shall call 'propositional or truth value symmetry'. The point is simple enough, though it has been either neglected or missed by most of those who have defended falsifiability. The difficulty is that falsification of a universal generalization is logically equivalent to asserting a purely existential statement. We could thus falsify the negative universal 'Nothing has the property of being a unicorn' though the vasty of its denial 'There exists at least one unicorn' would not follow from any finite class of observation statements. We thus have a failure of parity of truth-value as the fallibility criterion licenses asymmetrical distributions of truth-value to statements which are logically equivalent. If we insist on ascribing a truth-value to a sentence only if it is falsifiable by a finite set of observations, then while we will be able to ascribe truth values to universal generalization, as they are finitely falsifiable, we will not be able to give a truth value to their negations, since they are existential generalizations, and thus not finitely falsifiable. We can hold on to falsifiability but only at the cost of violating a fundamental law of logic; namely, if a proposition P is true, then not-P is false and if P is false, then not-P is true.

But let us suppose that by some feat of conceptual prestidigitation we could dispel our qualms about the exact formulation of a criterion of testability. The problem is that the relation between experience and the hypothesis to be tested will itself be problematic. On the view we are here adopting it would be a mistake to think that discordant data will serve, or indeed should serve, always to falsify an hypothesis. One reason for this peculiar resistance to falsification involves the way in which hypotheses intermesh in complicated truth-value patterns the measure of the theory they constitute. On the Quinean account of theory construction, a theory can most profitably be represented as a web of beliefs, a collection of hypotheses corresponding to reality not in the form of individual isomorphs, but in the form rather of a collective relation (Quine, 1953, p. 8, Y 2ff). The total web of belief or theory is thus under-determined by the tribunal of experience, since the collective nature of the system of belief affords a variety of internal revisions in the face of discordant data. There is considerable latitude regarding the way in which the discrepant experience distributes over the entire network of hypotheses and the strain of discordant data is borne by re-adjusting the truth-value considerations which influence the equilibrium of the total belief system. On this view virtually any hypothesis can be held true, even in the face of conflicting evidence, if sufficiently radical adjustments are made elsewhere in the system.

The consequence of all this is that the falsity of a particular hypothesis is not guaranteed by observational data which conflict with the expectations characteristic of the hypothesis. An interesting example of the character of hypothesis intermeshing is provided by K. Klein in his book *Positivism and Christianity* (1974, pp. 58ff). Klein points out that our general belief in the continued existence of the stars that form the constellation Orion is not falsified simply because of the disappearance of that constellation from the skies of the far-northern hemisphere during the summer months. The conflicting evidence is explicated by appeal to a separate hypothesis, the earth's axial tilt, which in turn supplies the prediction that the constellation will appear during the summer months in the skies of the southern hemisphere. Oddly enough, however, the hypothesis of the earth's axial tilt needs to be supplemented by yet another hypothesis, the heliocentric hypothesis which in its turn serves to yield this last prediction.

What we see here is something of the complex manner in which a conjunction of hypotheses are amalgamated into a theory. Recalcitrant observational data may rationally oblige internal adjustments, but such adjustments are essentially rational measures for avoiding falsification. Discrepant experimental data may reflect a failure of truth in one of the conjunctions of hypotheses constituting the theory, but as the boundary conditions of a theory are not unequivocally determined by experience, one cannot always deduce from the data alone which of the constituent hypotheses is false. There is thus a process of relatively continual re-evaluation of the logical connections between the constituent hypotheses, but the process of adjustment should not be assimilated to a falsification rubric. It is not as if particular hypotheses can be lined up with particular experience in virtue of which they are determined to be truth-carrying. The unit of cognitive significance has shifted from the hypothesis to the theory. This being so, the role which traditional falsification actually plays in science must be far less than is claimed for it.

Again, the history of science is abundant with examples that demonstrate that resistance to falsification is part and parcel of the scientific methodology. The scientist, like nearly everyone else, assumes a principle of tenacity which dictates a certain level of conceptual resilience in the face of conflicting evidence. If the scientist consistently relinquished a hypothesis whenever it conflicted with experimental observations, it would be virtually impossible to formulate constructive theories of even the simplest kind. A classic instance of the importance of the principle of tenacity emerged in the context of quantum investigations concerning beta-decay of the nucleus. The main problem was that experimental data relating to beta-decay ran contrary to the expectations logically associated with the law of conservation of energy. The experimental results were consistent, but rather than relinquish the law of conservation of energy as those results would have required, an auxiliary hypothesis was introduced to accommodate the discrepancy. The auxiliary hypothesis in this case marked the postulation of the neutrino, though at the time there was no independent evidence for its existence.

Contrary to much of the conventional wisdom about the reliability of scientific investigation, observational testability is not in itself sufficient to establish knowledge as theory-free. The epistemic reliability of the observational foundations of science are more publicized than they are actually demonstrated. We tend to remember only the successes, not the failures of science; yet we remember only the failures not the successes of non-science. But even if we are misguided in our view that the epistemic justification of the observational methodology of science is not proportional to the degree of reliance placed upon it, there is a more intractable problem confronting the myth of knowledge as value-free. Indeed, we would suggest, that had it been fashionable to direct society's resources and energy into the pursuit of the arcana and fringe domains, the discrepancy between the efficacy of scientific and non-scientific investigations would either be negligible or non-existent. There is no epistemic parity in comparing the methodological sophistication of an enterprise in which money and social status have been invested with an enterprise in which neither of these things has been invested. We preserve our judgment that the observational basis of science reigns supreme only by comparing incomparables.

The second point depends upon a closer inspection of the way in which science itself proceeds. It is clear that science has at various times in its history relied profitably upon precisely those domains which have traditionally stood outside of science (Feyerabend, 1978, pp. 100ff). Certain of the important achievements of modern science have been obtained only as a result of incorporating into the body of science, theory-components drawn from domains which were regarded unambiguously as non-science. Without making use of the unscientific pontifications of Philoaus concerning the character of motion, for example, Copernicus would not have achieved the astronomical advances attributed to him. It has also been observed that while astronomy reaped significant benefits from Pythagoreanism, medicine clearly profited from herbalism, wandering druggists, witches and wise men. It was by reverting to ideas which, at the time, were viewed as non-scientific that Paracelsus was able to contribute significantly to medical development (ibid., p. 105).

But it is not our purpose to pursue this divagation here. Enough has now been said to suggest that the observational language of science is not nearly epistemically sound as the conventional wisdom supposes. We have seen both that the concept of 'fact' is problematic and that observational procedures do not in themselves suffice to ensure that science is theory-free.

The Value-Ladenness of Knowledge

Not only is knowledge 'theory-laden', it is also 'value-laden', and it is the value-ladenness of knowledge which exerts the greatest influence on the institution of education and the social structures that arise out of and support it. To appreciate this point consider first that whatever else education may be, it at least involves the transmission of knowledge. This in itself is an interesting recognition, since we 'know' so little about knowledge. We are taught knowledge, but we are taught very little, if anything, about what knowledge is. Consider the story of the teacher who inquired of her class of young children 'What is the distance from Cambridge to Oxford?' After several children volunteered quite incorrect replies, one 7-year-old surprised the teacher with the reply, 'The distance between Cambridge and Oxford is 84 miles, but could you tell me one thing Miss, What is distance?' The education we have imbibed has bequeathed us a form of understanding knowledge which is not unlike this child's understanding of distance. She could produce an admirable number of instances of distance but she was never clear what she was producing instances of when she did so. Similarly, we often do not understand the things we know. We may know, for example, how many metres high Mount Everest stands, but we undeniably do not understand how high it is, if when go to climb it the next morning we are still wearing our shorts and haven't packed a lunch. Just as there is a difference between knowing and understanding, there is a difference between knowing and *understanding what knowing is*.

There are many things which could be said about the concept of 'knowing' that students — even university students — do not ordinarily know and understand, and one of the most important of these things concerns the extent to which knowledge is value-laden. Common to the various categories of knowledge formulated by western institutions of education is a value which both motivates and defines knowledge, and is the value we place upon knowledge as a *form of power*. According to the view to be advanced here, knowledge enshrines the values which prompt and motivate its discovery. Inasmuch as knowledge is motivated by our insatiable appetite for power, the search for knowledge recapitulates the preoccupation with power which holds our culture captive. What we have in western culture come to accept as knowledge, in other words, is determined presuppositionally by whether what is known provides some advantage to the knower.

It was perhaps Sir Francis Bacon (1561–1626) who can be credited with having formulated an aggressive creed to define the science of knowing. In his *Novum Organum* (1620) he explicitly stated that 'knowledge' is power over nature'. The point of knowledge is the power it provides for the material advancement of humankind. The science of knowing and learning, he urged, must proceed with this goal in mind. Bacon argued that power over nature could never be realized by relying on definitions of knowledge as truth as held by the philosophers of old. The so called 'wisdom' that Aristotle, Plato and most other Greek philosophers held was to him, 'contentious' and void of action. Their 'wisdom', he unabashedly wrote, '. . . abounds in words but is barren of works. . . . For fruits and works are as it were sponsors and sureties for the truth of philosophies.' (Bacon, 1960, Book 1, Aphorisms LXXI_LXXIII). Although he considered the ideas of Democritus and other ancient mechanists to be possessed of theoretical significance for the 'new science' he, nevertheless, dismissed as otiose the passive metaphysical approach to knowledge (what he called the 'why of things') and replaced it with the 'active how' (the 'facts' and 'works') of things.

Bacon's impact on the concept of knowledge as power has been monumental. Because knowledge is a form of power, knowledge becomes a form of control, and the more control we have, the more secure we become, or so Bacon and his followers supposed. Bacon's cherished hope was that knowledge provided power though the acquisition of predictability. The more readily the behaviour of the things of nature could be predicted, the more readily they could be controlled. Technologies born out of this value-laden form of knowledge as power will themselves replicate through their own interventions in nature the obsession of our culture with domination and subjugation.

Technological control on the service of human advantage traditionally depends upon recasting the face and the things of the earth in a form which makes their behaviour predictable in ways which suit our needs and desires. The process by way of which technology achieves this measure of control depends upon what we shall call '*transformative subjugation*'.

The technological process of control through *transformative subjugation* involves taking the vital things of nature and converting them into the utilitarian things of mankind. Technology thus gives us power over nature by systematically synthesizing and reconstructing it. Technology is the tool we have created to recreate nature.

The subject matter of educational knowledge is increasingly predictable because it is increasingly synthetic. Our technological interventions are designed predominantly to gain us control over nature by taking things which are natural and transforming them into things which are unnatural. Technology is by its very nature the process by which, if you like, we re-order God's creation into our own creation. Strangely when we do this, we recast the face of the earth definitely not in God's image (however that may be construed theologically) and certainly not in our own image (as perverse as that might be), but rather in the image of our technology. We have committed ourselves to a form of technology, sustained by a form of knowledge, the remit of which is to turn the natural environment into an artificial one, over which we have great control. We thus literally surround ourselves with our technology. We embrace the things we manufacture, along with the machines we have made to manufacture those things. And as we have seen in the previous chapter, we also all too often unwittingly embrace the toxic of by-products of the industries that produce the artefacts which adorn the new environment we synthesize for ourselves.

The prophetic destiny of this value-laden knowledge is fulfilled by its legacy of domination and control. We have indeed been bequeathed the power of giants. But what is the kingdom over which we have gained power? Technology achieves its promise of control and subjugation by taking the living things of nature and transforming them, without conscience, into the dead things of our own creation. Every application of a technology of power results ultimately in converting something which is living into something which is dead. The process of a technology of power does this because the less alive something is, the more predictable and thus controllable it is. This is the sense in which technological transformations are also subjugations. The more chemically inert a thing is the easier it becomes to subsume that thing under the aegis of mathematical laws designed to quantify its behaviour in countless circumstances of our interactions, both personally and by way of our machines, to do it. The more alive and conscious something is, the more incalculable its behaviour becomes. This being so, the world of technological control determines that the world be reconstituted by things which have by way of technology had the very life within them systematically withdrawn from them. Technology has indeed made us powerful, but the world over which it has bequeathed us power is a world of dead things. The technological world is a world we may, to a large extent control, but the world we control is paradoxically in essence a world of death and conformity. Driven by the lust for power, the form of knowledge we have selected to propagate in our educational institutions shapes, informs and conditions the form of technology which grows out of it. Our argument is that technology is thus as value-laden as is the concept of knowledge underpinning it and in the sense of transformative subjugation specified above, antithetical to environmental goals of respect for, and cultivation of, the living earth.

Towards a Theory of Transformative Subjugation

In the previous chapter it was argued that western society's unbridled commitment to technological development has led almost ineluctably to catastropic disruptions to the patterns of the earth's reproductive capacities. It has been the burden of the present chapter thus far to trace the roots of the environmetal crisis confronting society to a system of education sustained by a form of knowledge driven by western culture's preoccupation with power and control. It was observed that inasmuch as educational knowledge is motivated by power, the forms of technology to which it gives rise will, by their very logical character, manifest power through domination, expropriation, exploitation and subjugation. Technology is not a neutral concept, awaiting our application of it to judge whether it is used for good or bad. It is to be conceeded from the outset that some applications of technology may be more heinous than others. The point of our deliberations, however, has been to show that the lust for power is the precondition or presuppostion which conditions even the most beneficial applications of technology. It is the logical character of a technology driven by power to transform the world of nature into increasingly synthesized and artificial environments. To achieve this end virtually every application of technology of power results in the systematic conversion of living things into dead things which admit of greater control and predictability than the living things from whence they came. Technology subdues nature by transforming it and it is this sense of deprecatory conversion that is depicted by our expression 'transformative subjugation'. Having laboured the foregoing connections between the particular form of knowledge propagated in our schools and the technologization of the earth which results from this propagation, we are now in a position to reflect upon the extent to which the educative commitment to technology has disenfranchized us from nature.

Part of the covert rationale for the technologization of nature is that technology will transform the world in such a way that it becomes progressively shaped to suit our every purported need. This being so, our interaction with nature has been confined largely to our attempts to dominate and control it by reconstructing it to make it adapt to us. It is in this sense that we have, as a culture, sought total control and mastery over the environment. By controlling nature, we have been misled, however, into thinking that we have thereby made ourselves more secure. If night falls, we use the technology of power to turn night into day. If our homes or workplaces are too hot, we use the technology of power to convert warm air into cool air. When our food crops do not grow fast enough or as abundantly as we would like, we coax them to obey our will through chemically fertilizing the soils or genetically engineering the plants themselves. If our produce does not travel well, we engineer it to make it travel better, and if goods do not have a long enough shelf-life to make marketing them worthwhile, we either irradiate them or dose them with preservatives which inhibit their demise or take from them their most living parts (as when the food industry takes the germ from the kernal of wheat) to ensure that our foods are converted into products so inert that they are almost invulnerable to decay.

The way in which technology achieves this control is not only to transform things which are natural into things which are artificial, but further to take the things which have been synthesized and convert them into things which are even more artificial. What also happens in the context of transformative subjugation is that we surround ourselves progressively by the dead things which our machines produce or by things such as our machines themselves which are dead.

The problem is not just the obvious one of environmental degradation — the much discussed despoiling of our rivers and lakes, our toxic assault upon the sea, the pollution of the air we breathe and the mindless rape of the land. What we are endeavouring to bring into bold relief is that the environmental crisis confronting the world globally is far more subtle and relates to the philosophy of nature to which we have unwittingly been committed by virtue of the concept of knowledge we embrace.

Whatever the problem nature presents and wherever a conflict of interest emerges between our interests and those of the environment, the outcome is almost always the same. We rely on technology to control nature by using it to transform it. The more we seek to control nature, the more transformed and artificial it becomes and the more detached we ourselves become from nature. This has led to one of the most serious and neglected aspects of the environmental crisis confronting us, namely, its adverse and peculiar impact on the health of the community. To see that this is so, one need only consider the systematic transformation of our personal environments. The workplace is a case in point.

Most large office buildings are still designed so that they imperialize and dominate the environment rather than harmonize with it. Standing as fortresses against nature, their internal environments benefit little from the resources which nature is capable of providing. By virtue of their very architectural structures, these buildings need to be artificially lit, artificially heated in winter and artificially cooled in summer. The floors of our workplaces are almost invariably covered with synthesized materials, including carpets of synthetic fibres, linoleum or tiles. The tables at which we work and the chairs on which we sit are usually made of metal and plastic. Drapes and other furnishings are often made of synthetic materials, as are the paints with which we colour our walls. In addition to the electrical wiring which encircles us, we are exposed to fumes and levels of electromagnetic radiation different in kind from, and sometimes many millions of times greater than, the 'normal' background levels found in nature. Photocopiers, fax machines and computers, and even microwave ovens in staff kitchens, combine to contribute to the unwitting transformation of the natural environment into an artificial one. That living plants are unable to grow successfully in our workplaces is an important clue to which we pay little or no attention. That we are able to adorn our offices only with plastic and silk plants, or living plants which only survive by being removed on a regular basis for resuscitation, is in itself a revealing but sad commentary on the suitability of internal environments for living things. An excellent example of the transformative subjugation of our internal work and living environments is the recently identified form of environmental pollution known as 'tight building syndrome'. Given the importance we place in our argument on the sometimes subtle but serious adverse impact of synthesized environments on human health, a brief divagation to explore the gravity of the problem will be apposite. This pattern of transforming the natural world into an artificial one is virtually ubiquitous — it can be found in almost any example of our interaction with nature. We interact with nature largely to destroy it in the form in which we find it.

Today much of our time is spent indoors, whether it be at home, at work or in transit. The extent to which we have synthesized the environments of our homes and workplaces is in one sense an indicator of technological progress. What we have yet to learn is that the price of progress can be high. Whether we actually improve the quality of our lives through the creation of highly synthesized, artificial environments, is a question we can no longer afford to ignore. The risk of environmentally induced illness (EI) also known as the 'tight building syndrome', is a reminder that something has gone badly wrong.

In the name of progress, timber, instead of being sawn into boards, is now chipped into fragments and reconstituted with plastic glues into boards for furniture and flooring. Plastic polymers replace wool and cotton to form the fabrics of our clothes, floor coverings and curtains. Plastic sheeting replaces leather on our furnishings and shoes. Our homes and offices are insulated against the temperature cycles of nature with plastic foams. These plastics also form the basis of cushions, mattresses and toys. Most of these materials, chemically manufactured, exude trace amounts of unreacted monomers, plasticizers and other chemicals into the air, especially soon after manufacture or when new. The concentration of these substances is commonly less than one part per million and has in the past been regarded as insignificant by the industry and most health boards. The possibility that chemicals at the levels found in the indoor air environment could provoke illness was recognized by T.G. Randolph in 1970 (pp. 223–65). Since that time the spectrum of symptoms of the tight building syndrome has grown to include 'attacks of headache, flushing, laryngitis, dizziness, nausea, extreme weakness, joint pains, unwarranted depression, voice impairment, exhaustion, inability to think clearly, arrhythmia or muscle spasms' (Rogers, 1987, p. 195).

The cases of over 1000 patients with undiagnosed chronic symptoms were examined by S. Rogers in the early 1980s. Rogers found that patients were often able to associate the onset of disease with the purchase of new carpeting, furniture, beds, cabinets, renovation of the home or office, moving into a new dwelling or insulating with urea formaldehyde foam insulation (UFFI) (ibid.).

Of the many chemicals released, one of the agents now known to trigger the above symptoms is formaldehyde, a chemical exuded by many glues, resins and UFFI. In the United States, measurements of ambient levels of formaldehyde have shown that new mobile homes, newly constructed homes with particle-board subflooring, offices recently renovated with paneling or prefabricated walls, new clothing, or even new carpeting or new furnishings, and homes with new beds and cabinetry can accumulate as much formaldehyde, as a result of offgasing, as a UFFI home.

In the early 1980s, a survey of homes revealed that the average level of formaldehyde found in residences without UFFI was 0.03 ppm and 0.12pp for houses with UFFI (both with and without health complaints). Some mobile homes had levels up to 0.4 ppm and the mean level for several hospitals was 0.55 ppm (ibid.). These levels are particularly significant considering that formaldehyde has been shown to produce cancers in laboratory animals at levels as low as 6ppm (Nelson and Levine, 1986, pp. 23–35).

As discussed earlier in this chapter, another aspect of the indoor environment–health connection has been the concentration of people in large buildings to meet the demands of limited space and its efficient utilization, urged upon us by technological progress. The impracticality of incorporating a sufficient number of windows which open, has made it necessary to control the environment of the inner regions of these mega structures with air-conditioning. One problem with air-conditioning, however, is that it tends to circulate contaminated air and bypasses the sterilizing effect of sunlight that would otherwise purify the air. In one instance investigated by the Australian Goverment Analytical Laboratories (AGAL) in the early 1990s, a 'quick response' crew was suffering from headaches, sinus and respiratory tract problems. Evaluation of the room revealed a high concentration of airborne moulds. In another case, staff at federal electoral offices were complaining of lethargy, headaches, sinus problems and coughing. An investigation by the Occupational Hygiene section of AGAL found that there were high dust levels, incorrect temperature and humidity control, and high levels of volatile organic compounds (VOCs) in the building (see The Australian Government Analytical Laboratories Newsletter, 1996, pp. 1, 3).

It is now believed that indoor 'air pollution' in modern buildings exposes humans to both a wider ranging and a higher concentration of VOCs than any other source. Common sources of VOC emissions include synthetic carpets, tiles and flooring, contact adhesives and sealants, paints and varnishes and office furniture. The compound 4-phencylocyclohexane (4-PCH) has been identified as the major source of 'new carpet' odour. VOCs emitted from carpets include vinyl acetate and propane-1, 2, -diol. The health effects of these VOCs when present at low concentrations over long periods, are unknown (Scheirs and Bigger, 1996, pp. 261–4). A common plasticizer in vinyl flooring is diethylhexylphthalate (DEHP) which can be 30 per cent by weight of the vinyl. If the vinyl is overlaying damp concrete the DEHP can hydrolyze to 2-ethyl-hexanal which has a sickly odour. Other VOCs released from flooring materials include toluene and xylene from adhesives, phenol and trimellitic from floor leveling resins. This latter compound is considered to be extremely toxic as it causes immunological sensitization and severe respiratory irritation (ibid.).

The gradual breakdown of polystyrene-base adhesives that are used to secure bathroom tiles can result in toxic vapours of the chemical benzaldehyde.

Wall paints are well known for producing high levels of VOCs. Water-based acrylate paints release significant levels of butyl methacrylate and contain glycol ethers. These latter compounds are not readily detected by the human olfactory system due to their high odour threshold. However these compounds have been found to persist in the indoor air for up to six months after the application of the paint (ibid.).

Office and home furniture such as chairs, sofas and mattresses can emit volatile irritants that originate from the sponge rubber padding and upholstery. Polyurethane foam has been known to emit over 70 different chemical compounds after manufacture including aldehydes, chloroform and chlorobenzene.

In certain situations, much higher levels of VOCs can be produced. In bathrooms, where chlorinated water is used chloroform levels may be in the range 50–250 micrograms per cubic metre. Fresh magazines may cause room toluene concentration to rise to 3800 micrograms per cubic metre. Recently dry-cleaned clothing may emit from 100 to 10,000 micrograms of tetrachloroethylene per square metre of clothing per hour (Brown, S., 1997, pp. 10–13). Dry building construction products such as plastics, rubber, flooring, carpet and wallpaper can typically emit from 1000–10,000 micrograms of VOCs per square metre of surface each hour. Wet products such as polishes, cleaners, disinfectants and deodorizers used to clean and maintain walls and floors may emit up to 1,000,000 micrograms of VOCs per square metre of surface each hour (ibid.).

S. Brown from the Commonwealth Scientific Industrial Research Organization (CSIRO) Division of Building, Construction and Engineering has pooled the measurements of VOCs in buildings from a number of studies. For established dwellings the average total VOC concentration in indoor air was 1130 micrograms per cubic metre, while for buildings less than three months old, the total VOC level was much higher at approximately 4000 micrograms per cubic metre. Brown points out that these values were the geometric means of a large pool of data. For a proportion of buildings the concentrations were substantially greater. For example, the 90 percentile total VOC concentrations were 4600 micrograms per cubic metre in established dwellings, while for new dwellings and offices the total concentrations in the indoor air was a massive 18,000 micrograms per cubic metre (ibid.). These values are considerably in excess of the maximum indoor air concentrations for total VOCs recommended by the Australian National Health and Medical Research Council (NHMRC) of 500 micrograms per cubic metre (NHMRC, 1992). In poorly air-conditioned buildings these VOCs can accumulate or be circulated throughout a number of rooms and offices.

There are thus many aspects of aggravated health conditions and specific health problems arising from air-conditioning. A tragic example of one such problem was drawn to public attention by way of a meeting at the Belle Vue Stratford Hotel in Philadelphia in 1976. A convention of the American Legion was in progress when 182 of the war veterans attending contracted what was then an unknown form of pneumonia, 29 of the legionnaires died. This was the first recorded outbreak of what has since become known as legionnaire's disease. Research undertaken on this condition has revealed that it is mainly associated with poorly designed or improperly maintained air-conditioning systems. Another outbreak in the west end of London in 1988 claimed the lives of five people, along with a further 28 suffering from pneumonia (Purkis and Wilson, 1989, p. 34). Legionnaire's disease, just one of many diseases induced by so-called technological progress, serves as an incisive example of the truth expressed by Florence Nightingale's celebrated statement,

'There are no specific diseases — there are specific disease conditions' (cited by Dubos, 1959, p. 148).

In addition to the transformative subjugation of the external environment we also synthesize the foods we eat and the liquids we drink. In this context, for example, we have used technology to convert natural foods into artificial foods by adding dead things to them in the form of preservatives to increase their shelf-life. Similarly we add other chemicals to enhance the flavour or colour of the foods we eat. Because we have largely destroyed both the nutritional value and flavour of our foods by processing them, we end up having to try (in futility) to restore by fortification the nutritional value we have already robbed from them. In other words, to cover up for the loss incurred by the former technological transformations of our food, we perpetuate the viscious circle by increasing the level of techno-logical interventions, making our food look more like a non-living machine than the living emblem nature once was. Just as we surround ourselves with dead things, we thus also unwittingly welcome dead things within our bodies every day of the week.

The modern refining and processing of foods affects the dietary patterns and human nutrient intakes around the world to an extent appreciated by few. The vegetable oils we consume are refined, our sugar is refined, and our major cereals (wheat, corn and rice) are refined. The size of the food refining industry is enormous. For example, in India, the second largest producer of rice in the world, approxim-ately 75 per cent of the 80 million tonnes produced is refined by removing the bran. This bran, which constitutes nearly 8.5 per cent of the rice grain, is actually highly nutritious being rich in natural oils (including essential fatty acids), protein, minerals and vitamins. Yet much of this bran is further refined with organic chem-ical solvents used to make some edible oils for margarine manufacture, with the larger portion being used for soap production and other related products (refer to *Journal of the American Oil Chemists Society*, 1989, pp. 620–3). From this one example alone, it can be seen that nearly 60 million tonnes of a whole food has been split up into its components with important balance trace nutrients removed and largely destroyed. Furthermore, this processing involves the use of thousands of tonnes of organic chemical solvents which eventually have to be discarded into the environment.

Another aspect of the processed food problem is the huge range of everyday foods (and particularly the so-called 'fast foods') which are simply combinations of refined fats, and refined sugar with water, colours and processing chemical added. An examination of the 15 largest multinational food companies in the world reveals that the majority of their products are based on combinations of the refined food groups mentioned above. In 1989, the sales from these 15 companies alone amount to more than 1000 billion dollars annually (Gaynor, 1989, p. 35). Yet this is but a small fraction of the income derived around the world from the sale of nutritionally deficient refined foods.

In the United States, the food processing industry has an enormous impact on the economy with the sum of direct and induced effects giving a total industry output, reported in October 1996, as being greater than US$1.8 trillion annually (Roberts, Dillon and Siebenmorgen, 1996, pp. 65–8). In Australia, the food and beverage industry is one of the largest manufacturing industry sectors with a turnover of US$35.6 billion and employing 867,000 people in the 1992–3 financial year (Desmarchelier, 1996, pp. 668–77).

Fast foods: Costly to Our Health and the Environment

In Japan, western processed foods such as hamburgers and other 'fast foods' are replacing traditional diets particularly in highly industrialized areas such as Osaka-Kobe. These dietary changes, in turn, appear to be having a seriously adverse impact on the health of the Japanese people who have adopted them. In 1984, 46 per cent of people in the Osaka-Kobe region passed physical checkups, compared with only 21 per cent in the 1994 health survey (Hadfield, 1995, p. 5). Across the country, the Japan Hospital Association has found that the number of people with kidney and cholesterol problems also doubled during the 10-year period (ibid.).

Western fast-food companies are also changing India's eating habits, affecting not only the health of those who can afford the foods but undermining the nation's agricultural industry. Maneka Gandhi, a former minister for the environment in India's parliament, believes that the intensive farming of poultry and other livestock which fast-food restaurants encourage will have serious implications for India's ability to feed itself.

In a paper submitted to India's parliament in 1995 Gandhi warned that using food crops such as maize to feed chickens was a poor use of resource. Grain could feed five times as many people if consumed directly rather than being given to animals to be transformed into meat, milk and eggs. In addition, she pointed out that around 1700 litres of water were consumed in the modern commercial production of half a kilogram of chicken meat. This amounted to 20 times the amount of water 'a normal Indian family is supposed to use in one day — if it gets water all' (Patel, 1996, pp. 14–15).

In many western countries, children face a daily barrage of advertisements for processed junk food on television. A 13-country survey carried out by Consumers International found that children in Australia, the United States and the United Kingdom see more than 10 advertisements per hour during children's television viewing times (Coghlan, 1996, p. 8). Heavily processed and refined foods such as sweets, breakfast cereals and fast foods accounted for more than half the food advertisements in the survey.

On British television, nearly 95 per cent of the foods advertised were high in fat, sugar, salt or fixtures of these ingredients, and advertising for non-processed foods such as fruit and vegetables was virtually non-existent (ibid.). In Sweden and Norway, where television advertising directed towards children is banned, young people rarely see food advertisements. Consumers International fear that this type of advertising may undermine advice on healthy eating. A survey of fast foods by the Australian Consumers' Association found that fast foods tend to be high in fat, low in complex carbohydrate and high in sodium. This is not the recipe for a healthy diet. A well-balanced diet is low in fat and sodium, and high in complex carbohydrates and fibre (see also, *Choice*, April 1994, pp. 7–9).

Not only is food technology being used to add economic value to food that is often nutritionally poor, but part of the financial return from the sale of these foods is used, in turn, to promote other processed foods which are nutritionally inferior to the ones provided by nature. The public are lured into buying more and more processed foods which generates more commercial revenue and encourages more sales, thereby setting in motion a vicious circle which spirals towards ill health. Refined foods are favoured by food companies because their properties are more predictable in manufacturing processes. The technique of separating basic food into components and then recombining them with flavours and colours and manu-factured shapes also gives endless possible combinations for new products. It is known that consumers will tend to consume more of a product, for example, if is produced in a variety of shapes or colours (Rolls, 1986, pp. 68–71). Thus the potential for increasing sales via new products is almost unlimited. However, the point that has been lost amidst the fray is that very few of these manufactured foods are beneficial for health, and some, as we have seen, may be dangerous to health.

Modern, large-scale food processing, particularly of fast foods, is also increas-ing the risk of major outbreaks of food-borne disease. In the United States, a multi-state outbreak of food poisoning was traced to the use of pre-frozen meat patties which were later served in hamburgers at a chain of hamburger restaurants. Ac-cording to reports, 583 people were affected across four states. In all, 171 patients required hospitalization, and 41 developed a particularly serious condition known as hemolytic uremic syndrome (HUS) (Bettelheim, 1996, pp. 20–6). The illness was produced by an *Escherichia coli* (E.coli) bacterium described as serotype 0157.H.7. This bacterium can produce permanent illness including kidney failure, brain damage and diabetes. Dr K. Bettelheim from the Victorian Infectious Dis-eases Reference Laboratory in Australia believes the multi-state outbreak in the western United States occurred only because the meat patties were prepared in bulk in one plant and shipped to many restaurants. The meat for these patties came from a variety of abattoirs, which drew their supplies from many farms. Since meat offcuts are used in hamburger meat production and modern machines produce tonnes of thoroughly mixed mince meat at a time, it is possible theoretically for a single hamburger patty to contain meat which has come from thousands of different animals. Dr Bettelheim suggests that:

> The extensive development of fast-foods and the sale and storage of frozen foods, and the use of microwave ovens to heat foods rapidly may all contribute to the provision of new niches for potential pathogens to enter or survive in the food chain. (ibid.)

The interconnection of human food production, with other human activities such as sewage treatment is illustrated by Bettelheim's suggestion that:

> A simple path for the spread of a pathogen like E.coli 0157 to a new environment
> could be that an individual carrying it jets to the new areas, his/her faeces enter the
> sewage, which is inadequately treated before discharge into the sea. The E.coli
> infect the sea birds. When the weather at sea is rough, they feed and defecate on
> pastures where cattle and sheep graze. The route is then short from the pasturing
> animals to human infection. (ibid.)

Strong support for Dr Bettelheim's hypothesis has come from a British study published in March 1997 which found that 3 per cent of 700 samples of fresh gull faeces collected from beaches where they feed contained *E.coli 0157* (Brown, P., 1997, p. 11).

At the annual meeting for the American Society for Microbiology in May 1997, members were told that dangerous viruses are being spread around the world through the sewage held in aircraft. A study by researchers from the University of North Carolina found that from 40 samples of sewage pumped from international flights landing at United States airports, 19 contained infectious viruses that had survived exposure to disinfecting chemicals in the aircraft's sewage tanks. The leader of the study, Mark Sobsey, commented that the range of illnesses that could be transported by the world's airlines is 'quite worrisome'. Furthermore, even when aircraft sewage is pumped into local municipal sewage treatment works, only about 90 per cent of viruses are eradicated. The remaining 10 per cent of the viruses survive and are discharged into the environment (Coghlan, 1997, p. 7).

A recent survey of pollution levels at several of Sydney's popular beaches, which are not far from where treated sewage is pumped into the sea, found very high levels of pathogens. For several of the beaches, including the famous Bondi Beach, 98–100 per cent of water samples taken over a two-year period had faecal coliform counts greater than 1000 coliforms per millilitres (refer to State of Environment Advisory Council, 1996, pp. 8–11).

In January 1995, Australia experienced its first outbreak of hemolytic uremic syndrome (HUS), which was associated with the consumption of contaminated fermented sausage in the state of South Australia. There were 23 children hospitalized and one died (Goldwater and Bettelheim, 1996, pp. 152–3).

The intensive farming of cattle where protein concentrates sometimes containing meat offal are fed to animals which are normally vegetarian is also linked to the spread of disease. Since the early 1980s, sheep processing wastes were incorporated into animal feed concentrates for cattle. In 1986 'mad cow disease' or bovine spongiform encephalopathy (BSE) was first diagnosed in British cattle. The sheep offal (brains and spinal cord) contained scrapie, a long-standing disease among sheep. By 1996, 10 Britons aged from 18–41 years had died from a type of Creutzfeldt–Jakob disease (CJD) which was probably caused by eating beef contaminated with BSE (Pearce, 1996b, p. 5). A total of 40 cases of CJD had been diagnosed altogether. Because modern mass production processes were used in producing this unnaturally high protein animal feed, thousands of cattle were infected and, by 1996, 158,000 cattle had died (Pain, 1996, p. 6). Despite widespread publicity about the problem, contaminated high-protein animal feed was also being fed to pigs and chickens up to March 1996, even though a feed ban for cattle was introduced in 1988 (Pearce, 1996a, p. 5). Evidence that cows can pass the disease to their calves has also led to some fears that women might pass on the deadly disease to their children before showing the symptoms themselves (ibid., p. 5).

Modern meat production has introduced other possible disease exacerbating factors. For example, many intensive farming methods may reduce the proportion of available polyunsaturated fatty acids in food and increase the proportion of saturated fats (Denton and Lacey, 1991, pp. 179–89). Modifying the fatty acid profile of animal products through feedlot technology alters the fatty acid profile in the blood of humans consuming these foods which may in turn affect their susceptibility to heart disease and cancer (Noakes, Nestel and Clifton, 1996, pp. 42–6). Since the 1940s many farmers have given their livestock antibiotic growth promoters. It was found that antibiotics improved the animal's feeding efficiency so that the animals need less food to reach marketable weight. There is now growing concern, however, that this practice could promote the emergence of bacterial strains which have genetic resistance to antibiotics. The hypothesis is that antibiotic-resistant bacteria could then cause diseases in humans that would be untreatable with conventional antibiotics.

In 1983, there was an outbreak of food poisoning in the United States which involved a strain of the bacteria *Salmonella* that was resistant to a number of antibiotics. The strain was linked to hamburgers made from the meat of cattle fed on the antibiotic chlortetracycline (Bonner, 1997, pp. 24–7).

Not everyone is agreed about the best way to resolve the problem. Some researchers believe, for instance, that if the use of low-dose antibiotics in animal production is stopped, there will be an increase in the incidence of diseases in farm animals which require other drugs to control them, or alternatively farm animals will simply die. Supporters of this view site, for example, the situation where following the ban on the use of all antibiotic growth promoters by Sweden in 1986, an extra 50,000 pigs died of 'scours' diarrhoea (ibid.).

Part of the problem is that antibiotics treat only the symptoms, not the causes of diseases. The National Research Council in the United States in its comprehensive review *Alternative Agriculture* correctly reminds us that many of the animal diseases that farmers currently confront are a direct consequence of the intensive animal breeding measures now used by farmers, which forces animals to be raised in highly unnatural and confined conditions. The National Research Council refers to a number of studies which have shown that proper hygienic care of animals with access to fresh air, sunlight, clean pasture and water, together with proper waste disposal, substantially reduces disease in farm animals and the associated dependence on antibiotics (refer to National Research Council, 1989).

Nature's blueprint for health applies to animals as well as to humans. As we recognize that the earth's resources are limited, the use of animals for food must be urgently reviewed in favour of more sustainable forms of food production, (Smith, 1977) along with food production techniques such as permaculture (Mollison, 1992).

In the United States, approximately 200 million tonnes of maize are grown annually (Myers, 1985, p. 34) the bulk of which is fed to livestock to produce beef for hamburgers, and plump chickens for fast food. In the 1980s in Central America and Amazonia, cattle ranchers burned at least 2.5 million hectares of forest each year, mainly to clear land to raise beef for lucrative export markets in the developed world (ibid.). Much of the land is now incapable of sustaining even a crop of corn.

In Australia clearing land, together with overgrazing, have led to massive destruction of soil structure as well as extensive salinity problems in some areas (refer to State of the Environment Advisory council, op. cit.). Given the destructive nature of western livestock corn production on the soil, (Smith, op. cit.) together with its high fertilizer and pesticide/herbicide requirements, (refer to National Research Council, 1996, pp. 40–8) it is clear that meat, and especially beef, should be considered a luxury food in terms of the environmental costs required to produce it, not an expendable for fast foods.

Furthermore, some observers have noted that modern production methods may mean that up to 100,000 litres of water have to be used to produce 1 kilogram of beef compared to say 2000 litres to produce 1 kilogram of soy beans (Pearce, 1997, p. 7).

Nature's own fast foods, fruits and nuts, not only contribute in most cases to a sustainable environment (trees build up the soil, prevent erosion and contribute positively to the oxygen–carbon dioxide balance) but are in harmony with nature's own blueprint by providing optimum nutrition (Drecker, Maher and Kearney, 1996, pp. 241–5).

Health Implications of Refined Foods

In general there are two important aspects of refined foods that have a direct bearing on health. Firstly, there is the removal of essential nutrients during refining, and secondly the subsequent addition, in most cases, of chemical additives, flavours and colours to make the 'new' food more desirable. Both these aspects are inextricably interwoven with the diseases of civilization.

Let us now consider some of these health implications in more detail. We now know that there are at least 14 essential trace elements required for human nutrition, ranging in quantity from a few micrograms to milligrams per day (Mertz, 1981, p. 1333). The elements perform unique functions, often acting as catalytic or structural components of larger molecules which are essential for specific biochemical pathways. For example, chromium is required in microgram quantities for proper metabolism of glucose or sugars (ibid., p. 1336). White sugar and white flour, which are ultimately a source of glucose for the body, are refined to the extent that they no longer contain chromium. Furthermore, chromium deficiency is now implicated as a significant risk factor for cardiovascular disease (ibid., p. 1337), illustrating simply one of the many mechanisms linking refined foods with heart disease.

Another example is the element zinc. More than 90 zinc-containing enzymes have now been identified, including at least one in every major enzyme classification (Sanders, 1979, p. 35). Moreover, zinc appears to have a major role in nucleic acid metabolism, protein synthesis, normal development of the outer horny layer of skin and sexual maturation. Zinc deficiency can also cause impaired immune response (ibid., p. 36). The nutritional requirements for this metal are particularly high in children (refer to Committee on Nutrition, 1978, p. 408) and deficiencies have been linked with foetal abnormalities (Halmesmaki, Elikorkala and Alfthan, 1985, p. 1470). However, substantial quantities of this element are removed by the refining of sugar cane and the milling of wheat (Committee on Nutrition, 1978, p. 408).

In 1929, *The Australian Journal of Diseases of Children* published a case where:

> A boy aged 12 had been termed by psychiatrists and psychologists a 'nervous hyperkinetic child'. To use his own words, 'I have to keep on going and be doing something . . .'. His diet was meagre in meats and vegetables and rich in candy and cookies. (cited in Kruesi, 1986, p. 150)

Since that time there has been a lively debate linking refined sugar to hyperactivity (ibid.) and antisocial behaviour (Harper and Gans, 1986, pp. 142, 146) although the latter claims are especially controversial. What is arguable, however, is that foods and food constituents can adversely affect human health and behaviour (Lieberman and Wurtman, 1986, pp. 139–41) which raises very serious implications and new responsibilities for the food-processing industries.

For example, we know that nutrients are intimately involved in the regulation of brain function through their cofactor and precursor roles. However, as C.E. Leprohon-Greenwood and G.H. Anderson at the University of Toronto Faculty of Medicine point out:

> The role of vitamins and minerals in metabolic processes in most body cell type has been well described. However, their role in the nerve cell, particularly in the process of neurotransmission and view of current developments in neurochemistry, requires considerable elucidation. Furthermore, there has been relatively little examination of the effects of marginal deficiencies on brain metabolism and function. (Leprohon-Greenwood and Anderson, 1986, p. 132)

In addition to this relative uncertainty of the biochemical role of vitamins and minerals in neurotransmitter metabolism, the question must also be raised as to whether the brain has any special ability, relative to other tissues, to preserve its metabolic and neurochemical activity during nutrient deficiencies (ibid., p. 133).

The refining of carbohydrate foods, such as sugar cane and cereals, involves not only the removal of vitamins and minerals, but also the removal of dietary fibre. More than 20 years ago Burkitt and Trowell presented a powerful case from the available research directly linking refined carbohydrate foods and diseases of civilization, such as bowel cancer, ischaemic heart disease (IHD), diabetes, gallstones, constipation, appendicitis, diverticular disease, hiatus hernia, dental caries, periodontal disease and obesity (Burkitt and Trowell, 1975). Their pioneering work had been inspired by the seminal ideas of a British naval doctor, T.L. Cleave who, in

1956, upon reflecting on his naval experience, was led to conclude that most of the diseases listed above could be attributed to the excessive consumption of refined carbohydrate foods and of refined sugar in particular (ibid., pp. 37–8). In the meantime, evidence has continued to accumulate establishing the protective role of whole food components and certain dietary fibre in heart disease, cancer and diabetes (Baghurst, Baghurst and Record, 1996, pp. S3–S35).

One of the most recent studies confirming the importance of dietary fibre, and particularly whole foods, was the Health Professionals Study by Dr Walter Willett and colleagues at Harvard University. The researchers found that men who ate more fibre, especially fibre from cereals, suffered fewer heart attacks (Rimm, Ascherio and Giovannucci, 1996, pp. 447–51). The dietary fibre from oats (Kahlon *et al.*, 1993, pp. 435–40) rice (Hammond, 1994, pp. 752–4) and legumes (beans, peas and lentils) (Kritchevsky, 1994, pp. 219–24) have been found to significantly reduce blood cholesterol levels, a major risk factor in heart disease, which accounts for 44 per cent of all deaths in Australia every year (Ramsey, 1996/1997, pp. 8–11).

Dietary fibre appears to protect against colon cancer by increasing stool bulk and/or decreasing intestinal transit times and thereby reducing exposure of the colon to carcinogens (Baghurst, Baghurst and Record, 1996). Sufficient levels of fibre in the diet also enhances the production in the colon of one important short chain fatty acid, butyric acid, which is believed to inhibit the growth and proliferation of certain tumours (ibid.). Sufficient fibre in the diet may also serve to reduce the risk of breast cancer in premenopausal women by lowering the circulating levels of oestrogen. Other evidence suggests that it may be that the oestrogen-lowering effects are due to other components of whole foods such as lignands or isofavonoid compounds which occur in very close association with dietary fibre (ibid.).

A newly emerging aspect of our modern refining and processing technology is the often lower glycemic index (GI) of processed foods. The GI of a food is a measure of how quickly a food is broken down during digestion into simple sugars and in particular into glucose. Fibre present in foods slows down the absorption of food components and the foods remain in the digestive system longer. Reducing the dietary fibre content of food by milling and processing increases the GI value.

High GI foods are believed to be a significant factor in the development of mature onset diabetes, one of the modern diseases of civilization (Brand Miller and Colagiuri, 1996). In many countries, including Australia and the United States, the number of people with non-insulin-dependent diabetes mellitus has reached epidemic proportions. In the early 1990s there were an estimated 7,000,000 diabetics in Australia and about 10 million diabetics in the United States where the estimated cost of the health care to the economy was US$90 billion (Zimmet and Cohen, 1995, pp. 116–17). Traditional foods in their least processed state generally have the lowest GI values. In contrast, highly processed foods such as white bread, cornflakes and rice bubbles have high GI values (Brand Miller, 1995, pp. 871S–93S). It is revealing that unprocessed natural bush honey has a lower GI than commercial processed honey.

The growing epidemic of diabetes and the economic cost to the community of this, one of many health problems associated with processed foods, casts serious doubts on the perceived value to our economy of the food processing industry.

Another aspect of food refining and food processing which has been essentially ignored by both food technologists and nutritionists is the destruction of the original masticatory properties of the original whole food. As machines and chemical processes are used to extract food components from the original whole food matrix, the need for chewing, in most instances (especially for any length of time) has been done away with. Yet the act of chewing provides mechanisms for maintaining good health.

After reviewing the literature relating to dental caries and periodontal disease, A.K. Adatia found that unrefined food is chewed for a longer period, and protective factors which are extracted during mastication remain in the mouth in a high concentration for a relatively longer period (cited in Burkitt and Trowell, 1975, p. 266). Furthermore, there is evidence to suggest that during compression of food between the cusps of teeth water-soluble protective factors were incorporated into enamel. Adatia goes on to suggest that vigorous mastication may help to resist dental caries and periodontal disease in other ways by pointing out:

> Foods which require to be chewed for a long period are cleared from the oral cavity more thoroughly than those not requiring much chewing. Refined carbohydrate foods such as white bread are retained for longer than whole wheat bread . . . Secondly, mastication not only encourages salivary flow, which would have a flushing effect on teeth, but also saliva of a high buffering power . . . Thirdly, vigorous mastication would wear and flatten the cusps of teeth, reduce the depths of the fissures and eliminate potential stagnation areas on the teeth . . . Finally, vigorous mastication of firm fibrous foods would remove debris from the exposed areas of the teeth and help to maintain the gingival tissues in good tone. (ibid., p. 268)

Mastication of firm, fibrous foods also stimulates optimum growth of the jaws. For example, children who regularly chew sugar cane not only usually have caries-free teeth but have perfect orthodontal development as well.

The consumption of refined foods also tends to promote over-nutrition, particularly excess consumption of calories which ultimately leads to obesity and many associated diseases. C.W. Binns wrote in 1989:

> Since these early days [of European settlement] the nutritional status of the colonizing peoples has improved dramatically to our present situation where overnutrition and imbalance of nutrient intakes are the major problems. (Binns, 1989, p. 27)

G.B. Gori, a deputy director at the United States National Cancer Institute, had suggested a decade earlier that:

> It is plausible that nutritional deficiencies and/or excesses influence metabolic processes that, after many years of insult, result in the appearance of certain forms of cancer. (Gori, 1979, p. 50)

Thus K. Heaton, after reviewing the relationship between food ingestion and disease, concluded that:

> ... carbohydrate refining makes the consumption of starch and sugar quicker, easier and less satisfying. As a natural obstacle to food ingestion, fibre adds effort to eating. Nutritionally, the role of fibre may be to act as a natural preventive of overnutrition. (Burkitt and Trowell, 1975, p. 61)

Unfortunately these properties of whole foods are rarely, if ever, considered by food technologists when refining and recombining foods. Thus nature's inter-meshed mechanisms to sustain health are thrown into disarray by the ignorant processing and refining of foods.

This nutritional vandalism does not stop here. Numerous food additives are combined with the refined remnants of food. Many of these are inimical to health, often in ways which are subtle or indirect. These additives include colours, flavours, sweeteners, preservatives, emulsifiers, thickeners and hundreds of specific food-processing chemicals. There are so many food chemicals used that, in the words of Arnold Bender, then Professor of Nutrition at Queen Elizabeth College in London, 'The trouble is that we're using so many of these additives that you couldn't possibly test them all — not in the next 100 years' (Saxon, 1978, p. 14). Add to the list of synthetic substances in our foods the highly synthesized highly processed chemicals we ingest by way of prescription medicines, food supplements, vitamin and mineral pills, aspirin, not to mention the chlorine, fluoride and aluminium in our toothpaste, soft drinks and municipal water supplies and you get a sense of the magnitude of the transformative subjugation.

Yet another facet of transformative subjugation is our direct skin contact with synthesized chemical environments. With few recent exceptions women and men have unwittingly covered themselves with the technologically deadened chemical products of nature. Consider for example the daily routines women undertake to cover their faces with various forms of make-up, just as men spread chemical creams on their faces to make the human beard more susceptible to the razor's edge. The arsenal of cosmetics is almost unlimited. These are chemical cleansing creams, moisturizers, foundations, anti-wrinkle creams, pimple and blemish creams, body powders, depilator creams, mascara, hair dyes, artificial tanning creams, lip-sticks, along with a barrage of deodorants, perfumes and body fragrances. Men fare little better with their daily contact with colognes and deodorants, not to mention the chemical substances in soaps and sunscreens, sometimes applied to the skin several times throughout the day by both sexes, especially in hot climates.

Mind Control

In addition to the adverse effects of transformative subjugation on our bodies, there are also other aspects of the technologization of nature that deserve our attention. Sufficient examples have now been provided to demonstrate that western society's insatiable appetite for power leads to the systematic fabrication and reconstruction of the whole of nature. What we have yet to consider is the extent to which the pattern of transformative subjugation extends to the field dimension of the human mind. Just as we synthesize the world of nature, both surrounding ourselves and literally consuming the lifeless products of our technology, so we synthesize even our experience of the world and open our minds to the multifarious images of death (violence set in the context of news, murder mysteries, action films, real-life videos of police encounters and even documentaries, to name only a few). In the presence of TV, videos, film and now even the Internet, we experience much of life vicariously, through the scripts of those who have reconstructed social reality for us.

We willingly receive unto our minds not only the synthesized images of people, either dead or dying, but we also open ourselves to the deadened images of people tormented and broken by the misfortunes and adversities of life. What we witness are broken promises, broken relations, broken hearts and broken lives. We are tempted by the advertisements to adopt what must approximate a religious fervour for as much information as possible on the vicissitudes of soap-stars, as if their TV lives were real. Not only are we distracted by this medium from experiencing life directly, but much of what we experience vicariously is itself a scripted unreality. Here we have yet another synthesized environment but this time it is the environment of mind which has fallen prey to the process of transformative subjugation.

One way in which we convert our experience, or what may be called our 'endemic experience', of nature is through technologies of visual and experiential media such as the virtual reality computer which present ever more powerful images of synthesized experiences as if they were actual. In this sense the synthesized world of virtual reality is tantamount to a whole new technology for the control of the mind. Moreover, because so much information can be processed at once, cybertechnology also provides new ways of exploiting and expropriating the precious resources of the earth at phenomenal speeds. Rifkin suggested that 'information theory' and 'cybernetics' used as a model for explaining nature's evolutionary advance, only 'provides humanity with an updated rationale for its continued manipulation of the environment' (Rifkin, 1989, p. 215).

Transformative Subjugation and Conformity

There is another dimension of the ramifications of transformative subjugation which impacts subtlely and directly not only upon health and environmental education but also upon education in its most comprehensive expression. Given our unbridled commitment to the technologization of nature, it is perhaps unsurprising that the systematic transformation of living things into dead things in the service of predictability and control leads to staggering conformity. Living things constitute dynamic systems which constantly change, adapt, interact and engender diversity. This is one reason why it is difficult to predict and control the behavioural exemplifications of living things. Driven by its obsession with predictability, technology converts living things to dead things in ways which maximize control through conformity.

It is easier to mass produce commodities which are the same than it is is to produce commodities which are different. The manufactures can more readily predict and control production rates, as well as the longevity of the product, its marketability and resilience. The price of this predictability and control, however, is depressing conformity at the expense of exhilarating creativity.

If one reflects from a different perspective our earlier examples of transformative subjugation in regard to synthesized environments, the extent of this conformity becomes palpably clear. Consider, for example, a typical lecture theatre, cinema, restaurant or other public buildings with substantial seating arrangements. The first thing to notice, beyond the fact that the immediate environment is likely to be made up almost entirely of the dead products of technology, is that the dead things with which we so willingly surround ourselves are respectively all the same. The sea of chairs before you, from 10 to 10,000, are likely all to be made of plastic and metal, constructed in exactly the same shape and painted exactly the same colour. Cast your eye to the light fixtures, they are likely to be all of the same size and shape, with exactly the same artificial light globes. The drapes will be the same, as are the tiles or linoleum on the floor, the size, colour, shape and even the pattern of the bricks on the wall. If you move to an adjacent room, you will likely discover a mirror image of the room which you just left behind. Everything is the same or so close to it as to be negligible, even the carpets, overhead projectors and white boards. If you were not certain that you had just walked from one room to the next, there is little or nothing in what you actually see, other than a different number or name on the door, to convince you that you had even moved. Not only do we surround ourselves with dead things but the dead things with which we surround ourselves have lost their identity and individuality. We re-order God's creation by reconstructing the living things of nature into the dead things of man, and in so doing, expose ourselves to environments constituted not only of death but of monotonous and meaningless commercial conformity.

As far as we are able to ascertain from the literature, no one has explored the adverse impact of such artificial and boring conformist environments not only on human health but on the human spirit and the creative imagination of the mind. How can we be maximally stimulated to cultivate our own or our children's creativity if we voluntarily surround ourselves and those we love with death, images of death, and conformity? Why should we expect the human mind to be awake, alert and alive to learning if the environment in which it finds itself by its very design and nature not only fails to stimulate these virtues but through deadness and conformity discourages them? Extend this pattern of the technological production of synthesized conformity to education's current obsession with the computer. Consistent with our earlier scenario of the conformity which fills our immediate work and learning environments, the addition of computers to the desktops of classrooms is itself but the addition of another piece of conformist furniture. The appearance of each computer in the room is almost assuredly to look exactly as every other computer looks. Not unlike the desks on which they are perched, every computer is made of the same artificial materials, is exactly the same shape, same colour and same size.

As if the conformity which results from surrounding ourselves with the deadness of our machines is not enough, consider the conformity of what we educationally prescribe as the newest mandatory form of knowledge acquisition in our schools via the computer. The educational ideal pursued in this regard is that every school student should have daily access to a computer for increasing periods as students advance through the grades. What seems not to be acknowledged about this recent development in knowledge skills and acquisition is that just as all the computers are the same on the outside, there is an important educational sense in which they are all the same on the inside. To put this less provocatively, there are a limited number of computer learning programs available in schools, written by a small number of people (compared to the population of computers users) who reflect a particular, dare we say, technological way of seeing the world and thus of organizing human experience. No matter how valuable that perspective and associated ways of thinking may be, they represent only a small portion of the spectrum of ways of thinking about the world. What has happened almost imperceptibly as a consequence of the national and global proliferation of educational computers is a philosophical shift to institutionalized intellectual conformity. We and our children are being coaxed, cajoled and forced into thinking about the world of ideas in ways which can be accommodated by the small number of computer programs, if not generally available, then actually used in schools. If education by way of knowledge acquisition stands for anything worth preserving, then it must at least protect its commitment to the continual enhancement of the intellectual imagination. By obliging school-children around the globe to think primarily and increasingly in ways that are circumscribed by machines, we have created learning environments which inadvertently encourage the conformity of thinking about the world in *machine-like* ways. Through the process of encouraging a progressive movement towards intellectual conformity, eduction has inadvertently encouraged progressive movement towards the death of the mind. If there is a difference between indoctrination and education, it must surely lie in the different things we do either to stimulate and nurture the intellectual imagination or to stifle and diminish it.

Thinking in the context of the computer is in essence a binary process of reasoning and one kind of reasoning amongst many kinds of reasoning. Just as education has revealed its bias in favour of promulgating a particular form of knowledge (an act of conformism in itself), so it is by way of its commitment to universal computer-learning betraying a bias in favour of the promulgation of a particular form of reasoning, an act of educational conformism no less pernicious than the commitment to knowledge as power and control.

One central philosophical problem with our mindless commitment to the computer, is that the kind of imagination which is required for the liberation of nature, the human spirit and the human mind is systematically excluded from the binary process of computer technology. Thinking in ways which are primarily delimited by the binary processes that characterize computer thinking, serves both to inform and to condition the way in which students perceive and interact with nature. While it is no doubt possible to think with computers in a range of interesting ways, the framework domain of the scope and limits of those ways of thinking are quite rigidly circumscribed by the nature of the programs which can actually be utilized by computers. In other words, there are certain structural boundaries to the creative imagination which are endogenous features of machine-like ways of thinking. In essence what happens is that the structure of the computer process of reasoning serves in the end to delimit the boundaries of human thought in ways which transform living thought into synthesized exemplars of mechanistic reasoning. In a bizarre sense, the metaphor of the computer as 'artificial intelligence' thus turns back on itself as it transforms the boundless domain of natural intelligence into the artificial confines of a synthesized one. The dynamics of this process unfold themselves, on the one hand, by encouraging conformity of intellectual response, while on the other hand, institutionalizing a form of life outside our schools which requires that students must be computer literate to survive in it.

The mordant irony of all this is that the very concept of knowledge we have put as the centre-piece of our learning is the very form of knowledge which gives rise to our technologies of transformative subjugation. And the more we turn to a form of knowledge driven by our insatiable appetite for power, the more destructive of the living things of nature our technologies will become. Amidst our seemingly endless technological transformations of the natural world into an artificial and highly synthesized environment, we have created an environment inimical to the health of the human organism and the ecological integrity of the environment. Having systematically transformed the world of living things into a world of dead things, the environment we have reconstructed for ourselves to live in is constituted largely, as we have seen, of dead things of conformity and artificiality. We have also observed that the technologization of nature, based on the concept of knowledge as power, has led to the reconstruction of natural environments into artificial and highly synthesized environments, in respect of which the human organism is well-adapted neither psychologically nor physiologically to live in. In our efforts to make it easier to live in the world which nature originally provided for us we re-order and reconstitute it in many ways which may well make it impossible to live in the environment we create for ourselves.

By hoping to satisfy our insatiable appetite for dominance and the subjugation of the world in which we live, we have separated ourselves from nature and thus made it easier to exploit and degrade it without conscience. We have failed to see that the idea of rectifying the disastrous side-effects of scientific technology by developing more sophisticated forms of it is rather like trying to put out a fire by pouring petrol on it, simply because petrol is a liquid.

The problem is, that preoccupied by the desire for power and dominance, technological intervention will continue to be fundamentally alienating and destructive. The commitment to a technology of power may turn us into giants, but the loss of vision will ensure that we are giants who are truly lost. The paradox of progress is that our best efforts to make ourselves infinitely strong have, in the end, made us infinitely weak and therefore on the very brink of extinction. The paradox we face can be likened to the giant earth God Anteus from Greek mythology, whose source of strength is his bond with the earth. The myth goes that whenever Heracles tried to defeat Anteus, he was bound to fail because Anteus had the strength of the earth to sustain him whenever his feet remained firmly planted on the earth, that is to say, his own strength was the strength of the earth. Later on, Heracles reasons that he can only defeat Anteus 'by raising him in his arms' off the surface of the earth, and this he does, thus defeating him (Grimal, 1973, p. 143). Not unlike Anteus who was wrenched by Heracles from the source of his strength in the earth, transformative subjugation robs us of the source of our strength, our health and the integrity of the human spirit, as it manifests in our bond with nature.

The extent of our alienation from the earth is well-illustrated by the fact that we use the terms 'dirt' and 'soil' pejoratively. Dirt, after all, is the substance of the earth, as is the variant expression 'soil'. We depend upon dirt/soil as the womb of the earth within which the planted seed (through being nurtured by the earth) grows into the fruits, vegetables and grains so eagerly harvested every season. Despite the obvious truth that we are totally dependent upon the earth (i.e., its soil/dirt to provide the source of nourishment, not unlike the dependency of a breast-fed child upon its mother), we cavalierly take the names of the earth in vain. We say of someone for whom we have contempt, for example, that he is a 'dirty bastard' or a 'dirt bag'. In some cultures it is sometimes said of a woman who has lost her virginity before marriage that 'she has been soiled', and we often say of a person who treats another person badly, that he 'treats her like dirt'. These usages of dirt and soil betray at a very deep level of human psyche the extent to which we have, through the technologization of nature, been disenfranchised from the earth. The negative connotation we associate with these words is a sad commentary on our separation from and lack of gratitude for the source of our life in the earth.

We have also observed the extent to which the process of transformative subjugation applies educationally to the development or lack therein of the human mind. If our commitment to the technologization of the earth results in conformity of intellect, the question arises whether we thereby witness not only the death of intellectual imagination but the death of education as well. In the next chapter on indoctrination, we shall explore this question more determinately.

References

'Putting fast food to the test' (1994) *Choice*, April.

'Rice bran offers India an oil source' (1989) *Journal of the American Oil Chemists Society*, **66**, 5.

'Services improve occupational health and safety' (1996) *The Australian Government Analytical Laboratories Newsletter*, **4**, Summer.

ABEL, R. (1976) *Man is the Measure*, New York: The Free Press.

BACON, F. (1960) *Novum Organum, The New Organon and Related Writings*, ANDERSON, F.H. (trans.), New York: Bobbs-Merrill Co.

BAGHURST, P.A., BAGHURST, K.I. and RECORD, S.J. (1996) 'Dietary fibre, non-starch polysaccharides and resistant starch — A review', *Food Australia*, **48**, 3.

BETTELHEIM, K.A. (1996) 'Enerohaemorragic Escherichia coli: A new problem, an old group of organisms', *Australian Veterinary Journal*, **73**, 1.

BINNS, C.W. (1989) 'Editorial: Into our third century', *Australian Journal of Nutrition and Dietetics*, **42**, 2.

BONNER, J. (1997) 'Hooked on drugs', *New Scientist*, 18 January.

BRAND MILLER, J. (1995) 'International tables of glycemic index', *American Journal of Clinical Nutrition*, **62**, 4.

BRAND MILLER, J. and COLAGIURI, S. (1996) *The G.I. Factor*, Sydney: Hodder and Stoughton.

BROWN, P. (1997) 'Seabirds dirty diet spreads disease', *New Scientist*, 22 March.

BROWN, S. (1997) 'Volatile organic compounds in indoor air: Sources and control', *Chemistry in Australia*, January/February.

BURKITT, D.P. and TROWELL, H.C. (1975) *Refined Carbohydrate Foods and Disease: Some Implications of Dietary Fibre*, London: Academic Press.

COGHLAN, A. (1996) 'Junk food ads target the young', *New Scientist*, 30 November.

COGHLAN, A. (1997) 'Jetsetters send festering faeces round the world', *New Scientist*, 17 May.

COMMITTEE ON NUTRITION (1978) 'Zinc', *Paediatrics*, **62**, 3.

DENTON, M. and LACEY, R.W. (1991) 'Intensive farming and food processing: Implications for polyunsaturated fats', *Journal of Nutritional Medicine*, **2**.

DESMARCHELIER, P.M. (1996) 'Foodborne disease: Emerging problems and solutions', *Medical Journal of Australia*, **165**, 2/16 December.

DRECKER, M.L., MAHER, C.V. and KEARNEY, P. (1996) 'The traditional and emerging role of nuts in healthful diets', *Nutrition Reviews*, **54**.

DUBOS, R. (1959) *Mirage of Health*, New York: Harper and Row.

FEYERABEND, P.K. (1978) *Science in a Free Society*, London: N.L.B.

GAYNOR, M. (1989) 'Multinationals kick up their heels', *Food Business*, 10 July.

GOLDWATER, P.N. and BETTELHEIM, K.A. (1996) 'An outbreak of Hemolytic Uremic Syndrome due to Escherichia coli O157:H-: Or was it', *Emerging Infectious Diseases*, **2**, 2.

GORI, G.B. (1979) 'Food as a factor in the etiology of certain human cancers', *Food Technology*, December, 50.

GRIMAL, P. (1973) (ed.) *Larousse: World Mythology*, New York: Hamlyn.

HADFIELD, P. (1995) 'Japanese swallow western diseases', *New Scientist*, 2 September.

HALMESMAKI, E., ELIKORKALA, O. and ALFTHAN, G. (1985) 'Concentrations of zinc and copper in pregnant problem drinkers and their newborn infants', *British Medical Journal*, **291**.

HAMMOND, N. (1994) 'Functional and nutritional aspects of rice bran extracts', *Cereal Foods World*, **39**, 10.

HANSON, N.R. (1958) *Patterns of Discovery*, Cambridge: Cambridge University Press.

HARPER, A.E. and GANS, D.A. (1986) 'Claims of antisocial behaviour from consumption of sugar: An assessment', *Food Technology*, January.

HARRIS, K. (1979) *Education and Knowledge*, London: Routledge and Kegan Paul.

KAHLON, T.S., CHOW, F.I., KNUCKLES, B.E. and CHIN, M.M. (1993) 'Cholesterol-lowering effects in hamsters of b-glucan enriched barley fraction, dehulled whole barley, rice bran, and oat bran and their combinations', *Cereal Chemistry*, **70**, 4.

KLEIN, K. (1974) *Positivism and Christianity*, The Hague: Martinus.

KRITCHEVSKY, D. (1994) 'The rationale behind the use of diet and dietary ingredients to lower blood cholesterol levels', *Trends in Food Science and Technology*, **5**, July.

KRUESI, M.J.P. (1986) 'Carbohydrate intake and children's behaviour', *Food Technology*, January.

LEPROHON-GREENWOOD, C.E. and ANDERSON, G.H. (1986) 'An overview of the mechanisms by which diet affects brain functions', *Food Technology*, January.

LIEBERMAN, H.R. and WURTMAN, R.J. (1986) 'Foods and food constituents that affect the brain and human behaviour', *Food Technology*, January.

MERTZ, W. (1981) '*The essential trace elements*', *Science*, **213**, 1333.

MOLLISON, B. (1992) *Permaculture: A Designer's Manual*, Talgum, Australia: Tagari Publications.

MYERS, N. (1985) (ed.) *The Gaia Atlas of Planet Management*, London: Pan Books.

NATIONAL RESEARCH COUNCIL (1989) *Alternative Agriculture*, Washington, DC: National Academy Press.

NELSON, N. and LEVINE, R.J. (1986) 'Contributions of formaldehyde to respiratory cancer', *Environmental Health Perspectives*, **70**.

NHMRC (1992) *National Indoor Air Quality Goal for Total Volatile Organic Compounds*, Canberra.

NOAKES, M., NESTEL, P.J. and CLIFTON, P.M. (1996) 'Modifying the fatty acid profile of dairy products through feedlot technology lowers plasma cholesterol of humans consuming the products', *American Journal of Clinical Nutrition*, **63**.

PAIN, S. (1996) 'Ten deaths that may tell a shocking tale', *New Scientist*, 30 March.

PATEL, T. (1996) 'Bhajis not burgers for India', *New Scientist*, 3 August.

PEARCE, F. (1996a) 'BSE may lurk in pigs and chickens', *New Scientist*, 6 April.

PEARCE, F. (1996b) 'Ministers hostile to advice on BSE', *New Scientist*, 30 March.

PEARCE, F. (1997) 'Thirsty meals that suck the world dry', *New Scientist*, 1 February.

PURKIS, T. and WILSON, J. (1989) 'Cleaning up the cooling towers', *New Scientist*, 16 September.

QUINE, V.O. (1953) 'Two dogmas of Empiricism', *From a Logical Point of View*, Cambridge: Harvard University Press, p. 8, Y 2 ff.

RAMSEY, A. (1996/1997) 'Eat to your heart's content', *Ecos*, **90**, Summer.

RANDOLPH, T.G. (1970) 'Domiciliary chemical air pollution in the etiology of ecologicmental illness', *International Journal of Social Psychology*, **16**.

RIFKIN, J. (1989) *Time Wars: The Primary Conflict in Human History*, New York: Simon and Schuster.

RIMM, E.B., ASCHERIO, A. and GIOVANNUCCI, E. (1996) 'Vegetable fruit and cereal fibre intake and risk of coronary heart disease among men', *Journal of The American Medical Association*, **275**.

ROBERTS, T.A., DILLON, C.R. and SIEBENMORGEN, T.J. (1996) 'The impact of food processing on the US economy', *Food Technology*, October.

ROGERS, S.A. (1987) 'Diagnosing the tight building syndrome', *Environmental Health Perspectives*, **76**.

ROLLS, B. (1986) 'Why we choose what we eat', *Proceedings, World Sugar Research Organisation Ltd., Scientific Conference*, Sydney, Australia, 10–13 August.

SANDERS, H.J. (1979) 'Nutrition and health', *Chemical and Engineering News*, 26 March, 29.

SAXON, M. (1978) 'What are we eating?', *Scientific Australia*, March.

SCHEIRS, J. and BIGGER, S.W. (1996) 'Volatile organic emissions from polymeric materials', *Chemistry in Australia*, June.

SMITH, J.R. (1977) 'Tree crops', *A Permanent Agriculture*, Old Greenwich: The Devin-Adair Company.

STATE OF ENVIRONMENT ADVISORY COUNCIL (1996) *Australian State of the Environment*, Collingwood, Victoria: CSIRO Publishing.

ZIMMET, P. and COHEN, M. (1995) 'The diabetics epidemic in Australia: Prevalence, patterns and the public health', *Medical Journal of Australia*, **163**, 7 August.

Chapter 3

Educational Ideology and Indoctrination

In the previous chapter it was argued that one much neglected consequence of transformative subjugation is the systematic production of intellectual conformity. Given that our educational institutions are the state sanctioned vehicles by way of which society's commitment to the technologization of nature is promulgated, the question naturally arises whether education is itself a form of indoctrination. This being so the present chapter will be concerned to explore the issue in greater depth, with an aim to showing that education has indeed become a public forum for the ideology of science in its commitment to transformative subjugation. Lest we be misunderstood let us make plain at the outset that it is not part of our purpose to inveigh against the concept of science in its use as a process of reasoning under-taken in the service of intellectual curiosity. Our claim is rather that inasmuch as science has seized upon a particular concept of knowledge designed to enshrine a pernicious preoccupation with power, which in turn fosters technologies of trans-formative subjugation, science has become sectarian and education has become indoctrinative.

It seems generally to be accepted among philosophers and sociologists of education that indoctrination is a dead issue. Having accumulated a considerable literature (see for example Pittenger, 1941; Hollins, 1964; Scheffler, 1960; Peters, 1963; Archambault, 1965; Snook, 1972) particularly during the course of the past two decades, there is indeed a strong motivation to regard the matter as having been 'analysed to death'. This being so, the temptation is to become complacent by assuming that we have answers to questions that we have not yet begun to ask. While it is not our wont to engage in post-mortem polemics, we shall submit there is still much work to be done to expose the subtleties of indoctrinative education in relation to transformative subjugation.

In order to make explicit what has for far too long been an implicit feature of educational knowledge we commence this chapter by rehearsing briefly the use to which the conventional approach to the problem has helped to illuminate the debate. It would be presumptuous and naive to suppose that a perfunctory survey of such a large body of literature could possibly do justice to the range of important insights contained within it. Let us thus make clear at the outset that our aim is not so much to reconsider the minutiae of conceptual debate on indoctrination, as to show that the conceptual tools employed in its resolution have by their very nature *limited* the breadth of educational vision. The conventional debate has, for the most part, approached the question of indoctrination in terms of the logical relations between concepts, and in so doing, has prematurely delimited the range of the possible answers. In what follows, we shall argue that when the problem — or the whole tangle of problems — surrounding indoctrination is set in the context of a critical theory of genetic epistemology, the issues are still very much alive. Accordingly, we shall in the second part of the chapter, be concerned to anatomize the conceptual face of educational knowledge in terms of the ideological infrastructure within which it has become entrenched.

Although the term 'indoctrination' admits of a dictionary rendering which has no ostensible pejorative connotation, there has since the 1920s been a progressive inclination on the part of many theorists of education to use 'indoctrination' as a term of censure. The problem, of course, has been to specify in unequivocal terms just what it is about indoctrination that makes it objectionable. Attempts to specify indoctrination as a term of denigration have located three foci of conceptual orientation. Indoctrination has traditionally been analysed as:

1 a certain method of teaching;
2 a certain context of teaching; and
3 a certain aim in teaching.

These are now familiar shibboleths, but an examination of the pattern of their logical interstices will provide the point of this chapter's departure from them.

The claim that indoctrination is a certain method of teaching can be more formally represented as follows: in respect of some propositional belief or set of such beliefs ('P') one individual (In_1) indoctrinates another (In_2) if In_1 brings it about that In_2 comes to endorse P, otherwise than by enabling In_2 to understand the grounds requisite for its endorsement. So construed, indoctrination was deemed to be unavoidable.

Inasmuch as the education of children, particularly young children, entails the inculcation of beliefs, the grounds of which may be incomprehensible to the child, if not to the teacher, indoctrination will to some extent be an unavoidable feature of the educative system. Such an admission, however, clearly constituted a difficulty for the proponents of the method account, since its rationale depended upon being able to employ 'indoctrination' in such a way as to mark a definitive contrast with 'education'.

In addition to the discomfort of antimony generated by the recognition that indoctrination would have to be regarded as a necessary feature of the educative system, there arose a more fundamental difficulty as to whether the definition of indoctrination as a certain method of teaching could possibly bear the weight of the distinctions it was meant to sustain. The hypnopaedia example brought this problem into bold relief. If the *same* method, say hypnosis, could be used to instill different beliefs, certain of which we would properly regard as indoctrination and others of which we would not, it could not be the method of teaching which alone defined the concept of indoctrination, for the same method was being similarly employed; what differed was the content. The question of *what* was taught, not *how* it was taught thus became the central issue, and the content account of indoctrination was advanced as affording a deeper understanding of the scope and limits of the concept of indoctrination.

According to the content account, indoctrination occurs when an individual
(In$_1$) brings it about that another individual (In$_2$) endorses a belief or set of beliefs
(P) otherwise than by enabling In$_2$ to comprehend the grounds for the endorsement,
where P is a doctrine or disputatious area of belief. Here, the reiteration of the root
word 'doctrine' is important, as it places a restriction on the range of educatively
admissible beliefs. While considerable discussion ensued concerning the definition
of doctrines, it seemed generally to be agreed that doctrines were beliefs which
if not false, were not known to be true. Since this definition still let some metaphysical camels through the eye of the curriculum needle, however, it was further
stipulated that such doctrines must be constituents of a wider ideological system.

Despite gestures towards a coherent account of the connection between doctrines and ideology, the initial clarity of the content account emphasis on *what* is
taught diminished in proportion to the palpable obscurity of the explication of its
ideological implications. Whether it is possible to delimit the class of controversial
or doctrinal subject matter in a way required by the content account is after all,
itself, problematical. In any case, the ardent proponents of the method account still
persisted in their view that it was possible to teach even doctrinal content in a
legitimate or non-indoctrinatory way, and the debate went on.

Some educational researchers, finding themselves unpersuaded by either the
method or the content account, proposed the alternative that has come to be known
as the intention account. The suggestion here is that an individual (In$_1$) indoctrinates
an individual (In$_2$) in respect of a propositional belief or set of beliefs (P) if In$_1$
deliberately brings it about that In$_2$ endorses P in such a way that In$_2$ is, despite
otherwise compelling evidence, unable subsequently to endorse not P. The intention account defines indoctrination in terms of the process of influencing the mental
state of an individual such that a particular belief disposition is ensured. On this
account, the indoctrinator is concerned to inculcate a permanent conceptual bias
in respect of the subject matter under consideration. Consistent with this interpretation, it has been argued elsewhere (see for example, Laura, 1981a, pp. 1–13
and Laura, 1981b) that indoctrination is tantamount to a paralysis of intellectual
imagination. The mind becomes closed on those issues which are fundamentally
open, and the inability to imagine things as they are not imprisons the human being
in the world of things as they are.

Clearly, the intention account does serve to exhibit something of the extent to
which indoctrination is dehumanizing. The intellectual components of our individual autonomy are eroded by a narrowing of the mind's eye such that we 'see'
only those things which others want us to see. The value of the human personality
is subverted by the affirmation of other values such as power and wealth which are
made to take precedence over it. In this sense there is an implicit challenge to the
very value and purpose of what it is to be a human being.

Although the intention account does seem to assist in identifying what it is
about indoctrination that leads to our regarding it as pernicious, the concept of
intention is itself by no means pellucid. Indeed, it is arguable that by defining
indoctrination in terms of the teacher's intention, we simply substitute one obscure
concept, 'indoctrination', for another even more obscure concept, 'intention'. As

has been made evident by the impressive body of literature deriving from the philosophy of mind and action theory (see for example, Brown, 1974; Glover, 1976; Guttenplan, 1975; Honderich, 1973), one of the essential problems concerning intention depends upon being able to articulate the logical character of intentional states or episodes, while also showing in what way such episodes could be connected to intentional might, for example, be disposed to act in ways which would be regarded as highly anomalous by another individual who expressed the same intention. If this point is accepted, it would of course prohibit a determinate inference from the teacher's intention to the teacher's method. On the other hand, if the teacher's intention is taken as an occurrent or non-dispositional predicate in the way in which the concept of 'resolving' admits of analysis as a limiting case of intending, the occurrence of which itself constitutes an act of intending, then it is difficult to see how the reference to the teacher's intention could serve to delineate the necessary praxis for interpreting the actual teaching situation. For those who wished to avoid indoctrinating would not — on the occurrent account of intentions — be supplied with any relevant prescription of behavioural predicates for determining what they *should do* in order to educate.

At this point, however, it may be salutary to remind ourselves that our task in this first section has not been to tease out the conceptual details and logical impediments of the standard accounts of indoctrination in terms of method, content and intention. The burden of this section has rather been to rehearse the general arguments with an aim to showing that the conceptual analysis of indoctrination in these terms has not yet been firmly grounded in an epistemological framework sufficiently comprehensive to give the specific concepts employed their deepest sense. Having now rehearsed these traditional arguments, our present objective is to determine the extent to which the introduction of a comprehensive epistemological framework can alter our perception of both *what* indoctrination is and *how* it might be avoided. To achieve this end, we shall endeavour to integrate aspects of evolutionary epistemology with critical theory. Lest we be misunderstood also on this point, however, let us post a logical caveat. Since the death of Charles Darwin, there has been extensive use and abuse of evolutionary theory as a tool in the service of epistemology. The philosophy of knowledge we espouse is sponsored on the assumption of a fallibilistic realism, and we have no wish to assume the posture of the recrudescent evolutionary epistemologist. The position of evolutionary epistemology is not without its logical difficulties and any pervasive philosophic commitment to it without their resolution would doubtless be foolhardy. On the other hand, we find ourselves in sympathy with Stephen Toulmin's observation that the dominant tradition in twentieth-century philosophy remains inimical to evolutionary approaches to knowledge, reflecting an excessive preoccupation with the genetic and psychologistic fallacies. This being so, we shall seek to show that the assumption of an evolutionary account of knowledge is at least compatible with the version of fallibilist realism that we do hold. The explication we give of this position will go beyond conceptual analysis in that we make use of our theory of transformative subjugation to show that the very concepts of analysis are themselves conditioned by the comprehensive epistemological structure in which they take their life.

Wittgenstein had enough respect for Darwin's theory of evolution to include in the *Tractatus* one dismissive reference to it. In *Tractatus* 4.11.22 he wrote: 'Darwin's theory has no more to do with philosophy than any other hypothesis in natural science' (Quine, 1969).

In setting the logical limits for what can be thought, philosophy was capable of influencing, indeed delimiting the biological domain, but biology on Wittgenstein's view had nothing to contribute to the determination of a philosophy the foundations of which were laid in logic. Logic cannot be regarded as the evolutionary product of biological and socio-psychological transformations, for logic is transcendental. Being perfectly independent of experience, logical truths are not conditioned by it: the world of experience is neither a condition of the expression of logical truths nor a condition of their revision. Subject to neither the vicissitudes of history nor the caprices of mind, logic defies the very categories of description which evolutionary theory must by its nature make use of.

The standard rejection of evolutionary epistemology is grounded in an acceptance of the conjunction of the above theory of logic and the theory of knowledge deriving from it. Logical truths are immutable and epistemology reduces to a regimentation of the logical relations obtaining between language and reality. If 'to know is' *to know what is true*, the genesis or evolution of knowledge is — on this view — irrelevant to what knowledge is. To think otherwise is to commit the genetic fallacy.

It has in large part been an exaggerated reverence for the genetic fallacy that has kept conceptual analysis insulated from other philosophical developments capable of enriching it. In regard to evolutionary epistemology, there is a sense in which flouting the genetic fallacy simply means that the eating of one's cake is precisely what it means to have it. While there is a proper reverence to be shown for fallacies of the genetic kind, we want now to argue that epistemic elucidations are better served by setting the analysis of concepts in a wider framework of the phenomenology of perception and experience. Indeed, we are suggesting that the epistemological enterprise involves a subtle interplay between the analysis of concepts and the construction of the phenomenological basis of their origin. The view which we develop here is thus antagonistic to those who would content themselves with conceptual analysis as their only philosophic tool and also to those who would deny the importance of conceptual analysis as a philosophic tool.

The version of fallibilist realism which we hold postulates an external world which exists independently of what is said or thought about it. To say anything about what that world is like, however, requires a set of descriptive concepts of some alternative symbolic system sufficiently rich to express the logical relations which obtain between what there is and what we know. What we know is conditioned by the concepts of knowledge, but 'what there is' does not dictate unequivocally the concepts in terms of which its appropriate description can be certified. We can thus be mistaken in our claims to know what there is, though we could of course give grounds of such a kind that what we claim to know is the best possible explanation of what there is. Although the external world exists independently of what we say or think about it, there is a sense in which the realities of the external world depend very much upon what we say and think about it. We not only perceive the external world; we shape it and we contribute to it. In this sense, the concept of 'the external world' and the concept of 'reality' are not in our view coterminous in extension. The external world is what there is independently of what we say or think about it; reality is what there is once our sayings and thinkings have *altered* the form of what there is. Not all our sayings and thinkings do alter the form of what there is, but some do or might. We believe that this distinction can be extended to dissipate much of the tension between traditional realist and idealist accounts of knowledge, but it would be extraneous to our present consideration to pursue this divagation here.

We have thus provided the skeleton of this fallibilist realism, but the concepts it employs now need to be fleshed in more specific terms. We hold the view that the propositions of logic can be regarded roughly as limiting cases of the propositions of epistemology. Not all logical propositions have the same status, however, in that some are, in our view, primitive while others are derivative. The most basic features of our conceptual framework are characterized by logical primitives which in turn sustain and accommodate the propositional fragments of our epistemic structures. It has elsewhere (see for example, Laura, 1978 and 1980) been argued that the epistemic relations which obtain between logical and epistemic primitives are definitive of the bounds of reason within specific frameworks, so we shall not address this aspect of the analysis. Although we shall later in this chapter reconsider the matter of epistemic primitives with special reference to indoctrination, we shall content ourselves here with an elucidation of the status of logical primitives. We urge that the evolutionary character of knowledge is compatible with fallibilist realism and that logical primitives need not be immune to revision as a response to experience. If we are correct in this, the suggestion that logic is itself part of the process of knowledge would have much to recommend it.

In the philosophical classic, *Two Dogmas of Empiricism* (Quine, 1953, pp. 20–46) Van Orman Quine showed himself to be one of few philosophers bold enough to propose that the truths of logic were not immune to revision in the face of empirically discrepant date. Quine was not simply denying the crude empiricist doctrine that logical truths are sacrosanct no matter what. The annals of philosophical logic already contained references to the possibility of there being familiar statements of meaning such as future conditionals and systematically vague statements concerning which a classical law of logic might not admit of application (see for example, Geach and Bednarowski, 1956). Quine's radical challenge superseded the admission that logical analysis could be used to circumscribe the boundary conditions of otherwise acceptable logical truths. The revolutionary impact of his pronouncements lay in the suggestion 'not' that logical truth was impermeable to philosophic analysis, but that logical truths were susceptible of revision 'as a response to experience'. In the face of contradictions resulting from the application of classical laws of quantum mechanics, Quine urged that there was sufficient warrant for the revision of the law of excluded middle.

In more recent works (Quine, 1970, pp. 83–87 and Quine, 1969) Quine recants the revisability thesis on two grounds. Employing the 'change of meaning' argument, he first insists that the denial of a law of logic is either a contradiction in terms or a failure of meaning. If the meaning attached to the constants and logical operators is consonant with the classical logician's formulation, then the contradiction would result in denying precisely what was being affirmed. If the meaning attached to the constituents of the logical formula represents a variant on the classical formulation, the interpreter would not be denying anything affirmed by the classical logician. The dispute would be terminological, reflecting no more than a logical change of subject.

Quine's second ground of hesitancy derived from his account of theory construction. Confronted with evidence contrary to the expectations logically associated with a particular belief or belief constellation, he avers that a revision of physical theory will always be less disruptive to the total system of belief and thus *always* to be preferred to a revision of a law of logic.

We do not find this feature of Quine's argument entirely convincing. It implies an infelicitous *à priori* commitment to the status of logical truths as inviolable, though the criterion for revision is supposed, in Quine's own terms, to be construed in accord with the degree of disruption to the system. How one could know in advance of systematic examination whether a revision of physical theory will be more disruptive than a revision of logical truths must surely be regarded as an impossibly ambitious anticipation of the infinite transpirations of possible worlds.

While we accept that there is a presumption in favour of the non-revisability of logical truths on the ground of extensive systematic disruption, it does not follow that the preservation of a putative logical truth in the face of accumulated experiential anomalies always provides the path of least disruption.

Indeed, entertaining the negation of a non-logical truth such as 'I have got a body' may have disastrous consequences for the entire network of empirical propositions whose pattern of conceptual significance depends upon them, but the radical degree of disruption does not entail that such a belief is now and forever invulnerable to disconfirmation.

Let us now revert to the celebrated 'change of meaning' argument which Quine uses to support his recantation of the revisability thesis. The argument was that logical truths are unrevisable in the sense that their definitional meaning is the exhaustive condition of their truth. If you understand the statement, in other words, you cannot deny it, since your denial would constitute a vitiation of the very possibility of your having comprehended it.

It seems strange that Quine should so cavalierly in this context dismiss the difficulties concerning concepts such as 'definition', 'synonymy' and 'interchangeability' to which he has himself so convincingly drawn to our attention in other contexts, and upon which the 'change of meaning' argument depends. Although we remain confident that the attempt to define analytically in terms of the class of true sentences comprising the truths of logic along with all sentences reducible to them by substituting synonyms for synonyms is riddled with problems, we shall not here be concerned to remind Quine of the points he has previously made which he would now, it would seem, wish to forget.

Our purpose here is rather to challenge the thesis that logic is immune to revision as a response to experience by trying to show that the expression of the truths of logic rests upon an experiential base which implicitly determines the validity of their expression. To explain this let us consider the way in which Wittgenstein's account of logical truths as limiting or degenerate cases of truth-functions can be realized in the propositional calculus. It is a feature of propositional logic that all the 'possible worlds' denumerable by means of a given supply of atomic sentences Pi (i=1, 2 . . . , K), we see 'possible worlds' described by a series of conjunctions such that for each, the denumerable description contains either P, or its negation exclusively, but not any other members.

Given that each consistent sentential denumeration of propositional logic possesses a notational form which is a disjunction of at least some of the conjunctive constituents, every sentence will express certain of the possibilities implied by the conjunctions, but exclude the rest. Up to the logical limit of associated truth-functions, the degree of sentential informativeness is proportional to the extent to which possibilities are shut out. The logically true sentences of the propositional logic are thus those which, according to Wittgenstein, admit all the possibilities listed by the constituents and exclude none. The propositional logic generates the limiting case for true sentences by ensuring that such sentences are descriptively uninformative.

If we extend this analysis to the account of logical laws and the 'change of meaning' argument in defence of them, we see that the incontrovertibility of logic is far more problematic than Quine has led us to suppose. Upon reflection, it is not at all clear that the law of excluded middle expresses an eternal and immutable truth, nor that experience plays no role in preserving the truth it alleges to express.

To stay with the propositional calculus, the law of excluded middle is cast as 'P v P'. Unfortunately, the principle so stated is equivocal, for there is a strong and a weak interpretation of it. On the strong interpretation it formulates as 'Every closed proposition is true or false', and on the weak interpretation as 'Every closed proposition is true or not true'. In classical logic the weaker formulation is entailed by the law of contradiction, though the abandonment of the principle of double negation by Brouwer under the banner of 'Intuitionist Logic' would deny the entailment.

The 'change of meaning' argument hides the fact that logical laws do not contain within themselves the criteria for either their present interpretations or their future applications. The sign-post does not stipulate its proper interpretation. This being so, the meaning we actually attach to the propositional constituents of logical truths will depend upon the comprehensive conceptual framework in which certain postulates about the organization of experience are agreed upon. Although this agreement is a condition of language, not a conferred concensus, it does not follow that logical truths are autonomous in the sense of being semantically self-sufficient. Logic arises out of our language and is itself a part of it. Logic is not antecedent to language; it is rather the very organizational pattern which makes its coherent expression possible. Language is itself a response to our experience of the world, and the regulative principles of logic represent the conceptual form of that response. It is not so much the laws of logic that are inexorable as the way in which we apply them. Informally expressed, the law of contradiction, for example, says that for every proposition 'P', it is not the case that 'P' can both have and lack the same property. It is the application of this principle to a specific propositional context that yields the formal truism 'not both P and not P'. It is worth observing that the logical truism is constructed in such a way that it cannot be false; it is true in virtue of the meanings of its constituents.

Presumably, our justification for an explanation of truth in terms of component meaning rests upon the postulate that it is logically necessary that the conjunction of contradictories is false, and it is the law of contradiction that tells us this. We thus appeal to the law of contradiction to justify our judgment that the conjunction of admittedly contradictory propositions is necessarily false. But what then is the justification for our reliance upon the law of contradiction? It is certainly not tautologous in the sense that the propositional calculus notation is, for the law of contradiction is a generalization over all propositions, not a closed sentence whose truth can be derived solely from the meanings of its constituents.

There is no celestial necessity which guarantees that logical laws are immune to revision. Of course, 'given that' we accept certain logical 'truths' 'as inexorable', the truths which derive from them will be necessary in the sense of being true in all possible worlds. To concede this, however, is to concede that their necessity is conditioned by that acceptance. What we are trying to bring out is that the analysis in terms of truth-functional exclusion and possible world instantiation is underpinned by a frame of reference which has more to do with our projected needs and interests than with analysis of meanings in the search for the ontology of immutable truths. The 'change of meaning' argument assumes that logical truths can be assessed in isolation of their origin. We submit that the way in which they originate is essential to their assessment.

Once the foundations of logic are challenged in this way, it is easier to appreciate how tempting it is to complete the story with the help of an evolutionary epistemology. Clearly there is no reason why the human cognitive functions should escape the underlying mechanistic forces of evolution. The growth of knowledge would thus be regarded as the collective manifestation of a series of organic/mentalistic adjustments within the human species to environmental circumstances. The history of epistemology and the logic which sustains it would be seen as attempts, more or less successful, to advance the position of the species in relation to the environment. Notice that once again the driving force behind the development of knowledge is the drive for power and control. The more knowledge one has, so the theory goes, the greater the degree of power over nature and one's consequent control of it.

Contrary to the evolutionary view of knowledge, truth is not in the view of fallibilist realism we advance here, simply a presence of absence of a biologically expedient adjustment to external states of affairs. While we believe that knowledge and intelligence are directed partly by the inveterate drive for survival and are instrumental for the perpetuation of the species, the account of truth which best makes sense of this is not to be defined by evolutionary pundits.

This is an important point, as the logical difficulties confronting those who would wish to hold that truth amounts to saying that things are as they really are have served to discourage philosophers from saying just these things. The evolutionary approach to truth might be adopted for just the same sceptical reasons. It may be tempting to think that while we may succeed in making truth claims which perpetuate the survival of the species, there is no point in trying to describe things as they are. This is a temptation to be resisted. Indeed, the evolutionary epistemologist cannot do without the realist perception of truth. The evolutionary epistemologist must, to avoid a vicious infinite regress, be willing to admit that a particular claim about the world does *in fact* assist in securing the survival of the species. Whether the claim itself does or does not correspond to reality is irrelevant; what is relevant is that the evolutionary epistemologist is constrained from reducing his own claim to the claim that there is survival value in postulating survival value and so on. It must be acknowledged at some point, that is to say, that the hypothesis about survival value is an accurate description of how things are and this, of course, presupposes a concept of truth which is not to be explained away in terms of its survival utility.

But what has all this to do with the concept of indoctrination and transformative subjugation? We have been intimating that the structure of knowledge is far too complicated to think that we provide an adequate account of indoctrination by the provision of a conceptual analysis that does not reflect the complexity of that structure. We are now in a position to show that a better understanding of this structure will afford a better understanding of indoctrination in the context of educational knowledge.

As we have already seen from our earlier discussion of fallibilist realism, all our thinking takes place against the background of certain propositions which dictate the domain of coherent conceptualization. This basic background comprises laws of logic such as the principle of contradiction and the law of excluded middle, the propositions to which we have referred as 'logical primitives'. Consistent with the radical form of fallibilism presented here our view is that such propositions need not be regarded as immune to revision in response to experience, and we have argued that their revisability may well be consonant with the general thrust of evolutionary epistemology. Of all our beliefs, the laws of logic would seem to be most resistant to revision, their abandonment causing maximum mutilation of the total belief network which depends upon them. The logical laws feature within the comprehensive system of belief as the regulating principles in virtue of which epistemic beliefs are generated. The laws of logic do not determine the content of a specific epistemic belief, but they do circumscribe the domain of legitimate contenders.

Following on from laws of logic and the array of logical truisms which derive from them are what we call 'epistemic primitives'. In regard to indoctrination, the point to be made here is that the preoccupation with power which undergirds the dominant concept of knowledge cannot be justified by appeal to evolutionary epistemology. Moreover, to treat the concept of knowledge as power, as having a monopoly on knowledge, is to attribute to the concept a primitive role in the framework of logic from which it derives that it could not have. This will become clearer as we elaborate our concept of epistemic primitives.

Suppose one were to advance some proposition 'p' and that the sceptic counters by asking what justifies the assertion of 'p'. Presumably, one could reply by adducing another proposition 'q' which is taken to support 'p'. To this our sceptic then demands the justification for 'q', and so one responds by adducing 'r' in support of 'q'. The sceptic is still not satisfied and will repeat the move *ad infinitum* or *ad nauseum*, depending on one's stomach for such matters. He hopes to show that we cannot produce an adequate justification for our claims to knowledge. If the sceptic were correct, of course, his thesis would establish that nothing can be known, because no claim to knowledge can be satisfactorily justified evidentially.

Rather than reply directly to the sceptic, let us exploit the sceptic's remarks to advance a different case. If what constitutes an adequate justification of our claims to knowledge is that they require evidential support of the sort we have seen in the infinite regress argument, there is a sense in which the sceptic sustains his claim. But there is another move open to us. We might be better advised to concede that our concept of justification in terms of supporting propositions is not entirely satisfactory (for the general argument, see Wittgenstein, 1969) or as we should prefer to put it; there comes a point in our chain of reasoning at which one finds propositions for which no further grounds can be adduced beyond the data which they are supposed to monitor. In putting the matter this way, it is also tempting to think that in the end there are no grounds for our lower level beliefs (Malcolm, 1977, pp. 143–57). This is yet another philosophical temptation to be resisted. Our claim is simply that certain beliefs are related logically in such a way that we reach a belief in our chain of reasoning which is of such a kind that the grounds we can at the time provide for or against it are no surer than it is itself.

To characterize certain of our epistemic beliefs in this way is to say something about the logical role which these beliefs play in the language. In the required sense they are not testable propositions at all. We are enumerating a special class of propositions which we affirm without testing. That is to say, such propositions are themselves the very foundation of our testing; they inform the nature of our tests. They remain invariant under testing because they are epistemic fragments of the conceptual framework within which our testing acquires its significance. To ask whether such propositions are susceptible of empirical validation is to misunderstand the peculiar role which they play in the language; they are themselves a condition of a certain kind of testing. Or, to put the point in terms of 'evidence', such beliefs are themselves features of the framework to which we appeal to determine what counts as evidence and what does not. Accordingly, one might view these propositions as epistemically fossilized. To adapt a metaphor of Wittgenstein's, they lie apart from the route travelled by enquiry. They figure logically as the primitives in virtue of which enquiry proceeds.

We now have the skeleton of the view, but it obviously needs to be fleshed. Let us first consider an example of a belief drawn from science which while not directly testable, we should clearly wish to regard as significant. One convenient example is to be found in pathology. Pathology proceeds on the assumption that every disease has a cause; it is characteristic of the enterprise that pathologists trace the causes of particular diseases. But the causal principle itself is not a proposition which the pathologist is concerned to establish. She does not test the causal presupposition, for it constitutes the very ground of her testing. If some particular disease does not admit of a cure, say cancer, the pathologist does not conclude that her implicit belief in causal connections between diseases and their genesis is mistaken. The pathologist could relinquish many beliefs and still be said to be doing pathology, but the causal presupposition is not one of them. In this case, giving up one's belief in causality is tantamount to giving up one's belief in pathology. This is the sense in which one might speak of 'causality' as a constitutive concept.

A second example of this kind can be drawn from our general belief in the uniformity of nature (i.e., the belief that nature exhibits at least some regularities that hold over a long enough period of time for us to formulate them). We do not maintain our belief in the uniformity of nature as a consequence of our ratiocinations. The proposition which expresses this belief cannot be properly construed as the result of a felicitous inference or proof. Nor is it something we learn as a consequence of our investigations. It would be less misleading to say that a belief in the uniformity of nature is something we imbibe as a consequence of what we learn. Our belief in the uniformity of nature could not be undermined by appeal simply to observational grounds, for to rely on observation is, in any case, to presuppose it. A belief in the uniformity of nature is held in such a way that it is no longer dependent simply upon a particular connection between various natural events; rather, our belief in the uniformity principle is itself the basis for a particular understanding of how various natural events are connected. In this sense it is not to be construed as a provisional hypothesis; it is one of the beliefs in virtue of which it becomes possible to frame our provisional hypotheses. To what extent then can the concept of knowledge as power be construed as an epistemic primitive?

How one answers the above question — or indeed whether one has an answer at all — depends upon the relation between the epistemological primitives or presupposition and the system of propositions to which they belong. It would clearly be a mistake to analyse the relation as one of logical entailment constitutive of an 'Axiom system'. From entailment thus specified it would follow that scientific hypotheses would be related to the primitives of the system as consequences to postulates in a deductive system. But this deductive relation would make 'p' presuppose 'q' equivalent to necessitating 'p', and this is obviously too strong for the relation we have in mind. The law of induction may restrict the range of possible theories, but it does not dictate unequivocally which of the possible theories is true.

We suggest that the connection between the primitives and the propositions they license is better assimilated to quasi-formal relation which we shall call 'presuppositional implicature'. To forestall misunderstanding let us confess that our aim here is only to sketch what the relation might be like without insisting that the sketch is itself an adequate anatomization of the relation. If one states that 'all metals expand when heated' one can, under normal circumstance, infer that one believes that one has good grounds, or at least that good grounds are to be had, for making the claim. Whether one is aware of the fact or not, the reference to good grounds can be sustained only if one subscribes implicitly to induction. While the statement 'all metals expand when heated' is not logically incompatible with the statement 'the future resembles the past', there is a logical tension between one's belief that 'p' and one's disbelieving 'q' where 'q' is a presupposition of 'p'.

We shall thus define 'presuppositional implicature' as the relation that holds between the belief which is expressed by a statement and the belief or range of beliefs to which a sincere utterer subscribes in expressing it, such that one cannot consistently affirm the statement 'p' and deny the belief or range of beliefs which is implied by it. The inconsistency is not a logical contradiction in what is said, but a pragmatic contradiction in what is done in saying it. Presuppositional inconsistency would, of course, ensure a self-refuting performance, but the sort of performance ensured should not be confused with the pragmatic contradiction involved in affirming a claim such as 'nothing we assert is true', for in this case, the occasion of utterance is sufficient to falsify the proposition uttered. That is, the intelligent and correct use of its constituent symbols prohibits their being used to say something the utterer knows to be false.

In contrast to pragmatic contradiction, presuppositional inconsistency depends upon a conflict between the evidential components which attend the affirmation of a belief and the concomitant denial of the belief or range of beliefs which underpins it. To affirm 'p' and at the same time to deny 'q', where 'q' is a presupposition of 'p', is to frustrate the evidential force possessed by each of the conjuncts. The denial of 'q' amounts to denying the evidential support one has for 'p' and this is clearly self-stultifying.

We are now in a better position to appreciate the extent to which the value of knowledge as power cannot be assimilated as a logical feature of the class of epistemic primitives. Our analysis does not commit us, that is to say, to holding that epistemological primitives feature necessarily as part of the theories to which they give rise. It thus follows that the epistemic primitives cannot serve to guarantee their own truth. The elucidation of their logical role tells us what it means to say they are true and in what sense their truth consolidates the propositions which presuppose them. The epistemic primitives do not contain within themselves the criteria for preferring the system of propositions which they order to some other. This helps us to explain why the apparent universality of induction does not constitute a serious objection to the defence we have been enunciating.

This being so, it is clear that comprehensive scepticism is self-refuting. To claim that no statement admits of justification is, therapeutically speaking, incurably reflexive, the self-reference assuring the unacceptability of the referent. Comprehensive scepticism fails of truth, since the conditions of its truth undermine the conditions of its assertability. If our appetite for truth is to be satisfied, something more nourishing than comprehensive scepticism must be on the menu.

Although what the sceptic says shows that what is said is false, what follows is not that scepticism is false, but only that this particular version of scepticism does not succeed to truth. It is a central contention of this chapter that modified scepticism is tantamount to an epistemic repast which is substantive enough to warrant its inclusion in every epistemologist's diet. But, while it's seeming to someone that he or she thinks is itself an act of thinking, it's seeming to someone that he or she eats is not itself an act of eating. The time has come to cash the metaphor or go hungry.

In what follows we shall be concerned to show that the way in which we resolve the problem of scepticism, of whether scepticism is a problem that can be resolved at all, makes a considerable difference to what we are disposed to say about indoctrination.

Let it be conceded at the outset that if we are willing to allow the distinction between the character of reality and what we say about it, we are thereby committed to some form of scepticism. At the very least, we are bound to allow that our judgments about the world may be mistaken. There is no epistemic guarantee, that how the world is need coincide with our *statements* about how it is. Admitting this distinction, some philosophers have yielded to a scepticism which holds that we can never know the truth, while others have come to doubt whether such a concept even has meaning. Scepticism thus translates into something more radical than the traditional dispute over what we are justified in believing. Scepticism reduces instead to a dispute over whether any conditions could be satisfied such that their satisfaction would define what should be regarded in the first place as adequate reasons for belief. Scepticism on this level insists that what we regard as an adequate reason for belief depends upon our conceptual system. There is no way to extricate ourselves from this system, so the claim goes, to assume a neutral standpoint in virtue of which our own and other conceptual systems can be measured. Each system determines a standard of 'reason' and 'truth' appropriate to it. Our concepts are conditioned by our conceptual system and this implies that concepts do not depend upon the composition of reality; our concepts become the mechanisms by which the composition of reality is itself determined. As Professor Winch puts it in that often quoted passage:

> Reality is not what gives language sense. What is real and what is unreal shows itself in the sense that language has. Further, both the distinction between the real and the unreal and the concept of agreement with reality themselves belong to our language. (Winch, 1967, p. 13)

Let us now consider these issues closely. The semantic impetus to this epistemic relativism derives from Wittgenstein's later account of meaning, according to which the meaning of a word or of a sentence is the use to which it is put in the language (Wittgenstein, 1953, Part 1, Sec. 43).

The 'use theory', as we shall somewhat misleadingly call it, was proposed in marked contrast to Wittgenstein's *Tractatus* account in which the meaning of a word was the object it named. This is an important recognition, as it brings into relief Wittgenstein's admission that there was no uniform logical structure underlying the whole of language in virtue of which the limits of language were uniformly determined. The conditions governing language in general were so disparate that it seemed doubtful that there existed a monolithic logical structure to which they all could be reduced. Wittgenstein allowed that there may be limits to what can meaningfully be said, but he was inclined to think that they could be plotted only by examining language in the context in which it has its life. Language must be viewed in the socio-linguistic setting in which it has its use; or to put this differently, it must be viewed in the 'language-game' which is its home.

Consistent with this account of language was the suggestion that language admits of a multiplicity of uses. In one 'language-game' or system of beliefs the meaning of a piece of language might be different from its meaning in another. There is no one ultimate context, so to speak, in which the meaning of a piece of language can be determined once and for all. The meaning of a piece of language depends upon its logical function. But its logical function depends upon the framework assumptions and rules constitutive of the particular language-game. This conclusion represents a highly significant conceptual development in the history of philosophy. For neither the meaning of a sentence nor its assignment of truth-value any longer depends simply upon an independent correspondence between language and the world. Language is seen as belonging to and making sense only in the context of the particular socio-linguistic language-games which have no logical basis outside themselves. Language-games become the starting-point of the philosophical enquiry; they neither require justification nor do they admit of it. They determine both the meaning of their linguistic constituents and the terms of reference for their assignments of truth. Containing within themselves their own peculiar criteria for meaning and truth determinations, the language-games assume an autonomy of one another that can no longer be bridged by an external world against which they can be compared, for it is they that determine the nature of the comparison.

One need not labour to establish the connection between all this and the theory-ladenness thesis discussed in the previous chapter. To say an observation sentence is theory-laden amounts to saying that its production is not a consequence of a simple interaction between a language-user and the world. For given that the individual is a language user, the description of the relevant experience of the world is itself determined by reference to the theoretical or background assumptions characteristic of the appropriate language-game or belief system. Insofar as observation statements and the observation terms of which they consist derive meaning from the language-game in which they are expressed, they are meaning variant in respect of changes in the language-game and they are thus *epistemically idiosyncratic.*

It is this epistemic feature of the theory-ladenness thesis that militates against the use which is sometimes made of it. In the domain of any universe of discourse certain beliefs will feature peculiarly as propositional fragments of the framework in terms of which adjudications are made. While such beliefs usually go unarticulated, their enumeration isolates a special class of propositions which are primitive in respect of the epistemic judgments they license. They are foundational elements of the system in the sense that they determine the evidential ordering and priority of the propositions which derive from them. They are fossilized empirical propositions to the extent that the evidential relations which they order cannot in any straightforward way be used to shift them. That is to say, no proposition which a foundational belief licenses could in itself unseat that foundational belief, for the challenging proposition would presuppose the validity of the foundational item it was meant to call in question. To formulate the point more precisely: in respect of any standard belief there is a foundational belief so related to it than no proposition within the system of beliefs could plausibly be adduced to challenge the foundation of the system.

As we put this earlier, there comes a point in our chain of reasoning at which one finds propositions for which no further grounds can be supplied beyond the data which they are supposed to monitor. We reach a belief in our chain of reasoning that is *primitive* in respect of the reasons it licenses. The belief is thus of such a kind that the reasons that could be adduced either for or against it will be no better entrenched epistemologically than it is itself. The explanation of this is tied to the taxonomy of evidential priorities which the foundational primitive sustains. This being so, it is clear that no evidential item that could plausibly be alleged as a ground in favour of doubting the truth of the primitive would be regarded as evidentially more entrenched than the primitive. Indeed, it is characteristic of the primitive that it determines the degree of evidential entrenchment to be enjoyed by the propositions which it orders.

If we could not be certain, for example, that we have each got only one physical body, might we not lose confidence in everything our sensory faculties characteristic of a single body revealed? What I believe is of such a kind that the grounds I can furnish in its favour will be no more secure than the belief they are called to support. It is in this sense that these framework beliefs determine the nature of grounds, as well as the role grounds play in the system. The foundational items thus remain invariant under testing, for they are themselves the principles in virtue of which we characterize the way we test. We will not be less certain of having got only one body before than after we look down to see. In respect of epistemic primitives there is thus a sense in which there is no making sure, for it is they that determine when it makes sense to speak of making sure and when it does not. They are themselves epistemic templates of sensible doubt.

If the argument is left in this form, it is tempting to think that the logical extension of the theory-ladenness thesis must commit us to full-blown epistemic relativism. If epistemic primitives determine the semantic and evidential relations pertaining to a specific theory or sphere of discourse, it would no longer seem possible to discriminate rationally between 'conflicting' theories or spheres of discourse. Since these spheres of discourse are deemed to be logically autonomous, the respective epistemic primitives will serve to interpret any discrepant data in a way which is consistent with the evidential ordering of their respective belief systems. That is, if the presuppositions of theory T_1 and theory T_2 are primitive in the sense that they respectively license what the proponent of T_1 or T_2 will accept as reasons for or against T_1 or T_2, it would seem to follow that our rational grounds for arbitrating between T_1 and T_2 are thereby relinquished. There is no neutral standpoint in virtue of which a determination could be made concerning the adequacy conditions for the acceptability of T_1 over T_2. Neither framework will countenance as an adequate reason for doubt, a belief that depends upon assumptions which the framework does not itself license. We are now in a position to see that if the theory-ladenness thesis thus rendered is granted, its implications would undermine the possibility of rational discrimination between competing conceptual systems. When all is said, we would be obliged to concede that one educational or political theory is no more or less adequate than any other, and this is not a conclusion that we find palatable. The difficulty is that the relativist thicket in which we have become entangled deprives us of the objective standpoint from which any such arbitration between competing theories might be warranted. One cannot, in one and the same consistent breath, concede that there is no such thing as a 'proper perspective' and then go on to argue as if there were. The general point is well made by G.J. Warnock when he says:

> Much admirable philosophical work has been done upon the notion of 'ways of seeing', of angles of vision, of — to speak more ponderously — alternative conceptual systems. We have become familiar enough with the idea that phenomena may be viewed in more than one way, comprehended within more than one theory, interpreted by more than one set of explanatory concepts. It has thus become almost impossible to believe that some one way of seeing, some one sort of theory, has any exclusive claim to be the right way; the notion of 'reality' itself, it would commonly be held, must be given its sense in terms of some particular theory of view, so that the claim that any such theory reveals or corresponds to 'reality' can be given a circular justification which is also open, in just the same way, to quite other views as well. (Warnock, 1958, p. 144)

We thus conclude this first section by affirming that the implications of the theory-ladenness thesis are of such a kind that we cannot, without moving beyond an evolutionary epistemology of power, use it in the way in which it would need to be used to justify it educationally. If there really is nothing to which we can appeal to discriminate between the merit of believing T_1 and T_2, it would be rationally infelicitous to believe either, and this is bound to make you uncomfortable if you are concerned that what you believe is true.

In the subsequent pages we shall be concerned to demonstrate that though the general strategy we have enunciated can be employed in favour of a pernicious relativism, there is a version of the relativist argument that derives from a scepticism that is not pernicious. We propose to show this by:

1   arguing that the starting points in our chains of reasoning may be only temporary; and
2   arguing that a language-game or theory-relative belief system should not be construed as a comprehensive metaphysical system impervious to external assessment.

Let us commence this part of the disquisition by placing a logical caveat. In our consideration of the epistemic structure of conceptual systems we must not be seduced into thinking that the propositions which constitute these systems are a homogeneous corpus of propositions laid down once and for all. Propositions which have long belonged to the scaffolding of our reasoning may be dislodged and given a different role in our thought. A proposition which we now treat as something to test by experience can become transformed into a rule by which we test. While the propositions which feature as the framework of a conceptual system are treated as rules for judgement, it is not inconceivable that the sustained accumulation of anomalies to which they have themselves given rise might well erode their stability. It is, however, crucial to recognize that the conceptual shift of epistemic primitives is no casual matter. Essentially, the shift is a conceptual revolution, *alla Kuhn*, more or less dramatic, and the instantiation of new primitives will generate widespread revisions as well as the redistribution of truth values across the entire system. But the point we are really wishing to stress here relates to the transient boundary existing between the propositions which compose the system in virtue of which we make our assessments, and the propositions which get assessed in the context of the system.

At this point it may be objected that we are guilty of palpable contradiction. For it was earlier argued that at the root of reasoned belief lies belief which does not itself rest upon reasons. Doubt presupposes a proposition or set of propositions which we exempt from doubt. This view is incompatible, it might be insisted, with the view we are now espousing: namely, that even the epistemic primitives which feature as propositional fragments of the framework of our conceptual system can be shaken from their peculiar position of logical priority. It would thus seem that no epistemic primitive is intrinsically immune from doubt and indeed, this is what we would wish to say.

It may be possible to dissipate the feeling of antinomy here by observing that from the admission that doubt presupposes an acceptance of some proposition or set of propositions exempt from doubt, it does not follow that these propositions are *permanently exempt from doubt*. We can, in principle, subject to doubt any and every epistemic primitive, but we cannot doubt them all at one and the same time and from the same basis. On any particular occasion doubt must be sustained by some belief we do not question. What we are really contending is that the epistemic elements which go to constitute the framework of our conceptual system are not a specifiable corpus of undemonstrable presuppositions which mark the unchanging and ultimate foundation of our chains of reasoning. While there is — at any one time — a foundation upon which 'doubt' and 'knowledge' rest, it is neither ultimate nor unchanging.

In saying this we are of course, espousing a modified scepticism that amounts to fallibilism, and in the light of our earlier remarks about the self-stultifying character of comprehensive scepticism, we are not unaware that fallibilism comes perilously close to being paradoxical. If all beliefs are susceptible of revision, fallibilism must itself be susceptible of revision; and once this concession is made, one is bound to concede that it may not after all be the case that nothing about the world can be known for certain. Such a logical lament may not be without a point, but it is a point that is easily exaggerated. From the admission that fallibilism may be false, it does not follow that it is false. The fallibilist does not deny that an empirical belief may be well-supported, on the contrary, the supposition is that fallibilism is itself a well supported belief. What the fallibilist denies is that even the most impressive of well-supported beliefs admits of conclusive certification. For the fallibilist there are no indubitable items of empirical knowledge. While the range of statements to which the fallibilist dictum applies might include itself, the self-reference is innocuous, or at most tolerably self-enfeebling. The possibility that fallibilism may be false does not entail that a genuine alternative to what it claims to be true has actually been provided. To say that all beliefs are corrigible is not to deny that some beliefs may be justified. We discover that some beliefs are corrigible by appeal not to incorrigible beliefs, but to beliefs we deem more worthy than those they call in question. Fallibilism and justification are compatible; fallibilism and conclusive certification are not.

It would, of course, be mistaken to think that we are rationally obliged to relinquish an epistemic primitive as soon as it is found to generate anomalies. On the contrary, we submit that it is a feature of the rational process that we adopt, in the face of discrepant data, a *principle of tenacity* which assists in ensuring that our investigations are not prematurely diverted. However this may be, it is clear that an accumulation of anomalies cannot be tolerated indefinitely without putting the conceptual system under intolerable strain. In the end, even an epistemic primitive can be shifted from its position of logical priority, and it is in this sense that we assert that the starting-point of an enquiry may be only temporary.

Let us reiterate that the uprooting of an epistemic primitive is not a mere shift in language; it is a radical and fundamental shift in our conception of things. It is a shift which may occur when the accumulation of anomalies to which the primitive gives rise can no longer be accommodated without abandoning the supporting beliefs in terms of which the primitive was all along held fast. In this respect, one could say that the epistemic primitive has itself taken part in the conceptual shift to a new standpoint in which it is no longer included as a primitive. What has been contributed by the primitive in terms of understanding has been incorporated into a new system of belief in which the former primitive is regarded as so astonishing as to call itself in question.

Once it is conceded that the starting-point of a chain of reasoning, an epistemic primitive, may be only temporary, the force of relativism is considerably diminished. For if the presuppositions upon which a conceptual system depends are not wholly immune to doubt or totally resistant to revision, a conceptual system could not be as hermetically sealed as the relativist thesis requires. If the tenability of an epistemic primitive and assignments of truth-value were matters determined entirely within the system of reasoning which the primitive licenses, then it is difficult to see how, without a more comprehensive notion of 'reason' that epistemic relativism allows, primitives could ever be challenged.

Against all this it could be protested that our view rests on naivete; for the concept of truth is in any case systematically ambiguous. Consider, it might be argued, the status of a mathematical proposition, say, a theorem of geometry. In ascribing the predicate 'true' to such a proposition we are doing no more than reiterating what, within some system of geometry, is licensed as 'true'. In this case, our ascription of the predicates true or false reveals that the mathematical proposition or theorem could be proved true in one system of geometry and false in another. And what 'could be proved true' comes to here is simply that some particular mathematical proposition or theorem is derivable from the axioms of the system in accordance with the appropriate apparatus of transformational rules which that system stipulates.

Now it is clear that here we have an impressive paradigm for a concept of truth which at first sight appears to reduce unambiguously to what within some system is — in accordance with the relevant derivation rules — called 'true'. But while we do sometimes speak of truth as equivalent to 'truth within a system', it would be unwise to make too much of this admission. For to speak of truth in this way is a technical and a misleading way of speaking. Let us elaborate this.

Our basic dissatisfaction with the concept of 'truth within a system' arises from the recognition that it exhibits a radically different logical character from what might be called our ordinary concept of truth. This difference in logical character is brought out well by Mackie:

> Ordinary truth obeys the law of excluded middle; as soon as we have adequately specified a statement and its negation, one or other of them must be true. But it may well be that of a well-formed formula of a certain system, and its negation, neither is a theorem of the system, neither can be proved within it. (Mackie, 1973, p. 24)

Although he does not elaborate the point, we submit that the distinction between our ordinary concept of truth and the concept of 'truth within a system' could be amplified in the following way. If the ascription of the predicate 'true' depends on provability in some specific system, then 'true', 'false' will not constitute an exhaustive division of what can be stated in the system, and thus the law of excluded middle is deprived of its application. This may be clearer if we consider the construction of a mathematical system. In a formal deductive system such as Euclidean geometry what we see introduced are various primitive symbols, the rules for well-formed formulae, axioms. Given that 'negation' is present in the system, it is quite possible that there will be well-formed formulae which nobody has succeeded in proving or disproving. Consider as a possible candidate, for instance, the famous conjecture of Goldbach: that every even number is equal to the sum of two primes. Insofar as this particular case remains unsettled, however, it might be objected that what this putative mathematical anomaly reflects is not the peculiarity of the concept of truth which underpins it, but rather the boring fact that we are just not yet competent enough to resolve it, or if we are, we have not laboured hard enough on its resolution. But even if this objection is granted, it is still possible that there are well-formed formulae that can never be proved. Indeed, if recent investigations into the matter are dependable, it would seem that Pierre de Fermat's well-formed formula: 'For all n greater than two, there exist no integers x, y and z, not equal to zero, such that $x^n + y^n = Z^n$ would — despite Fermat's pretension to have proved it — be a case in point (see Waismann, 1951, pp. 130–1). But whatever the verdict arrived at on this matter, it is difficult to see how the technical concept of 'truth within a system' can escape the Godelain paradox that in any given formal deductive system which is sufficiently sophisticated to express arithmetic, there will be some propositions of elementary number theory which, while regarded as true, are paradoxically not provable within the system (Godel, 1970, pp. 87–107). In the end what 'truth within a system' seems to involve is the equation of 'true' with provable. And the point is that what this equation trades on is a *confusion between the syntactic and semantic notion of validity*. While it is one thing to say that a theorem is syntactically valid in following from certain axioms, it is quite another thing to say that it is semantically or model theoretically valid. On the assumption that truth is a semantic notion, to say that a theorem is true is to say that in every model on the intended interpretation of the sentence expressing the theorem, it turns out to be true.

It would lead us too far astray to pursue any of this further here. It is to be hoped, however, that enough has now been said to show that the technical concept of 'truth within a system' differs from our ordinary concept of truth in some very important respects. A salient feature of our ordinary concept of truth shows itself in the way our ascriptions of 'true' are restricted by the law of excluded middle once the specification of a statement and its negation are given. However, if truth amounts to nothing more than 'provable within a system', it is difficult to see how the law of excluded middle could unambiguously have application; for any such system would either be incomplete, in the sense that the totality of truths which the system is supposed to embrace can never all be reproduced, or else bankrupt, in the sense that it establishes a proposition as 'true' which might otherwise be false (see Quine, 1969, pp. 18–20).

Thus it seems that any attempt to generalize the concept of 'truth within a system' as the paradigm for what is meant ordinarily by the predicate 'true' would be misguided. So while we have no wish to deny that the particular conceptual system to which a statement belongs (e.g. classical physics, psychology, religion, etc.) may make an important contribution to what is meant by saying that the relevant proposition is 'true', we maintain that the question of whether a particular use of the term 'true' is acceptable cannot depend simply upon the truth-value configuration which the specific theory governs.

The relativist might reply to this by saying that to doubt an epistemic primitive is to question the conceptual system to which it gives rise. Although there may be a shift from one conceptual system to another, it would be a mistake to think that this shift is a consequence of some form of rational discrimination between conflicting conceptual systems. Such a shift is best described, in our view, as more akin to a conceptual conversion. While we agree that to doubt an epistemic primitive is in some sense to call into question the conceptual system which it sustains, we do not accept that the shift from one conceptual system to another is necessarily non-rational. But to show this we need to revert to our earlier claim that a language-game or conceptual system should not be construed as a comprehensive metaphysical framework impervious to external assessment.

There is clearly a grave ambiguity in the epistemic relativist's use of such terms as 'theoretical system', 'conceptual system', 'language game', etc., and we suggest that this is an ambiguity on which the relativist's argument trades. Epistemic relativists tend to construe these expressions generously, in accordance with their conceptual needs. So when the claim is made that no observations can be made independently of a theory, the term 'theory' is being construed as a closed, logically independent network of beliefs. Similarly, when the relativist is referring, for instance, to scientific or religious frameworks, the interpretation conveys the impression of a comprehensive and closed system of beliefs in terms of which an individual organizes his or her entire experience of the world.

We have no wish to deny that it is part of what it means to describe an individual as say, a theist, that such an individual is disposed to see the world in terms of God. But implicit in the believer's talk about the world in terms of God are foundational elements which are common to theists and antheists alike. For example, the theist's belief in God is not secured at the expense of his or her belief in the uniformity of nature. Thus among the beliefs which the theist does not call in question are primitives which transcend the religious language-game, so to speak.

A similar transcendence holds in the case of theory-laden observation claims. Therefore, theory which informs a particular observation statement need not be the theory for which the observation statement serves as an empirical test. We try to make sense of, and organize, our experience of the world, then, not in terms of a closed system of beliefs, formalized in the light of a single epistemic primitive, but in terms of a comprehensive conceptual system comprising epistemic primitives drawn from a whole host of specific language-games.

Against the relativist who must define, say, theism as a closed sphere of discourse with its own internal logic, we contend that the religious believer is an individual who shares in a diverse culture. That is to say, culture has not bequeathed him or her a monolithic intellectual history; the religious believer, like nearly everyone else, is variously educated. This is why religious believers are not less certain than unbelievers that human beings have only one physical body, at least one physical body at any one time. Our experience of the world is rendered in terms of a comprehensive world picture in which a variety of epistemic primitives are drawn from an array of specific language-games such as theism, science, morality, psychology and so on.

It is evident that when the relativist admits the possibility of conversion from one conceptual system to another, he or she cannot be referring coherently to a shift from one comprehensive world picture to another. For a conversion as comprehensive as this would require something far more radical than the 'persuasive conversion', concerning which some relativists have reverently spoken. Even 'persuasion' depends upon the possibility of communication, and it is hard to see how any sense can be made of 'communication' without allowing for the sharing of some percepts and concepts. For without minimal agreement of this kind, we should be unable to individuate any utterances when the situation of use could even be specified.

And if arbitration between competing conceptual systems amounts to no more than a terminological difficulty, then the relativist's dilemma loses its point. For epistemic relativism rests upon the supposition that alternative conceptual systems are not simply reducible to terminological disputes. The term 'velocity' would not be susceptible of relativization merely by switching units of measurements.

Given the distinction between a *comprehensive* conceptual system and a discipline or theory specific one, it is possible to subject a specific epistemic primitive to doubt without effecting an illicit transposition of primitives (whereby the primitives of one conceptual system have been used to judge another, when each conceptual system sets its own inviolable standards of assessments). When a specific primitive is called into question, the tribunal it faces is not a system of beliefs unacceptable to the proponent of the primitive, but the *comprehensive system of beliefs* in which the specific primitive is just one component. In the context of this comprehensive metaphysical system, rational arbitration takes place between specific conceptual systems, each of which plays a role in defining the logical character of the comprehensive system. We can indeed doubt only in the light of some propositions which — at the time — we exempt from doubt, but on the view we are proposing, the totality of these propositional primitives that are, in the required sense, exempt from doubt constitute our comprehensive conceptual system.

When the matter is put this way, we deprive the relativist's notions of *from within* and *from without* the language game of much of their initial force. In order to doubt a theory specific primitive we do invoke criteria of assessment which were not themselves all originally licensed by the primitive under scrutiny. Construed on the proffered model, the idiom *from without* is thus inappropriate, for the origin of our doubt derives *from within the comprehensive* conceptual system in which the theory specific primitive is an element.

Whether a theory or discipline-specific primitive rationally deserves to be countenanced depends in part upon its compatibility with the repertoire of primitives that feature comprehensively. If reflection reveals that the specific primitive is consistent with the comprehensive enumeration of primitives, then it satisfies what we take to be the minimal rational requirement of its acceptability. If a theory or discipline-specific primitive turns out, upon reflection, to conflict with the comprehensive array of primitives, it is the conflicting primitive that will normally require revision. The rational individual is under some logical obligation to ensure that the propositional fragments which feature as framework components of the comprehensive conceptual system are consistent with one another. The consistency condition asserts that it is not permissible to accept all of a system of propositional primitives, once we are cognizant of the fact that within the system some propositions are contradictory.

For a contradiction without our comprehensive conceptual systems implies that at least one of its constituent primitives must be false. And it is the nature of an epistemic primitive that a condition of its acceptability is it being true. It is no part of our purpose to suggest that it is easy to determine which of our conflicting beliefs, if any, must be abandoned or revised in order to restore consistency to the system, in a way that disturbs the system least. Nor are we suggesting that the rational individual will in fact assent to no propositions which contradict one another, for this would imply omniscience. The point is simply that once an individual is cognizant of a contradiction between propositional primitives, he or she is required rationally to reflect upon the system with an aim to restoring consistency. From a rational point of view the fewer inconsistencies within a conceptual system the better.

Once the concept of epistemic primitives is thus assimilated into the context of our fallibilist realist ontology, the concept of indoctrination takes on a much broader interpretation than the analytic account, canvassed at the beginning of this chapter, allows, and we are now in a position to attend to its elucidation.

Let us now consider the traditional accounts of indoctrination in terms of such a scheme. The method account speaks of teaching in such a way that belief is always accompanied by evidence. We wish to suggest in the light of the sketch above that even if the teachers were able to achieve this noble aim, indoctrination would not be avoided. The reason for this is that if what we regard as evidence is itself pre-determined by the framework of belief primitives, having evidence for a belief is no more a sign of intellectual freedom than making the sign of the cross is a proof of religiosity. The process becomes all the more pernicious when it is realized that we have, as educators, identified the provision of reasons as the cornerstone of critical thinking. On the contrary, general training in the provision of evidence does little more than serve unwittingly to promulgate the underlying ideological structures in terms that make them appear rational. The content criterion seems to us similarly in jeopardy. The problem is that the criteria of discrimination set out by the proponents of the content view simply beg the question in favour of one set of epistemic primitives as against another. One cannot talk about determinations of truth and falsehood independently of a specification of the specific epistemic primitives in accordance with which adjudications of truth are made. Once the specification is made, the question of arbitrating rationally between conflicting epistemic primitives is transformed into the incommensurability dispute, and the original criterion of 'content' amounts to little more than a nostrum of partisan epistemology.

The criterion of intention is also displaced as a true measure of the problem confronting the educator. It is one thing to fashion theories on the value of an open mind; it is quite another to become aware that what we are calling an open mind is itself conditioned by a form of scientific rationalism that has by its very nature closed our own minds on open issues. The educator who believes that indoctrination is avoided simply by ensuring that children can question everything they have been taught makes the mistake of assuming that the tools of enquiry are themselves free of ideological bias and insularity.

We tend to draw a sharp distinction between science and non-science on the ground that science proceeds on the basis of evidential ordering and induction, whereas non-science does not. It is as if we believe that science has a monopoly of rationality, being the only enterprise that makes use of evidence in support of its conclusion. There are at least two replies to this. First, the domains which we tend to regard as non-scientific (e.g. morality, religion, etc.) actually make far more use of evidential procedures than they have hitherto been given credit for. We spend so little time considering these other areas that we are lamentably ignorant of the methodologies which govern them. Only by cavalierly dismissing these other enquiries are we able to maintain our prejudices about their subjective status. Indeed, had it been fashionable to invest research energies and equivalent findings for the development of these subject areas over the past half century, the epistemic disparity between science and these supposedly non-scientific domains would doubtless have been minimized. The supremacy of science and the concept of knowledge as power which it enshrines in contemporary society cannot be regarded correctly as the result of a methodological enterprise signifying the best and only legitimate tool by which we come to understand the world. The dominance of science in the western world and the attitudes it fosters have become strangely self-serving. Scientific enlightenment in the form of technologies of power is a self-fulfilling prophecy of the rape of nature. We have crystallized science into a metaphysics and our vision has become myopic.

The pervasiveness of the scientific idiom and the sphere of its influence are undeniable.We claim that our research is scientific because we believe that its being so makes it more reliable and important than if it were not. Science has become a banner word, an accolade ascribed to allegedly successful aspirants of knowledge. Most of us are either scientists, or if we are not, we are treated in ways which make us sometimes wish we were. Amongst those in arts faculties, there are few who have not been made to feel self-conscious of the nature of their intellectual expertise, not infrequently having to defend their professional competence against the persistent charge of irrelevance or unscientific. The faculty of science is no longer just one faculty among many. In this era of the self-avowed scientist, science has become the measure of all faculties that we believe to be worth having. To be engaged in scientific enquiry oneself or to be associated closely with those who are, has become a status symbol. In a milieu of convoluted scientific imperialism it is no surprise that science has partisans everywhere. One need only canvass the names of (sundry) university departments to appreciate the extent to which the cultural domination of science has shaped our perception of ourselves and of what makes us valuable. The aegis of the natural or physical sciences has been palpably extended to include engineering science, computer science, medical science. The proliferation of partisan terminology is exemplified by recent discipline designations of title which witness the fact that university departments previously simply called the department of politics or the department of sociology are now called the department of political science and the department of social science, respectively. The attempt to legitimate the work of the university by making its areas of study more scientific is further illustrated by other new designations such as health science, behavioural science, horticultural science, food science, environmental science and even mortuary science.

The impetus to scientific conformity has not been without its benefits, but our acquaintance with these is not in question; indeed, it is a feature of the cultural dominance of science that this should be so. Admittedly we have in recent years become aware of some of the more undesirable side-effects of a scientific technology, as we have been forced to grapple with the reality of a rapidly declining environment. But the exercise has in an important sense been epistemically unproductive. For it has really been the scientist who has identified the ecological problems, and where this has not been so, it has been the scientist who has pronounced upon their resolution. That academic culture sees this problem-solving orientation of science as unexceptionable is in itself a measure of the philosophical problem with which we have been here concerned. Science has become self-perpetuating, furthering its dominance by capitalizing on the very objections that might otherwise have served to call it in question. The notion that improved technology will make everything better, including the things improved technology is bound to make worse, is a peculiar educational disease of our times which badly needs to be cured.

The problem is that the standard treatment is irrelevant, treating only symptoms and leaving the aetiology of the disease unattended. As long as amelioration is defined in scientific terms, we shall be unable to perceive the genesis of the process, the amelioration of which we seek.

These deliberations clearly have serious ramifications for any system of education which pretends to do more than guarantee that society is able to perpetuate itself. Our educational system has so assimilated science to an all-embracing world view that education has itself become partisan, or as we earlier put it, 'intellectually sectarian'. Let us now endeavour to explain this.

The posture we assume towards science has come to define implicitly the posture we assume towards education. So pervasive is the scientific world view that it inhibits the disposition to think in ways which we normally regard as unscientific, and this is clearly reflected in the content of the school curriculum. Given our reverence for science, we incline to the view that this constraint is a good thing. We suppose that science has proved itself worthy of our total commitment and thus that our reverence for the enterprise is justified. We have now seen that this supposition is an exaggeration. The epistemology of science is not sufficiently rich to establish its monopoly of objectivity. We thus wish presently to argue that our inability to break the hold that science has on our thinking has diminished rather than enlarged the sphere of intellectual imagination and that such a hold is itself a pernicious form of indoctrination. While science once served to liberate mankind from the tyranny of dogmatic religion, it has unwittingly imposed on contemporary thought a tyranny of its own. Science has become as oppressive to the imaginative faculty as were the oracular pronouncements of religion against which science has traditionally inveighed. In this respect science has itself been transformed into a dogmatic religion.

Because we have earlier intimated a sympathy for the place of religious education in schools, it is tempting to think that we stand to defend the tenets of dogmatic religion. On the contrary, our objection to dogmatic science is, equally, an objection to dogmatic religion. Neither has the power to emancipate the mind from the conceptual structures which each requires for the generation of new insight. Both dogmatic science and dogmatic religion constrict rather than enlarge the domain of intellectual freedom. Dogmas set authoritarian limits, not logical limits, to what it is permissible to think. To this extent dogmatic science and dogmatic religion close minds, and a closed mind is tantamount to the paralysis of intellectual imagination.

Most of us find it easy to conceive of dogmatic religion, but what, one might ask, is dogmatic science? Is not science by its very nature liberating? The answer to this is not easy, for there is a radical ambiguity in the use which the term science has. It is true that science has played an important historic role in breaking the comprehensive hold which religion once had over the mind. It achieved this venerable task by affording the opportunity of thinking about the world in ways other than those that had become ideologically entrenched in the institutional Church. This entrenchment meant that the received wisdom was institutionalized as a vested interest of those in power. One's identity was itself tied to the institutional form in which it was made manifest. To challenge an accepted belief was therefore to challenge the institution and by implication, those who had vested interests in its perpetuation. The reification of religion was thus expressed as a bureaucratic, or institutional, representation of truth. Any challenge to the institution, or to the bureaucracy that ensured its function, was registered as an objection to truth and the objectors were maligned as heretics. The science of the time obliged a questioning of inherited beliefs and undermined the authoritarianism of the monolithic conceptual structure that had been built in the name of God. This we believe was a salutary gamut, and one can appreciate how the term science and enlightenment came to be used co-extensively. Science began as a heresy, but the reflective model it stimulated was regarded a heresy of enlightenment.

It is crucial to recognize, however, that the equivalence between science and enlightenment is an equivalence of process, not an equivalence of content. What was enlightening about science, we suggest, was not so much the specific content of its doctrines, as that its doctrines forced reflection upon the corpus of inherited beliefs. That this is so is borne out by our earlier remarks on epistemic primitives and their admission of testability. Despite protestations to the contrary, the content of science is not guaranteed by its methods of acquisition. An hypothesis which has thus far survived all our tests may be rejected in the light of further experience, and similarly, an hypothesis which is degenerate and failed our tests may tomorrow be reinstated. Epistemologically speaking, the content of science is no more secure than the content of religion, if security is rendered in terms simply of reasoned beliefs.

The ambiguity in the use of the term 'science' has arisen as the consequence of the failure to distinguish between science as '*reflective enlightenment*' and science as '*content enlightenment*'. Science enlarges the scope of intellectual freedom to the extent that it provides the conceptual tools for liberating the mind from the tyranny of rigid and inflexible doctrine. Much of the confusion about the status and value of science derives from contemporary society's collapsing of the above distinction, transforming the content of science, including its methodology, into the criterion of its enlightenment. Where science was once a force against authoritarianism, helping to speak the spell of oppressive religious dogma, it has come ironically to cast an authoritarian spell of its own. While religious salvation was once the prerogative of the institutional Church, intellectual salvation has become the prerogative of the scientific establishment.

This being so our contention is that insofar as science has been institutionalized as an all pervasive world view, its content has ceased to be subversive. Science has lost its power to challenge inherited belief, because it is science itself that now constitutes the inheritance. Science does, as part of its natural evolution, question, modify and revise certain of its doctrines, but the questioning is almost invariably set within a methodological framework driven by power which is not itself questioned. This is true even in the case of conceptual revolutions, since paradigm shift is movement from one kind of science to another, not movement from science to a perspective which itself challenges movement in terms of technologies of power.

The challenge science presents itself, in respect of its content, is not the salutary challenge science formerly presented to religion, for the institutionalization of science has deprived science of the power to call itself in question, by virtue of challenging the insatiable appetite for power upon which its technological constructions have been built.

One need only look to the character of our education system to determine the extent to which science is embedded in and conditions learning. It is ironic that 'facts' of science are ultimately taught to children in as dogmatic a manner as were the 'facts' of religion. Consider, for example, the religious fervour with which the science of evolution is presented against creationism. What science is thought to offer is a body of knowledge, passed down to lesser mortals from those whose position in the system makes them almost more than mortal. Where this is not so, we have hypostatized the methodology of science, transforming a guide to strategy into a law of nature. The scientist has replaced the high priest of dogmatic religion, but he has certainly not relinquished the power and authority attached to the office. The establishment of science is sustained by vested interests much in the same way as was dogmatic religion. The myths are different but the philosophic disposition is the same. The more powerful the scientific establishment has become, the more it has to lose from those conceptual challenges that would deprive it of some of its wealth. We are told that there is no knowledge outside of science, yet we do not — as we tried to show earlier in the chapter — have even a tolerably coherent epistemic account of what it means to say that we have knowledge. Learning has never been more 'authority ridden' than it is now, though the form of authority has perhaps become more subtle.

We may do more, that is to say, to create the impression that we educationally nurture the critical faculties, and that our school children are now really 'thinking for themselves', but the context of reflection is so rigidly circumscribed by what is deemed respectable and permissible in terms of the ideology of power that the exercise is little more than a sham. Scientific heretics, like their religious counterparts, suffer considerable hardships. School, college and university examination sanctions have proved to be powerful weapons against those who would wish to reflect critically on the power-driven technologies which reflect the dominant posture of our scientific interchange with nature. One would be very hard pressed to isolate an examination question that provides a forum for exhibiting the scope and limits of the epistemic power-preoccupation upon which contemporary science is built and in terms of which such examinations are themselves set. We say that our educational programmes are designed to encourage children to think critically, but we preserve a system of exams which ensures that they will have no time or stimulus to do what we say we encourage them to do.

It is imperative to be clear as to just what we are and what we are not arguing. We are not suggesting that science has nothing to recommend it that would be absurd. Our objective is not to denigrate the technological achievements of science, but rather to put those achievements in a proper perspective which does not depend on a prior commitment to an epistemology of power to assess them. We are not suggesting that science has been unsuccessful. On the contrary, our point is that if anything, it has been all too successful in that science has itself become the measure of success. Because science has campaigned so vigorously and effectively against its unscientific competitors it is science that reigns supreme in contemporary society as the arbiter of truth and this, as we have endeavoured to show, is educationally pernicious. Our argument has been directed to showing that society's reverence for science as the only source of knowledge is neither epistemically justified nor maintained without considerable diminution of reflective and imaginative capability. If science is designed to enhance the critical imagination, its institutionalization has produced the contrary result. Having generalized science as an all-embracing world view, its hold over the mind is comprehensive and the values it fosters destructive.

Within this world view all rivals to science are assessed as ephemeral historical phenomena, but science is itself made exempt from this historical judgment. Science is construed on the model of a neutral activity untainted by the socio-historical factors that shape the myths of its competitors. Under the guise of neutrality and objectivity governments have invested billions of dollars in the establishment of science. Science has unsurprizingly become so closely aligned with the State that the perpetuation of western society and scientific progress feature essentially as one and the same thing. As the dominant cultural influence, science comes to function not as a critic of the status quo, but as one of its most ardent supporters. The dominance of science in education thus reflects an impoverished homogeneity of approach, for the only approach is deemed to be the scientific one. In the end we close minds on the pretence of opening them. We submit that we all have before us the momentous task of advancing education at a stage in its history at which it is clear that our efforts in the name of science may have contributed to its decline. This being so, the rather well-worn distinction between education and indoctrination is tantamount to a philosophic purgative, and this should be worrying, especially if you are one of those who tends to mistake purgatives for food.

References

ARCHAMBAULT, R.D. (1965) *Philosophical Analysis and Education*, London: Routledge and Kegan Paul.

BROWN, S.C. (1974) (ed.) *Philosophy of Psychology*, London: Macmillan.

GEACH, P.T. and BEDNAROWSKi, W.F. (1956) 'The law of excluded middle', *Proceedings of the Aristotelian Society*, Supplementary Vol.

GLOVER, J. (1976) *The Philosophy of Mind*, Oxford: Oxford University Press.

GODEL, K. (1970) 'On formally undecidable propositions of *Principia Mathematics* and Related Systems I', Cambridge, MA: Harvard University Press.

GUTTENPLAN, S. (1975) *Mind and Language*, Oxford: Clarendon Press.

HOLLINS, T.H.B. (1964) (ed.) *Aims in Education: The Philosophic Approach*, Manchester: Manchester University Press.

HONDERICH, T. (1973) *Essays on Freedom of Action*, London: Routledge and Kegan Paul.

LAURA, R.S. (1978) 'Philosophical foundations of religious education', *Educational Theory*, Fall.

LAURA, R.S. (1980) 'Epistemic Relativism: On the rational arbitration of conflicting conceptual schemes', Paper delivered at the Annual conference of the Philosophy of Education Society of Australasia.

LAURA, R.S. (1981a) 'Philosophical foundations of science education', *Educational Philosophy and Theory*, **13**.

LAURA, R.S. (1981b) 'Wittgenstein's doctrine of silence or does the philosophical investigations show less than it says?', *Prudentia*, Supplementary Number.

MACKIE, J.L. (1973) *Truth, Probability and Paradox*, Oxford: Clarendon Press.

MALCOLM, N. (1977) 'The groundlessness of belief', in BROWN, S.C. (ed.) *Reason and Religion*, Ithica: Cornell University Press.

PETERS, R.S. (1963) *Authority Responsibility and Education*, London: Allen and Unwin.

PITTENGER, B.F. (1941) *Indoctrination for American Society*, New York: Macmillan.

QUINE, W.V. (1953) *From a Logical Point of View*, Cambridge, MA: Harvard University Press.

QUINE, W.V. (1966) *The Way of Paradox and Other Essays*, New York: Random House.

QUINE, W.V. (1969) *Set Theory and its Logic*, revised edition, Cambridge, MA: Harvard University Press.

QUINE, W.V. (1970) *Philosophical Logic*, New Jersey: Prentice Hall.

SCHEFFLER, I. (1960) *The Language of Education*, Illinois: Thomas.

SNOOK, I.A. (1972) (ed.) *Concepts of Indoctrination*, London: Routledge and Kegan Paul.

WAISMANN, F. (1951) *Introduction to Mathematical Thinking*, London: Hafner.

WARNOCK, G.J. (1958) *English Philosophy Since 1900*, Oxford: Oxford University Press.

WINCH, P. (1967) 'Understanding a primitive society', in PHILLIPS, D.Z. (ed.) *Religion and Understanding*, London: Basil Blackwell.

WITTGENSTEIN, L. (1953) *Philosophical Investigations*, ANSCOMBE, G.E.M. (transl.) New York: Macmillan.

WITTGENSTEIN, L. (1969) *On Certainty*, ANSCOMBE, G.E.M. and VON WRIGHT G.H. (eds), PAUL, D. and ANSCOMBE, G.E.M. (transl.), Oxford: Basil Blackwell.

Chapter 4

The Reductionist Ghost in the
Educational Machine

Our burden in the previous chapter was to elucidate the concept of indoctrination by appeal to the conceptual dynamics of pedagogy which integrates a modified version of what we called, 'fallibilist realism' with a theory of knowledge based upon our account of 'epistemic primitives'. We observed that inasmuch as a power-driven form of knowledge has been institutionalized through the teaching of a form of science which enshrines that concept of knowledge, indoctrination is a far more subtle educational process than the traditional philosophical accounts reveal. It was argued that the concept of knowledge upon which this form of science focuses is proliferated educationally with an ontological priority not adequately justified in epistemic terms. The point of these deliberations was to show that insofar as the pedagogic reliance upon and priority given to the teaching of power-based knowledge is epistemologically gratuitous, the mandatory study of the form of science which enshrines knowledge as power should be recognized as the state-sanctioned, albeit unwitting, promulgation of an ideology of environmental destruction and degradation.

The main concern of the present chapter is thus to elaborate the implications of the knowledge as power paradigm for the current pedagogy which has given rise to environmental expropriation and social alienation. We argue that the obsession of educational knowledge with power gives rise to tools of technology which most aptly express and manifest it. To secure power over nature we are — as we earlier intimated — driven to eliminate the *qualitative* dimensions of nature from the *quantitative* associations of which they form a part. The more quantitative we can make the objects of our investigation, the easier it is to predict the outcome of our interaction with them and their interactions with each other. With every increase in predictability we enhance our hold on probability and this augments — or so the orthodox view would have it — our capacity for knowing. What the methodology of '*qualitative extirpation*', as we shall dub it, depends upon, however, is the reconceptualization of the things of nature into the things of technology. We thus perceive nature as a machine and create a methodology of reductionism to assist in the disassembly of nature into the machine-like parts of which it is composed. We hypostatize our detachment from the objects of investigation on the pretence of greater objectivity without recognizing that our method of interaction with nature is itself fundamentally alienating. We thus become progressively separated and distanced from the very world which our methodology was intended to help us understand. To begin our argument, we trace the ontology of our contemporary crisis to the methodological expression within science that sustains western society's technologies of power.

The Biography of Mechanism

Mechanism implies the idea that the universe is a machine made up of smaller and smaller parts, down to the smallest fundamental parts. It furthermore implies that there are certain laws or logical relations amongst the parts. This being so the idea is that if you can discover what these logical relations are, you will be able to decipher all there is to know about the machine. If the world and things which constitute it can be understood as a machine, knowledge is designed to afford the scientist the power to take the machine apart and reassemble it as required to fix up its internal workings when they deteriorate or dysfunction.

Mechanism dates back to the early Greek concept of *Atomos* (meaning: 'indivisible'). It was the Greek philosopher Democritus (460–370 BC) who developed the concept of 'atom' to represent the smallest indivisible part of the universe. The mechanistic model for understanding the world was thus explicated by means of a methodology of reduction whereby wholes are broken down into their atomistic components. The 'method', as outlined by Birch (1990):

> Consists in subdividing the world into its smallest parts, which at one time were thought to be atoms. The essence of atomism is that these parts remain unchanged no matter what particular whole they constitute, be it star or brain. Having divided the universe into its smallest bits you then try to build it up again, and of course when you do that you get a machine. The reductionist principle of atomism leads to the doctrine of mechanism — that the universe and all entities in the universe are machines. (Birch, 1990, p. 57)

It was not until the 'age of enlightenment' that a complete reductio-mechanistic world paradigm took shape. The birth of modern science in seventeenth-century Europe can be understood insightfully as the consequence of the clash between scientific thought and religious authority. More accurately, the advent of modern science reflected a paradigm change from one epistemic and ontic world view to another; from the monistic holistic philosophy (or science) of the Greeks and Stoics, who viewed the universe as a 'self-sufficient' living organism, to the dualist-mechanistic philosophy of Newtonian science. The emphasis of the emergent Newtonian mechanistic paradigm was to remove from the world, as it was then understood, all its 'qualitative'-'subjective' aspects so that the only aspects which remained were the 'quantitative'-'objective' ones. Qualitative extirpation would thus make the world amenable to analysis within the context of mathematics. The task of the methodolgy of this power-based epistemology was to analyse and reduce the world in such a way that what remained was simply a collection of quantifiable, analysable, 'dead' or inert objects devoid of any intrinsic value or purpose. In effect, western society had been duped into jettisoning its intimate bonds with nature in favour of technological interactions with the largely inorganic and mindless objects of scientific investigation.

Central to this paradigmatic transformation, according to Merchant (1990) were critical changes in the 'controlling imagery' of nature as 'female'. The ancient organic image of nature as a 'nurturing mother' was replaced by the image of a disorderly 'wild and uncontrollable' female in need of immediate subjugation. In Merchant's words:

> The metaphor of the earth as a nurturing mother was gradually to vanish as a dominant image as the Scientific Revolution proceeded to mechanize and rationalize the world view. The second image, nature as disorder, called forth an important modern idea, that of power over nature. Two new ideas, those of mechanism and of the domination and mastery of nature, became core concepts of the modern world.... (Merchant, 1990, p. 2)

The most notable 'architects' of this male-chauvanistic reductio-mechanistic power paradigm were the four seventeenth-century figures Galileo Galilei, Francis Bacon, René Descartes and Isaac Newton. Considered as the father of modern science, Galileo (1564–1642) initiated the combined use of scientific experimentation and mathematical language to 'deduce', what he believed to be, nature's mechanical laws. To understand nature, he maintained, you need to understand its language; and its language, he believed, could be reduced to mathematical symbols and geometrical figures — numbers, circles, triangles etc. Galileo's distinction between the things of nature which could be quantified (i.e., which could be weighed and measured) and those which were non-quantifiable (i.e., the values and qualities of emotion, love, smell, colour, taste, sound etc., the 'secondary', unimportant, 'subjective' properties) were to restrict the domain of learning to just that: the quantifiable and the 'objective' (Laura and Heaney, 1990, p. 28).

The second architect, Francis Bacon (1561–1626), formulated an aggressive creed for the emerging mechanistic world paradigm. He explicitly stated that 'knowledge' is 'power over nature'. Getting things done for the material advancement of man was at the forefront of Bacon's thinking. The science of knowing and learning, he urged, must proceed with this in mind. In his publication, *Novum Organum* (1620), Bacon argued that 'power over nature' would never be realized through the definitions of knowledge held by the philosophers of old. The so called 'wisdom' that Aristotle, Plato and most other Greek philosophers possessed was, to him, 'contentious' and void of action. Their 'wisdom', he would write, '... abounds in words but is barren of works.... For fruits and works are as it were sponsors and sureties for the truth of philosophies' (*Novum Organum*, Trans. 1960, Book 1, Aphorisms LXXI–LXXIII). Although he considered the ideas of Democritus and other ancient mechanists as possessed of theoretical significance for the 'new science', he nevertheless dismissed the 'passive' metaphysical approach to knowledge (the 'why' of things) and replaced it with the 'active' 'how' (the 'facts' and 'works') of things.

According to Merchant, the feminist interpretation of Bacon's commitment to knowledge as the enlargement of man's dominion over nature required a 'new method of interrogation'. In adopting the Baconian approach, scientists would be instructed in the art of constraining and dissecting nature. 'By art and the hand of man', nature can then be 'forced out of her natural state and squeezed and molded'. In this way, 'human knowledge and human power meet as one' (Merchant, 1990, p. 171).

To this she adds:

> Here in bold sexual imagery is the key feature of the modern experimental method — constraint of nature in the laboratory, dissection by hand and mind, and the penetration of hidden secrets — language still used today in praising a scientist's 'hard facts', 'penetrating mind', or the 'thrust of his argument'. The constraints against penetration in Natura's lament over her torn garments of modesty have been turned into sanctions in language that legitimates the exploitation and 'rape' of nature for human good. . . . (Merchant, 1990, p. 171)

By virtue of these macho-mechanistic images of nature, the new paradigm fosters the view that nature exists as an object of investigation and exploitation, as something to be subdued, subjugated and conquered. A new way of seeing the world gives rise to a new way of doing science which replicates the values we attach to the earth as a machine to be taken apart, rebuilt and controlled/exploited, as women have traditionally been controlled and exploited. As Merchant puts it:

> Scientific method, combined with mechanical technology, would create a 'new organon', a new system of investigation, that unified knowledge with material power . . . [U]nder the mechanical arts, 'nature betrays her secrets more fully . . . than when in enjoyment of her natural liberty.' . . . The interrogation of witches as symbol for the interrogation of nature, the court room as a model for its inquisition, and torture through mechanical devices as a tool for the subjugation of disorder were fundamental to the scientific method as power. For Bacon . . . sexual politics helped to structure the nature of the empirical method that would produce a new form of knowledge and a new ideology of objectivity seemingly devoid of cultural and political assumptions. (Merchant, 1990, p. 172)

Another way of construing this paradigmatic transition from an interactive to an expropriative relationship with nature is by re-introducing the distinction between the observer and the observed. Nowhere is this more evident than in Bacon's approach to science, for here the objectivity of science is somehow secured by virtue of the observer detaching himself from the subject of observation itself. In essence the very methodology of science is one which defines the observer in the position of alienated subject. On this point, Rifkin elaborates:

> The new method Bacon alludes to is the 'scientific' method, an approach that could separate the observer from the observed and provide a neutral forum for the development of 'objective knowledge'. According to Bacon, objective knowledge would allow people to take 'command over things natural . . .' Every school child is weaned on Bacon's method. From the time we are able to form a conception, we

are informed that there is in fact an objective world out there whose secrets can be discovered and exploited to advance human ends. We are encouraged to create distance between ourselves and the world, to detach ourselves so that we can sever our natural relationships with things and turn them into objects for manipulation. The scientific method ... reflects our consuming passion for predictability and order. We have transformed all of physical reality into a giant testing site and then attempted to discover predictable patterns of behavior that can be exploited over and over in such a way as to advance our control over the forces of nature. The more successful we are at imperializing our environment, the more secure we feel. The long history of Western consciousness, which reached its zenith with the flowering of the Baconian revolution, can be summarized as follows: Knowledge is power, power is control, control is security. (Rifkin, 1985, pp. 17–18)

The third architect, René Descartes (1596–1650), provided the emerging mechanistic paradigm with the metaphysical postulate for its rationale. The mind (*res cogitans*. 'thinking thing') is for Descartes truly separate from body (*res extensa*. 'extended thing'). After subjecting everything to doubt, his inability to doubt his own doubting mind provided Descartes with his 'first principle' of his metaphysics *Cogito ergo sum* 'I think therefore I exist'. Descartes goes on to conclude: '. . . this self, that is to say, the soul [the mind], by which I am what I am, is entirely distinct from the body, and even more easily known . . .' (Descartes, *Philosophical Writings* in Anscombe and Geach, 1966 Trans., pp. 31–2). The mind he believed to be pure and indivisible; and the body, plus all other 'corporeal or extended objects', he believed knowable only through analysing them into as many parts as possible (see his 'Meditations', p. 121; see also his 'Discourse', p. 41, 1966 Trans.). Appreciation of Descartes' concept of mind and body makes it easier to appreciate how his work set the stage for a reductionist methodology of science. From the initial analysis of the world into mind (spirit) and body (matter), everything consisting of matter i.e., both the human body and the rest of nature, could be reduced to its mechanical components.

To this day Descartes' dualist philosophy has served to encourage seeing the world in dichotomies. Consider for example: mind/body; spirit/matter; 'man'/ nature; subject/object; fact-objective/value-subjective; humanities-subjective/science-objective and so on (for other examples of Cartesian dichotomies, see Craige, 1988, Chapter 1). Through this dichotomous process a mechanistic paradigm of power, already alluded to in Bacon's writings, was forged. We see the idea of science and scientists being 'objective', detached, providing neutral or 'value-free' language for the elicitation of knowledge of the 'outside world'. Moreover we see, fully implied in Cartesian dualism, the Baconian assumption of our 'objective' separation from nature, justifying our utilitarian scientific power over it. 'As mind, infinitely separated from a world which is matter', the role of man can only be that of dominating his surroundings, of becoming 'master and possessor of Nature' (Sutcliffe, 1968, p. 21). The preoccupation of science with accumulating the 'facts' of matter encouraged methodologists more effectively to reduce nature to its non-thinking, non-living, elements which make it up apart from mind. Cartesian dualism provided materialist science with a concept of the world highly amenable to study and dissection. Even the trees and beasts were, for Descartes, reducible to mechanisms without spirit or purpose, other than the purpose man would give to them. The 'analytic method' of analysing or dividing the world into its parts was thus refined and processed into the method of reductionism.

When one speaks of Cartesian dualism, one also speaks of the mechanical mathematization of nature. It is to Descartes that we owe the original 'view of nature as a perfect machine, governed by exact mathematical laws'. Like Galileo, Descartes sought to provide the mathematical formalism for the description of nature. He believed that it was mathematics that would eventually unlock the secrets of nature, by way of cataloging laws and scientific formula.

Newton's famous laws of motion and his inverse law of gravitation provided a measurable and predictive description of both the celestial and terrestrial dimensions of nature and its course. The mechanical order of nature was revealed by the mechanical laws governing it. The universal secrets, so it was believed, could in principle be completely explicated with sufficient application of the laws of Newtonian mechanics. In his *Philosophiae Naturalis Principia Mathematica* (first published 1687; trans. Cajori, 1969) the laws of motion were stated thus:

> Every body preserves in its state of rest, or of uniform motion in a right line, unless it is compelled to change that state by forces impressed thereon.
> The alteration of motion [i.e., acceleration] is ever proportional to the motive force impressed; and is made in the direction of the right line in which that force is impressed.
> To every action there is always an opposed and equal reaction. . . . (Newton, 1969, p. 23)

The implication of Newton's mechanical laws of motion for western science and society was enormous. Hailed as the 'queen of sciences', Newtonian mechanics, engendered a completely reductionist and deterministic methodology of science. Nature was broken down into particulate matter, the constant motion, acceleration and rest of which could be measured or determined exactly in terms of external ('impressed') push/pull forces.

It was not long before Newton's reductionist disposition was crystallized by his followers into a full blown reductio-mechanistic paradigm. Working tenaciously within this Newtonian framework, the scientific reductionist would observe, isolate, divide, quantify and in essence kill his quarry. The ultimate intellectual hunt. Only that which could be weighed or measured, so it was reasoned, belonged to the realm of genuine knowledge. The Newtonian scientist was spurred on by the challenge of reducing all phenomena to elementary 'solid particles', so that the whole of the machine-like universe could be reconstructed from a sample of its parts.

Reductionist Transformative Technology

The power paradigm of reductio-mechanism has become institutionalized in western culture and society through the curriculum of schools and the organizational goals of industries. Since the time of the industrial revolution, the very concept of progress has covertly relied on the value of power for breakdown, separation, transformation, consumption, competition and specialization. The reductio-mechanist method of breaking things down into their composite parts, whether they be material substances, societies, or even psychological disorders, has been ubiquitous. To illustrate the enormous impact of this paradigm let us first consider the way in which the reductio-mechanist methodology has permeated our view of the human body, along with the diseases which afflict it and the treatments used to cure those diseases. Reductionism in medicine is just one of its varied manifestations, but nowhere is the process and consequence of breaking wholes into parts more clearly exemplified.

The Reductio-mechanist Medical Model

Contrary to the conventional wisdom, the genesis of medicine is to be traced not to the foundation of empirical science, but rather to the foundation of supernatural religion and ancient philosophy. In an attempt to manipulate the forces of nature, some of which all too frequently wreaked havoc upon them, it has been proposed that the ancients incorporated medicine as a component of their supernatural belief system (see, for example, Eliade, 1964). Common events such as famine and plague were thereby interpreted in the context of a presumption of a world populated by spirits and unwieldy demons. Endeavouring to make these impersonal forces more comprehensible and thus more tractable, the world of impersonal spirits was conceptually transformed into a world of personal gods, possessed of some of the same attributes as the human creatures over whom they were deemed to rule. While the savage force of the wind was without ears, for instance, it was at least possible to implore the god of tempest to calm the angry sea. It was at least possible, that is, to appease or to supplicate the gods and homage and sacrifice came to feature as the common modes of petition. Within this framework of belief, sickness and health depended primarily upon the caprice of the gods or their willingness to be entreated by their human subjects. Medicine and religion thus became progressively more culturally entwined. Although polytheism gave way eventually to monotheism, the nexus between medicine and religion was preserved. Living in accordance with God's law, often determinative in ancient times of the 'law of the land', came to function along with humble entreaty, as the way in which religion remained the cultural form for the expression of medicine.

Whether an individual had violated social or religious taboos, or even had nightmares, became relevant to the religious or supernatural explication of disease and its prognosis. In many cultures it was believed that disease was the punishment which the gods inflicted upon those who dared disobey them. Even the supposed bodily intrusion by evil spirits was often explained in terms of a violation of taboos or a straying from belief, thus incurring a loss of the personal protection otherwise provided by the gods. Unsurprisingly, the medical relevance of personal hygiene came covertly to be enshrined in religious prohibitions in connection both with the consumption of certain foods and the appropriate incantations or prayers in relation to their planting, harvesting and consumption (see Feuerbach, 1964). In this sense earlier cultures employed a concept of disease which was more comprehensive than an account of its biological causes.

The history of the relation between medicine and religion has in different places and in different times, of course, been decidedly ambiguous, and while there is no single logical progression in its development, a progression towards reductionism can nevertheless be discerned. Resolved to assimilate into medicine the spiritualist element of religious consciousness, for example, the Vitalist school held firmly to the role played in the workings of the human body by a 'life-force' independent of the material components of which it is constituted. On the other hand, there was the Mechanist school which affirmed resolutely the machine-like nature of the human organism, thereby fostering the working hypothesis that all illness was a result simply of a malfunction in the machine's parts. Intervention by the physician, a kind of sophisticated body mechanic, was the mechanistic way of repairing the human machine. The difference of philosophy marked by these two schools led ineluctably to a cleavage within medicine itself which contributed significantly to our present medical heritage (Singer and Underwood, 1962, pp. 143ff).

Although not entirely rejecting Vitalism, the Hippocratic conviction that natural rather than supernatural forces were the cause of illness gave rise to a causal mechanics of medicine which ensured that Vitalism was suppressed. Inasmuch as the proceedings of the gods and the individuals to whom they related were deemed to be exogenous to the appropriate considerations of the causal science of medicine, the role of religion in medicine was thus systematically diminished. The Hippocratic school was, in essence, articulating a new philosophy of medicine based upon a natural rather than a supernatural or religious understanding of the human organism. Disease and illness were thus made susceptible of scientific investigation and the method of science, not the faith of religion, came to be seen as the way of medicine. Hippocrates' own writings, however, set the scientific context of medicine sufficiently broadly to incorporate the role played by the environment and the interdependence of the mind and body in the preservation of health and the elimination of disease. Hippocrates' own theory of medicine did not restrict the explanation of disease or health to the causal breakdown of the body's mechanics. Such restrictions were the prerogative of Hippocrates' successors who focused upon the mechanistic aspects of the Hippocratic tradition. Acceptance of the mechanist theory, for example, gave rise to the notion that diseases have specific causes, a notion which, as we shall see later in this chapter, was ultimately reinforced and promulgated by reductionist epistemology.

It was around the second century that the causal mechanist model was advanced further with the advent of Galenic medicine. The vast writings of Galen were on the one hand philosophical and on the other hand descriptive, though some of his writings which have been regarded as strictly medical contain elements of both. Occupying a virtually unique position of pre-eminence amongst the medical scientists of his time, he espoused in his protracted treatise *Peri Apodexixeos* (On Demonstration) a theory of scientific knowledge which relied upon and amplified the causal mechanistic paradigm contained in Aristotle's, *Posterior Analytics*. Also influenced strongly by Hippocrates on whose work he wrote some 15 commentaries, Galen revived the Hippocratic doctrine of the humours and enunciated principles of anatomy which have survived in varying degrees as the authoritative basis of the subject even in recent centuries. While the teleological tenor of his theory of physiology was never altogether reconciled with his mechanistic theory of anatomy, his doctrine of scientific knowledge contained a predilection for a causal mechanics forceful enough to subsume his teleology (Venzmer, 1972, pp. 93ff).

With the collapse of the Roman Empire in the fifth century, medicine and medical education were thrown into chaos. The Middle Ages witnessed not only the development of Feudalism, but the rise of power by the Church Fathers. It was they who regarded themselves as the guardians of medicine, feeling somehow compelled to destroy the Library of Alexandria with its immense accumulation of medical literature, on the judgment that it was the product of pagan culture. The role played by religion in medicine came once again to predominate, and the aetiology of disease was traced to sin. It was the heretic to whom sickness was mainly attributed, and those who were sick were in some way or other heretics or sinners. The healer of heretics, acting on God's behalf, was the priest who saw the Church as his residential hospital. The pendulum had swung full circle. The official panacea for disease had shifted from medical intervention through science to repentance and self-flagellation through religion. Dissection was regarded as desecration, and the earlier forms of medical learning by discovery of the intricate workings of the human body were prohibited (see Sigerist, 1955, pp. 267–97).

Confronted by a social reality of plagues, fires, floods and famine, however, the people of the times often sought healing outside the aegis of the Church. In this context of desperation, the Church's determination to suppress 'unholy' forms of healing was bound to be abortive. Magic, witchcraft, astrology, along with belief in fairies, elves and amulets which either caused disease or prevented it, thrived and proliferated, but there was no systematic re-appearance of the Hippocratic tradition.

The wisdom of the Hellenic tradition, embellished by the medical heritage of Rome, survived in the hands of the great Arab physicians of the East. Nestorius was one of these physicians who in the fifth century, was banished for heresy from Constantinople which, upon the fall of Rome, had become the new axis of the Christian world and its domination (Easton, 1965, Secs. III and IV).

With the medieval adoption of the Hellenic tradition in medicine by the Arabs who maintained their fascination for alchemy, the first attemps to produce chemical analyses of living matter were conducted outside the Christian aegis of power. It was attempts such as these that laid the foundations of modern biochemistry, while concomitantly adding a strong reductionist component to the causal mechanistic medical paradigm. Having both a philosophical and empirical interest in medicine, Arab physicians such as al-Tabari and Rhazes in the ninth century and Haly Abbas and Avicenna at the end of the first millennium, promoted reductionist biology as the new philosophical underprinnings of the Hellenistic inheritance in medicine (Venzmer, 1972, pp. 100–6). In Avicenna's famous book, *The Cannon Medicine*, an explicit attempt was made to synthesize the writings of Aristotle and Galen in the service of a coherent mechanist philosophy of medicine (Venzmer, pp. 109ff). A conceptual framework was thus being re-estabished in which the science of medical understanding was made increasingly dependent upon the articulation of causal connections between diseases and specific pathological states.

It was not until the Renaissance, however, that the next stage in the emergence of reductio-mechanist medicine took place (Lyons and Petrucelli, 1979, pp. 369ff). Consistent with the interest in exploring new places and continents was a fervent desire among thinkers of the time to explore the human body itself. It was in this context of fervour that Michelangelo, da Vinci and other renowned artists pursued dissection to achieve a knowledge adequate for depicting the human body in its finest detail. In so doing, they inadvertently contributed to the development of new methods of medical research stimulated by their new methods of art.

The mechanist disposition within medicine was given an even stronger reductionist orientation in the work of Galileo (1564–1642) who, as we saw earlier, held that mathematical laws governed the functions of all nature, including the human body. All that was required to comprehend fully the mysteries of the nature of the human body, for example, was a mathematical theory of its anatomical workings. The possibility of the mathematical analysis, Galileo averred, depended upon restricting science to the primary or quantifiable properties of the phenomena under investigation (Galileo, Trans. by Drake, 1957, pp. 64ff). Secondary properties such as colour, taste and smell belonged, he thought, to the domain of subjective experience and therefore had no place in objective science (Singer and Underwood 1962, pp. 113–15). Nature was to be understood, and in turn controlled, by effecting its reduction to the basic mathematical, or more precisely, the geometrical relations of which it was constituted. Mastery of the human body was simply one aspect of this reduction.

To appreciate the full impact of Descartes' thought upon the philosophy of medicine, however, it is imperative to couple his epistemic reductionism with his doctrine of dualism. It was the separation of *res cogitans* from *res extensa* that made it possible for the first time to describe, without an embarrassing residue, the world of *res extensa* as a machine the workings of which could be reduced to mechanical laws. It was only by taking the mind or spirit out of matter that matter could be characterized in purely mechanical terms without reference to spirit. The ramifications of Descartes' dualism have been far-reaching. Not only has it transformed our perception of the material world and paved the way for the presentation of Newtonian mechanics, but it has also profoundly altered the attitude taken to the human body and the healing processes associated with it. As Fritjof Capra has put it:

> The Cartesian division between mind and matter has had a profound effect on Western thought. It has taught us to be aware of ourselves as isolated egos existing 'inside' our bodies; it has led us to set a higher value on mental and manual work; it has enabled huge industries to sell products — especially to women — that would make us owners of the 'ideal body'; it has kept doctors from seriously considering the physiological dimensions of illness, and psychotherapists from dealing with their patients' bodies. (Capra, 1982, p. 45)

Descartes' analytic method is in essence the method of divide and conquer. The method of analysis and the concept of reductionism have important similarities in medicine, as elsewhere, but they need not be equated. Analysis amounts to epistemic reductionism, for example, only when it is crystallized into dogma holding that the complexity of nature can be known exclusively by way of its analysis into its most basic parts. On this Cartesian interpretation, the theory of knowledge thus becomes perversely analytic, setting the precedent for scientific investigation in reductionist terms, with bio-reductionism functioning simply as one expression of reductionist epistemology. Although Descartes may not have intended that analysis be used in this way, it is clear that it has since been so used. The philosophical search for the foundations of knowledge may be paralleled within science by the search for the foundations of biology. Descartes unwittingly assured that bio-reductionism would not stand unsupported, for its analytic 'backing', so to say, was in Cartesian terms given by the reductionist theory of knowledge itself.

The transition from the Cartesian to the Newtonian picture of the world followed without philosophical encumbrance. As mentioned earlier, it was Newton who provided the systematic mathematical articulation of Descartes' mechanistic and reductionist vision of nature. Epistemic reductionism was given its most powerful expression in Newton's invention of the differential calculus. By means of its deployment Newtonian mechanics not only set the stage for the future development of the medical sciences for the next three centuries, it mapped the particular direction that development would take. The degree of development within the medical sciences was proportional to the degree of formalized epistemic reduction within them. Medical knowledge of the nature of the human body and its workings was thus a matter of a progressive revelation of the nature of its fundamental parts, and their contribution to the whole. The historical progression led medical science to analyse the body in terms first of its appendages, then its internal organs, and later to the cells of which those organs are constituted, and more recently, to the DNA components of which the cells are made, the ultimate building blocks, we are told, of all living organisms (ibid.). Incorporating the Galilean and Cartesian stress upon a reductionist mathematics, Newtonian mechanics transferred the Hippocratic reliance upon an empiricism of qualitative impression to an impiricism of quantitative analysis. Insofar as quantitative analysis favoured a science of mensuration, the reductionist programme claimed for itself an objectivity that could for the first time itself be measured.

In the seventeenth century anatomical progress within the reductionist model was impressive. The shift from the study of the external parts of the body to a study of its internal organs was facilitated by Wirsung's isolation of the pancreatic duct, by Glisson's analysis of the liver, by Stensen's work on the parotid gland and van Leuwenhoek's ophtalmological discoveries. But the truly outstanding medical scientist of the seventeenth century was perhaps William Harvey (1578–1657). Harvey was educated in Cambridge and in Padua, where the influence upon him of Galileo and Fabricius *ab Acquannendente* would be indelible (Lyons and Petrucelli, 1979, pp. 427–63).

It was the Galilean concept of motion, that is to say, which Harvey would employ in describing the body as a machine through which blood was moved by the heart in a systematic cycle through the body. The movement of circulation of blood was believed to be measurable, as were the specific factors which might serve to inhibit its cycle.

Following the causal model to its logical conclusion and coupling it with his own reductionist orientation, Rudolf Virchow in the nineteenth century postulated that the cause of all disease was to be traced to anomalies at the cellular level. The reductionist paradigm had thus been taken yet another step further: from the body as a whole to its parts, from its parts to its internal organs and glands, from its internal organs to the cells of which they are constituted. In this regard the invention of the microscope both represented, and in its own way reinforced, the cellular concept of disease. According to Virchow, the cell was the fundamental structural component in the human body. Where Morgagni had traced the lineage of disease to its organal ancestry, Virchow held that pathology reduced to abnormal cell physiology, and that the focus of the medical research should be redirected accordingly. The concept of the body as a machine was the same, but the principle of reduction led to what Virchow took to be its most minute structure, the cell (Venzmer, 1972, pp. 180–1).

The entrenchment within medicine of the reductionist paradigm finds its next expression in perhaps the most celebrated nineteenth century contribution to medical progress, the aetiopathic or 'germ theory of disease' (Lyons and Petrucelli, 1979, pp. 497–8). Anticipated in *obiter dicta* by earlier scientists such as Acerbi (1785–1827) and Bassi (1773–1856), the endeavour to link microbes or germs with disease culminated in the research of Pasteur, Koch, and von Behring. Concerned to save the French wine and dairy industries from ruin, Louis Pasteur (1822–95) discovered that lactic and butyric fermentations of alcohols were caused by either aerobic (oxygen requiring) or anaerobic (non-oxygen requiring) bacteria (Singer and Underwood, 1962, pp. 330–41). The causal nexus was thus provided for the reduction of disease to microscopic bacteria, and the development of the X-ray ushered in a whole new era of mensurable prognosis with charts, tables, case histories and pictures.

It was Robert Koch (1843–1910), however, who first enunciated the further reduction between a specific disease and a specific germ, when he identified a singular particular bacteria as the cause of anthrax. Koch went on to articulate a set of criteria in virtue of which the aetiology of particular diseases could be reduced to particular germs. 'Koch's postulates', as his criteria have come to be called, have remained an integral part of medical education to today' (ibid., pp. 326–41). Emil von Behring (1854–1917), one of Koch's pupils, continued the work of his beloved teacher and identified the causal relation between the toxins produced by bacteria and the body's production of antitoxins in its defence reaction against them. He earned the Nobel Prize in Medicine in 1901 for his development of the diptheria antitoxin, four years prior to the award of the same prize to Koch in 1905 (see Lyons and Petrucelli, 1979, pp. 557–8; and Singer and Underwood, 1962, pp. 411–12).

The reductionist principle had thus by the twentieth century become firmly established as the framework within which the theory and practice of medicine derived. While the Cartesian paradigm had served to elevate the concept of the body as a machine to heights unimagined even by the mechanists, the induction of nuclear physics in the twentieth century and the atomistic epistemology that accompanied it ensured the progression of medical science to depths of analysis that would probably have defied the credulity of even Descartes. In little more than a century the subject matter of medicine had shifted from the study or organs to the study of cells and their structure. As medicine became increasingly 'technicalized' by physics, physics became increasingly the technology of medicine with molecular biology as its subject matter. Access to hitherto biologically remote bacterial and viral structures was now procured with the aid of the electron microscope, and advances in treatment were made possible by radiation therapy, CAT or tomography scanners for the production of visual image X-rays of cranial and brain abnormalities, radioactive tracers, the cyclone knife or microtome, artificial organs and laser surgery. Microsurgery has in fact today become almost commonplace, and the electrocardiogram and the electroencephalograph have become familiar terms to many lay public.

To comprehend the further elaboration of reductionism as it unfolds at the genetic level we need first to discern the parallel between fire as a tool for the technologization of the earth and genetic engineering as a tool for the technologization of the body.

Pyrotechnology and Biotechnology: Reductionism in Nature

Through the practical application of reductionist science man has subtly transformed his environment from a natural one into an ever increasing artificial one. Firstly, with the use of pyrotechnology i.e., the power of 'fire', as a replacement for muscle power, man was able to break or melt down earth substances into their various elements and recombine those elements to form other stronger or more useful substances — the stronger the metal, the stronger the resistance against the forces of nature. The amassing of iron and steel led to the production of the first self-perpetuating machines. This in turn led to the era of instant energy in which vast amounts of natural resource were needed to feed energy guzzling dynamos (see for example, Laura and Heaney, 1990, p. 97).

The use of fire provides a good example of the extent to which knowledge, motivated by power, gives rise to a technology inspired by dominance. One crucial sociocultural difference between humankind and the animal world is that humankind has learned to use and develop the technology of fire. Not only is it the case that animals neither make nor use fire, but they are instinctively frightened by it. Knowing how to use and make fire has given man a power over the animal world which recapitulates his use of fire as a means of dominance over all things. The social history of mankind can in this regard be caricatured as man's all-consuming passion and torrid affair with fire and the power it produces.

The culmination in the technological evolution of pyrotechnics came with the breakdown of the atom itself. Capable of unleashing huge amounts of energy, atom smashing became man's pocket sized power over nature, with the nuclear bomb manifesting the ultimate symbol of fire-power. In its various megatonage guises of concentrated power, nuclear energy was applauded as being capable of lighting cities and effortlessly keeping battleships and submarines moving for years on end. In addition to its many heinous side-effects, the current stockpile of nuclear weaponry and waste is also capable of destroying all of humankind and the environment several times over. Despite the end of the cold war, the nuclear crisis we still face today defies assessment as an historical aberration. It is the logical outcome of our hunger and thirst as a culture for power. We have sought total mastery and control over nature, and the reductionist methodology which has led us to the technology of atomic energy and its nuclear weapons of destruction are consistent with that end.

Just as pyrotechnology provides the power to control and manipulate the inanimate components of nature, so the methodology of reductionism has led us to a new technology which provides the power to breakdown and recombine, to destroy and reform, the biological constituents of life itself. This relatively new technology is genetic engineering and its potential power for the genetic reconstruction of nature is mind-boggling. The reductionist methodology which underpins its conceptualization brings with it a value orientation which in the light of its sensationalist technology has virtually been neglected. Let us now consider this biological form of technological transformation. The extraordinary power genetic engineering provides to manipulate the biological programmes of living things is fundamentally linked to what Hallen referred to as 'Mercantile Mechanism'. She wrote:

> ... the exclusively reductionist tools of mechanism still dominate in genetic engineering. Nature is reduced to a pool of genetic 'raw materials' which can be spliced and recombined. Genetic engineering erroneously assumes that the reconstructed whole is the sum of dismembered and recombined parts. Participating in these implicit assumptions of mechanism, agricultural biotechnology (for instance) reduces the cultivation of life and living land to the factory production of chemical and biotechnological fixes in agribusiness ... Genetic engineering is big business ... Genetic engineering is enmeshed in the political economy of industry. The objective of the industry is not what is best for humans and the biotic community, but what will sell. (Hallen, 1991, pp. 38–9)

To appreciate the full and continuing impact upon society of the Biogenetic Revolution, it is essential to have some understanding of the philosophical assumptions which underpin it. Without making these assumptions explicit, the discussion of genetic engineering will rely implicitly upon certain of the very concepts which serve inevitably to distort it. The Biogenetic Revolution did not just happen serendipitously. Not unlike the development of pyrotechnology, biotechnology marks the culmination of a long and venerable tradition in science the thrust of which has been predominantly reductionist. Biological reductionism reflects the persistent disposition to reduce the biological functions of living organisms to their most fundamental chemical properties and to explain malfunctions of the human organism in terms of malfunctions of these properties. It is against the background of biological reductionism that the Biogenetic Revolution took place.

Dependent upon a paradigm in which the human organism is viewed as a machine, reductionism regards illness as a malfunction of the machine's parts. In embracing this picture of the body as a machine, the physician comes naturally to be regarded as a kind of mechanic whose job it is to repair the body, by intervening either to restore or to replace its parts.

Medical knowledge of the nature of the human body and its workings were thus a matter of the progressive revelation of the nature of its fundamental parts. The historical progression of the bio-reductionist orientation led first to an analysis of the human body in terms of its appendages, then its internal organs, and later to the cells of which those organs are constituted, and now to the DNA components of which the cells are made. DNA is the last stage in the reduction, we are told, for it marks the discovery of the ultimate building blocks of all living organisms.

The Power of the Gene: The State of the Technology

Although the techniques of genetic engineering were only introduced into molecular biology as recently as 1973 with the advent of recombinant DNA, a number of earlier developments in genetics heralded the possibilities of the diverse application of these techniques. As is well known, it was in 1953 in that now celebrated April 25th edition of the journal *Nature* that the American, James Watson, and his British colleague, Francis Crick, reported the discovery of the twisting double helix or spiral staircase microscopic structure of deoxyribonucleic acid, or DNA as it is now commonly known. The steps of the spiral staircase structure were constituted of what they called 'base units'. The base units were made up of a modest sequence of four chemical nucleotides, capable of assuming an almost infinite variety of patterns, each of which expressed a specific genotype. The further production of the particular protein structures responsible for the individual characteristics of all living organisms was said to be dependent upon the way in which the genes interact by way of their collective arrangements. Generally speaking the fewer the number of genes in concatenation, the simpler the resulting organism and vice versa. Depending upon the particular collective arrangement of genes, the result ranges from the simplest of life forms at one end of the spectrum to the most complex of life forms at the other.

The discovery of the structure of the salt of deoxyribonucleic acid was seen as a great victory for, and confirmation of, the reductionist tradition in science. With the discovery of DNA came both substantial government support for further research in genetics and a series of consequent discoveries that prepared the way for genetic engineering. Four years subsequent to Watson and Crick's discovery of DNA, for example, Dr Arthur Kornberg unravelled the mystery of the structual replication of DNA. On his account DNA undergoes a division into two separate strands, or 'unzipping', as he described the process, each strand of which, in turn, utilizes chemical substances from the immediate cell environment to reproduce its original structure. Kornberg's contribution did much to prepare the context for genetic engineering, as it provided the basis upon which techniques for the current synthesization of DNA have been implemented (Howard and Rifkin, 1980, p. 24).

The mystery of the genesis of all living organisms was in principle solved in reductionist terms, it was alleged, inasmuch as the fundamental genetic constituents of the simplest organisms were reiterated in the genetic components of the most complex. The secret of life revealed by the discovery of DNA was the blueprint not just for this or that life form, but for all possible life forms on this planet. Hidden within the structure of DNA lay the genetic information, or the determination of all living organisms that there are, of all that there have been, and of all that there could be. The impact of the reductionist revelation is thus staggering. From an understanding of the structure of DNA the biological sciences have progressed to the stage where it is now possible to manufacture and to manipulate life itself. This is the power of genetic engineering.

Recombinant genetic engineering refers to the techniques whereby DNA from one organism is recombined with the DNA or genetic material from a different and often unrelated organism. The discovery of recombinatory DNA thus permits the incorporation of genetic material from unrelated organisms by splicing DNA segments together in such a way that the grafted gene is established as part of the natural process whereby the engineering organism reproduces its own DNA. When the germ-line or sex cells are affected, the introduced genes can be transmitted to subsequent generations. 'Pronuclear' or 'zygotic' injection is one such genetic engineering technique which has been used successfully to double the size of mice and their offspring (affectionately dubbed 'supermice') by grafting together the growth hormone gene of a rat with the genetic material of the mice (see Bartels, 1983, pp. 257–62).

For the first time in human history, the human race achieved the potential power to control its own evolutionary future and destiny and thus the destiny of every life form on this planet. There is, when all is said, a mordant irony in the fact that along with Francis Crick a number of distinquished physicists abandoned their research into nuclear physics because they found it morally repugnant that the research in which they were engaged was potentially destructive of humanity. Little did they anticipate that as part of their migration to the life sciences, they would make discoveries capable of altering, beyond recognition, the living face of this planet. What they seemed not to realize is that there is no human activity which constitutes a sanctuary from moral responsibility.

We are now in a position to appreciate the full panoply of ways in which genetic engineering might impinge upon future directions in the re-organization of the living planet. There is no doubt, for example, that the elimination of genetically based disease will provide the first port of socially accepted entry. It is well known, for example, that mental retardation is caused by genetic disorders, and it is estimated that approximately 80 per cent of all mental retardation is linked to genetic diseases. Four main categories of genetic disease are employed in tracing the aetiology of mental retardation. The largest of these classes is made up of *Constitutional Disorders* and these are estimated to account for 14.8 per 1000 births. Diabetes mellitus and idiopathic epilepsy fall within this category. The next largest class is characterized by assorted *Congenital Malformations* which exhibit an incidence of 1 per 1000 births. Phenylketonuria or PKU, Tay Sacks disease, galactosaemia and X-linked mental retardation are examples of what are classed as *Single Gene Effects*, occurring in 11.2 affected births per 1000 births. Conditions such as Down's Syndrome, Klinefelder's Syndrome, Turner's Syndrome, and Cri du Chat Syndrome are included under the heading of *Chromosomal Abnormalities* and account for 5.4 per 1000 births (Hayes and Hayes, 1982, pp. 28–9).

One obvious application of genetic engineering to mental retardation can be seen in its service to genetic screening. At present prenatal diagnosis may involve collecting genetic data from family histories in the hope of identifying suspected carriers of genetic diseases, and where detection is successful, to provide genetic counselling as appropriate. In certain cases, a couple might be admonished of the complications of marrying, of having children, and in some cases where pregnancy has already occurred, of the effects on the future life of the child if carried to full-term. A reputedly more effective and relatively recent development in screening is amniocentesis. In amniocentesis a sample of fluid containing desquamated foetal cells is obtained from the amniotic sac during the early part of the second trimester of pregnancy. The foetal cell sample is obtained by passing a long needle into the sac and drawing off a small amount of the amniotic fluid. Utilizing recent genetic innovations in chromosome analysis, it is possible to detect more than 60 genetic abnormalities by means of this process. Inasmuch as there are some 1600 human diseases caused by defective genes, including congenital blindness and deafness. Genetic engineering could be employed to reduce further the incidence not only of genetically based mental retardation, but the incidence of other genetic diseases as well.

Consideration of the sundry applications of the techniques of genetic engineering to mental retardation, even in regard to genetic screening, lead ineluctably, however, to a discussion of *in vitro* fertilization or IVF. This is an important point, as it shows that the role which IVF plays in genetic engineering is pivotal, not peripheral. One can no longer sensibly regard IVF merely as a technique for overcoming some forms of infertility in those who would otherwise remain childless (Bartels, 1983, p. 257). It is IVF which itself provides the laboratory context in which various of the techniques of genetic engineering can be tested and introduced. In this sense IVF is a technological presupposition of genetic engineering and not just one separate expression of it. Thus to talk of the way in which genetic engineering can facilitate genetic screening inevitably involves appealing to IVF for its elucidation. In coming to appreciate this point it is to be hoped that we become less susceptible of failing to perceive the extent to which assumptions of value both inform and *are informed by* technological development. This is a matter to which we shall later return.

It is, in any case, clear that given the ostensible objectives of amniocentesis, genetic engineering can assist in achieving those objectives more efficiently. Using the *in vitro* fertilization environment as the screening context, for example, it is possible to extract — presumably without harm — cell samples from the early embryo for recombinant DNA analysis. What would be regarded as 'normal' versus 'abnormal' gene variants can be differentiated by the creation of 'gene probes', and it is envisaged that techniques of 'mapping' or 'marking' will soon permit the identification of any gene which exhibits genetic anomalies.

It is conjectured that most of the 1600 genetic anomalies could, in principle, eventually be tested in this way. If the DNA analysis proved to be satisfactory, the embryo could then be implanted, otherwise not. Since identification of the gender of the embryo can also be readily determined through chromosomal analysis, sex-linked inherited diseases, such as the Duchenne type of muscular distrophy and haemophilia, could be effectively reduced by ensuring that only zygotes of a certain relevant sex are implanted. In the case of the Duchenne type muscular distrophy, for instance, it is the sons of the heterozygous mother which risk a 50–50 chance of being affected. In the case of male haemophiliacs who produce children, it is the sons who are normal and the daughters who are heterozygous carriers. By implanting only female zygotes in the former case and male zygotes in the latter, the incidence of both types of genetic diseases could be considerably diminished. The adoption of *in vitro* fertilization, coupled with genetic screening, would thus have the putative advantage of reducing the numbers of so-called therapeutic abortions by making them unnecessary.

It is in connection with heterozygous carriers that the impetus to cloning is perhaps at its strongest. Cloning, as is well known, refers to the reproductive process which results from recombinant DNA manipulation utilizing a cell sample from the body of only one person. An individual or any number of individuals possessed of identical constitutions with each other and the parent cell source is the consequence of this quite remarkable feat of genetic engineering. Cloning is now a sophisticated engineering technique which has proved extremely successful in its application to amphibians and some animals. Utilizing the technique of cloning, a female carrier of haemophilia, for example, need not worry about having a son who stands a 50–50 chance of being affected. The genetic manipulations which constitute cloning would permit her to have a daughter whose genetic constitution would be identical with her own, a carrier of haemophilia, but not a haemophiliac sufferer. It is worth noting, however, that cloning would do little to overcome the problem which remains even when screening for heterozygotes is successful. For while the restrictions placed on the gender of offspring born to heterozygotes would serve to reduce the number of children born with genetic disorders, these restrictions would do little to diminish the incidence of the recessive gene which heterozygotes carry. Only a prohibition on the reproduction of heterozygotes or comprehensive gene therapy could achieve that aim.

In addition to the proposed benefits which genetic engineering affords for the screening of genetic disorders responsible for mental retardation, genetic engineering can also be combined with IVF techniques in the service of gene therapy. The possibilities of human genetic manipulation have been markedly increased by the introduction of IVF. Besides making the genetic material accessible for manipulation, IVF ensures that it is possible to identify (genetic screening) and to replace (genetic transfer) a defective gene at an early enough stage in embryonic development so that the non-defective DNA molecule can be incorporated into the germ-line (sex) cells as part of the normal integrative and developmental process of the zygote. Although genetic transfer is also possible at later stages of development, including adulthood, the ability to direct the non-defective gene for integration into the specific community of cells which manifest the defect is enhanced by IVF. The alternative procedure for removing from the body a sample of the defective cell population for recombinatory therapy and later for return to the body in the hope of genetic integration has thus far been only modestly successful, though considerably research continues to be directed to this end. Once again, it is evident that IVF provides the experimental context in which gene therapy can be effectively executed without undue social protest. If genetic manipulation of defective DNA is permitted, it then becomes possible to alter the genetic material of an otherwise defective zygote, thereby permitting its implantation, while thus further reducing the alleged necessity of therapeutic abortion. The technique of gene therapy would thereby also overcome the moral objections to withholding certain zygotes from implantation. Enough has now been said, however, about the technique of genetic engineering in the avoidance of genetically based diseases, and we are now in a position to consider some of the ethical issues which arise from its more general applications.

The Ethical Issues: How Brave a New World?

The range of ethical issues raised by the foregoing considerations is kaleidoscopic. Scientific concern, for example, expressed resolutely at the Asilomar Conference of 1975, was directed primarily to ethical issues of safety. Inasmuch as recombinant DNA research usually involves the transplantation of genetic material into a bacterial environment for propagation, there have been ethical worries as to whether the resulting bacterial strains could be pathogenic to humans. *Escherichia coli*, better known as *E. coli* and used as the common bacillus of recombinant DNA propagation, represents a laboratory strain of the same bacteria normally found in the colon and the human intestinal tract. While the gut strain of *E. coli* is not pathogenic to humans, it is unknown whether its laboratory counterpart is equally favourably disposed to life in the human intestine.

The anxiety is not simply conjectural in its source. It is known that varient strains of *E. coli* can be seriously disruptive of the multiplicitous functions of the human organism, causing diarrhoea, infantile meningitis and bloodstream infections, to name only a few of its deleterious effects. A bacterial strain resistant to antibiotics, moreover, could be seriously threatening for the survival of the human species. As a result of this concern, attempts have been made to produce weaker strains of bacteria, the prime example of which is the bicentennial bug bred in 1976 by Professor Roy Curtis of the University of Alabama Medical School (see Pouledge, 1981, p. 498). Nonetheless, the dramatic steps taken to make recombinant DNA research safe betrays — or so it would appear — a measure of just how unsafe it would otherwise be, or indeed in essence is.

Despite efforts to make recombinant DNA research safe, it has often been argued that a total moratorium should be declared on genetic engineering and its research. Given that we cannot predict the consequences of this relatively unexplored technology, it is possible that its negative utility to society is such that continued research constitutes too great a risk to bear. We do not wish here to engage in a protracted debate *in these terms* as to whether a total ban on genetic engineering is warranted, though we shall later in this chapter raise this question in a different way and in different terms. In the present terms of argument, however, it is not at all clear that the 'doomsday argument', as the risk objection against recombinant DNA research has come to be called, succeeds.

Although it is undeniable that even precautionary experimental research in genetic engineering could possibly have catastrophic consequences, it does not follow from this *possibility* that such research should be banned. We say this for two reasons. First, to have demonstrated the *logical possibility* of the catastrophic consequences of genetic engineering is not in itself to have provided any reason whatsoever in support of the likelihood of their *actual* occurrence. It is simply to have provided a coherent description of some possible event or events. Second, the fact that no assurance can be given of the non-zero probability of their occurrence is not an anomaly peculiar to research in genetic engineering. It is the same problem which confronts almost all scientific research and many commonplace activities as well. As Steven Stich puts it:

> It is, after all, at least logically possible that the next new compound synthesized in an ongoing chemical research program will turn out to be an uncontainable carcinogen many orders of magnitude more dangerous than aerosol plutonium. And, to vary the example, there is a non-zero probability that experiments in artificial pollination will produce a weed that will, a decade from now, ruin the world's food grain harvest. (Stich, 1981, p. 171)

The point of this traditional anti-moritorium argument is that if, on the grounds of *possible* catastrophe, we invoke a prohibition on recombinant DNA research we are equally committed to a prohibition on all research in general. The point this traditional argument in support of research into genetic engineering misses is that there are significant differences in the nature of the things which are manipulated by fire, as opposed to the things which are manipulated through genetic engineering. Indeed, these differences are not differences of degree, but of logical kind and they make a distinct contribution to how we understand the technology of genetic engineering. First, it is salutary to remind ourselves that the subject matter of genetic engineering, despite reductionist efforts to make it as chemically inert and predictable as possible, is the world of living things. As long as it is life which we engineer, the behaviour of the living form engineered will almost invariably be less predictable than the mechanical processes and outcomes of the actual engineering. This means that there will always be an element of unpredictability and incalculability not characteristic of the inanimate world. This leads to the second point of difference.

It is characteristic of living things that they move and migrate. This being so, the notion of keeping genetically engineered organisms confined to laboratories or particular natural settings is highly problematic. It is in principle extremely difficult to ensure that a genetically engineered organism can be forever confined. Third, virtually all living things reproduce or multiply, making control over their environmental impact even more unpredictable. Whether they reproduce with similar or different life-forms will be difficult, if not impossible, to predict as will be the possible mutations which may define the vicissitudes of their developmental processes. This being so, the traditional arguments in favour of open research into genetic engineering need urgently to be reconsidered.

The possible military, terrorist and other nefarious applications of the products of recombinant DNA research is another of the diverse issues raised, even by that body of research innocently and benevolently intended to reduce mental retardation by genetic engineering. The sinister uses to which malevolent governments, terrorists or the demented could make of a debilitating or lethal bacterial strain, accidentally or otherwise derived, are too heinous to contemplate. The imaginative but all too possible and provocative constructions of recombinant DNA chimeras have also served to stimulate ethical qualms for professionals and laymen alike. Is the human form inviolate? Can we ethically employ genetic engineering not only to improve the human species, but to transform it? Is it right, for instance, to exploit cloning to advance either the commercial or scientific interests of a society? Is it wrong, as Fletcher suggests,

> . . . to use cloning to produce legless people, dwarfs, individuals distorted functionally in various ways — for example, to man spaceships to Jupiter . . . Similar is a proposal to solve the fruit picking problem in a future leisure society by using a genetically 'designed' and then cloned submental people with prehensile tails to do the work. It can be countered immediately with 'Why not monkeys?' (which are already being considered by some orchards). (Fletcher, 1981, p. 496)

Yet the degree of difficulty in deciding these issues in the terms in which Fletcher decides them is shown by his own ambivalence as to what provides the criteria for the acceptable limits of cloning. Elsewhere in the same work he writes:

> There could also be reasons for the social good. Individuals might need to be selectively reproduced by cloning because of their special resistance to radiation, their small body size and weight, because they are impervious to high decibel sound waves; these things could be invaluable for professional flights at high altitudes and space travel, for example. In a stretch of imagination, a biologist could solve the weight problem by going alone to a distant planet with a supply of different somatic cells, and colonize it for a cloning start. (ibid., p. 495)

If the former case of cloning is wrong and the latter case right, as Fletcher suggests, to what could he appeal to justify the difference? Is it that in the former case we design the functional distortion, whereas in the latter case, it is an accident of nature? It is not at all clear why this difference, if it is a genuine difference, should be regarded as morally relevant. After all, why would it be right to clone an already existing legless person to produce many such legless persons to pilot our spaceships to Jupiter, but yet be wrong to design and clone legless persons? In both cases there is, in the name of the social good, a genetic proliferation of legless persons. Either both cases are right, it would appear, or both cases are wrong. Yet there is something awkward in putting the matter in this way, something ethically fulsome in the discussion itself. For in our deliberate efforts to seek the ethical principles by which to guide humanity, we have unwittingly contributed to the very conditions which make us less human. We shall in what follows try to give some sense to this presently obscure epigram.

In the first section of this chapter we were concerned to show that genetic engineering is the current culmination of a long and venerable tradition of reductionism in medicine, in turn underpinned by certain philosophical assumptions about the nature of reality and all that it contains. Genetic engineering is postulated on the assumption that human beings, indeed all living things, are essentially machines, the sum of their genetic parts, and perhaps nothing more. The precedent for engineering the environment, including plants and animals, to suit human needs and interest is deeply entrenched in the biography of the human race. Genetic engineering simply extends that precedent one stage further by establishing techniques to engineer the human race itself. The respectability of genetic engineering is thus powerfully expressed by its laudable objectives: the reduction and prevention of genetic disease, the alleviation of suffering associated with these diseases, and the more effective deployment and distribution of our health-care resources. While the standard way of putting the case for genetic engineering is attractive, its attraction is, we submit, at least partly meretricious.

It is true that as a race we have seemingly, from the beginning, engineered the world around us. What has also to be admitted, however, is that we have not always engineered it to the better. Our reverence for science and its technological inheritance, in combination with prevailing institutional interests for profit, have all too often engineered the environment for destroying and distorting it. We have treated the world like a machine the parts of which can be used-up and replaced, and our engineerings have brought about the natural holocaust of lakes and rivers dying from pollution, drinking water unfit for consumption, plant and animal life diseased and ravaged. Now that we have distorted the world so as to make it almost unlivable, genetic engineering provides the prospect of distorting us to allow us to live in it. Moreover, our adjustment to the world is sponsored on the pretence that it is not we but our biological imperfections that will be eliminated.

It is a strange coincidence, if it is a coincidence, that at the very time in our history when so much of the mindless prejudice against persons with genetic defects has finally been rooted out that genetic engineering should engender attitudes which only serve to reinstate it. For the more capable we are of preventing genetic defects, the more difficult it becomes to tolerate them when they exist. Genetic engineering may unfortunately give rise to the potential situation in which those who escape the detection of screening, or who as a result of foetal injury, mutation or accident are born defective, will be regarded as genetic mistakes, as those who need not have been and who, in being, are somehow less human in consequence. That we today sometimes treat those born with defects as second-class humans is symptomatic of this inclination. Consider, for example, actual cases in which children with Down's syndrome, who not infrequently also suffer intestinal blockage, are refused the surgery necessary to correct the condition, a surgery which would otherwise be given unhesitatingly to so-called normal children. Professor Kass makes a similar point when he writes:

> It is ironic that we should acquire the power to detect and eliminate the genetically unequal at a time when we have finally succeeded in removing much of the stigma and disgrace previously attached to victims of congenital illness, in providing them with improved care and support, and in preventing, by means of education, feelings of guilt on the part of their parents. One might even wonder whether the development of amniocentesis and prenatal diagnosis may represent a backlash against the same humanitarian and egalitarian tendencies in the practice of medicine, which, by helping to sustain the age of reproduction . . . has itself contributed to the increasing incidence of genetic disease, and with it, to increase pressures for genetic screening, genetic counselling, and genetic abortion. (Kass, 1981, p. 466)

Kass also recognizes that the language of genetic engineering creates the mistaken impression that the afflicted foetus or person *is* (in the sense of identity) rather than *has* a disease (ibid., p. 467). He laments, justifiably, that we flip far too cavalierly from the language of possession into the language of identity, from 'He has haemophilia' to 'He is a haemophiliac' or 'The foetus has Down's syndrome' to 'The foetus is a Down's'. Our use of language in this connection reflects an important matter, and discussion of its ramifications educationally have been teased out at greater length elsewhere (see Laura, 1982, Intro.). Suffice it to say here that inasmuch as the way in which we describe 'things' reflects our concepts of those 'things' it is clear that by identifying the person with the disease, we create the illusion of mitigating ethical responsibility by talking of the elimination of genetic defects or genetic defectives, rather than of the elimination or manipulation of persons or of human beings *with* genetic defects. This is particularly interesting in respect of the case of the use of the term 'mental retardation', as its predicative attribution has become embedded grammatically as a nominative structure. It is grammatically proper, that is, to use the reference of identity 'He *is* mentally retarded' in place of the grammatical impropriety 'He *has* mental retardation'. The linguistic structure tells us something about the way in which the description 'mentally retarded' has come to function conceptually as a substitute for what would otherwise be recognized as a person. Once the humanitarian concepts of description are eroded, we inevitably dehumanize our ethics in no longer being able to reflect the human concerns upon which we pass judgment.

In saying this we are not of course denying the laudibility of the ostensible aims of genetic engineering in the prevention of genetic defects, at least insofar as this is not equated with the elimination of persons afflicted with such defects. This is obviously a crucial difference (ibid., 1980, pp. 156–66). It should also be made clear that the concept of 'defect' is not itself a pellucid concept. Since each of us is alleged to have a minimum of between five and 10 genetic defects, the objective of eliminating all defects becomes puzzling, if not decidedly disconcerting. The question of what a defect *is* and of *what* defects will be eliminated is a matter of *who* is doing the defining and the eliminating. This raises unavoidably questions of power and control and the misuse of both.

The concept of 'defect' acquires its pejorative connotation when viewed as a condition we have no wish or need to tolerate. Inasmuch as the techniques of genetic engineering would, as earlier suggested, put us in a position technologically to have to tolerate less, progressively more traits would come to be regarded as defects. An IQ of 100, for example, might plausibly be viewed as a defect if we were able via recombinant DNA procedures, to increase standardly the IQ of all or most children to say, 150. The issue of the defect of the so-called 'supermale karyotype' is pertinent here. It is estimated that one out of every 800 men has an extra Y chromosome, and that although most of those who possess this XYY arrangement are law abiding, there is a better than average probability that those who possess this chromosomal arrangement will display aggressive and antisocial behaviour. Could not our blind commitment to the reduction of genetic defects commit us to the foetal elimination of all those with this defect, in spite of the fact that the majority will never exhibit the criminal behaviour associated with having the defect?

There is another approach to these questions which addresses them by enlarging the conceptual prism through which they are viewed. We earlier intimated that having used technologies of power to engineer our world to distortion, we are now ready to rely upon a new technology of power, genetic engineering, to distort our own being, the human form, to assist our survival in a distorted world. Let us conclude this chapter by elaborating this charge further. Genetic engineering and the particular bio-ethical questions to which it gives rise are symptomatic of a much deeper social ill than the traditional treatment of the bio-ethical questions has satisfactorily brought to relief. Bio-ethical questions are traditionally articulated as personal or individualistic dilemmas which are resolved by the provision of the right answer to the dilemma, derived from a fundamental principle or principles of action. Our ethical understanding, in other words is reductionist. We reduce the problems of genetic engineering to the specific problems of individuals, and we reduce the problems of ethics to specific principles of decision. Either we act, for example, on utilitarian grounds or we do not. The entire process is encapsulated as a peculiarly ethical problem. There is a weakness in this process, and it has in part blunted our ethical appreciation of the deeper questions of value presupposed by our institutional structures, customs and lifestyles. In accepting the terms in which genetic engineering casts the problem of ethics, we are encouraged to narrow our focus on the factors which contribute to their immediate or short-term solution. In so doing, our attention is deflected from a consideration of the underlying framework of assumptions which underpin the human activities whose adjudication we seek. This deflection is infelicitous; for it is in the light of these assumptions and their examination that our ethical vision can be re-directed to the long, rather than short-term solutions to the human problems we confront. Inasmuch as there is already a presumption in favour of the rightness of eliminating defective genes, the issue is joined at the level of conflicts of principle, say, between individual and community rights. To what extent, for example, can the State legislate the genetic engineering of defective foetuses? We have no wish to minimize the gravity of this conflict, but only to indicate that such questions do not arise in isolation and cannot thus be answered in isolation. In this sense there is no such thing as an uniquely ethical question. Questions of ethics are also questions about our emotions, attitudes, institutions, and customs. The problems of ethics are systemic problems, and their resolution is less a matter of juxtaposing one reductionist principle of decision against another, as a matter of showing the way in which conflicts of value arise out of, and are expressed by, the web of values we have ourselves created. This is why no fundamental ethical principle contains, or could contain, within itself the decisional criteria for all its future applications. To treat it as such is to treat it a-historically and in isolation from the web of beliefs, institutions and customs by which it is conditioned and defined. *'Holistic ethics'*, as we shall call them, are concerned to show that the answers to the questions of genetic engineering must be given in terms which are more comprehensive than those contained in the questions it raises.

In responding to the ethical problems of genetic engineering our answers must do more than perpetuate the conditions which gave rise to the problems in the first place. To reconstruct one's genetic heritage at the level of individualized genetic engineering is not to contribute one iota to the eradication of the conditions which caused it. In this sense genetic engineering is tantamount to a palliative.

> Although the US spends over $100 billion per year on health care, it ranks fifteenth among the nations of world in infant mortality and life expectancy. Part of the reason for this lies in the fact that our health-care system is structured for short-term treatment of illnesses rather than long-term prevention of them. Despite the fact that hundreds of reports and studies have concluded that the major causes of death and disease are preventable and related to occupation, environmental deterioration, nutrition, consumer products, and poverty, only limited government or private funds are put into programs designed to address the problem. (Howard and Rifkin, 1980, p. 217)

It is the bio-reductionist approach and the values it fosters which require challenging. To regard human beings as machines is to reduce our ethical inhibitions in respect of engineering human beings to ensure their efficiency and performance. As we earlier observed, it is the power-driven reductio-mechanist methodology that also encourages the interventionist disposition. Machines require mechanics, and the king of the mechanics is the engineer. If the problem is exposure to environmental radiation, why not alter the genetic programme of humans to be radiation resistant? This is, of course, a caricature of genetic engineering, but it exaggerates only the state of the technology, not its inspiration. Herein lies the rub.

Genetic engineering is a remarkably impressive technological development. Because it is impressive, however, it has the power via the institutions that have sponsored and sustain it, to distract us from the task of making ourselves more rather than less human. By holding out the promise of yet another technology of transformative subjugation, in this case genetic transformation as the panacea of our humanity, we lose sight of the myriad ways in which our engineerings of the world have made us less human. We have exploited the lands of the earth, its waters, its plant and animals, and more recently, even its skies. To what extent our genetic defects are themselves, either in their origins or in their manifestations, partly or wholly consequent of these exploitations is a question which is, we believe, fundamental to our humanity and to our educational expressions and possible suppressions of it. We can no longer just keep turning to ever new forms of technology to avoid having to turn to the question of whether we are living properly.

The time is long overdue to turn our attention to the prevention of the genetic conditions for which genetic engineering is one remedy. The laudable aim of eliminating genetic defects must surely be more than a technique for eliminating their appearances. The technologization of our lives has done much to depersonalize and to desensitize our culture. In our endless efforts to reduce things and people to their smallest parts, we have lost the sense of what makes them and us whole. An alternative hypothesis is that it is perhaps what makes us whole that makes us healthy and in turn minimizes our own defects, as well as those we bequeath in perpetuity. The technology of science may thus have transformed us into giants but little does it avail us, as we have urged elsewhere, if it leaves us as blinded giants (see Laura, 1981, pp. 1–13). Inasmuch as the promise of genetic reconstruction lures us from the humanistic task of social reconstruction, it functions inevitably to dehumanize us even further. In the end, the task of social reconstruction must be seen to be less as a matter of trying to turn back the hands of the clock, than as a matter of trying to make better use of our time.

We are now witnessing a parallel and corollary development to these notions of pyro and industrial genetic transformations in what might be called 'nanosecond' efficiency of technology. As Rifkin explains, the cybernetic revolution 'brings with it a new and more virulent form of reductionism' that is coming to replace the old Newtonian 'clockwork' image of nature (Rifkin, 1989, p. 218). Elaborating on this, he wrote:

> In the coming century our children are likely to redefine their environment using the language of information theory and cybernetics as they attempt to conjure up a view of nature that conforms with operational principles of the new computer technology. We are entering a new temporal world where time is segmented into nanoseconds, the future is programmed in advance, nature is reconceived as bits of coded information, and paradise is viewed as a fully simulated, artificial environment. (Rifkin, 1989, p. 218)

Whatever the image portrayed, the reliance that we place on the computer to analyse our data is in a way representative of the blind commitment we have to power and control over nature. The covert rationale, as we saw, for the reductio-mechanistic paradigm is that by controlling the environment and exploiting it, our environment will be an easier place to live in. This hope appears to be in vain, for it is this very lust for power that encourages technological transformations which not only place us closer to the brink of extinction, but which also depersonalize and dehumanize us as they desanctify the things of nature.

The Social Value of Knowledge as Power

Our final consideration of the implications of the reductio-mechanist paradigm relates to its development as a socio-cultural ideology. We saw earlier that educational knowledge has been substantially influenced by the architects of the reductio-mechanistic framework which despite its controlling imagery of nature as female, paraded falsely as a 'value-free' and 'objective' account of reality which in turn has been employed to legitimate our unfettered technological rape of the planet.

In the previous sections we have also observed that far from being value-free, the western orientation to knowledge contains within it a panoply of values which need badly to be made explicit and re-assessed. One facet of this re-evaluation concerns the development of the social theory of control which parallels the epistemology of technological power. After Galileo, Bacon, Descartes and Newton had provided the philosophical foundations for the reconstruction of a cold mechanical universe to be analysed with the tools of reductionist methodology, empiricists such as John Locke attempted, along the same lines, to provide order and control to human society. For Locke, 'civilized' society (as opposed to chaotic or barbarian society) consists entirely of individuals seeking 'self-preservation' and material self-interest. Nature, in this connection, he considered intrinsically valueless. He considered that nature in its unmolested state was 'shear waste', waiting to be exploited maximally by the 'labours' of civilized men.

In his *Two treatises of Government* (First published, 1690) Locke sets the agenda for so called civilized society. On *property* he wrote:

> ... Land that is left wholly to nature, that hath no improvement of Pasturage, Tillage, or Planting, is called, as indeed it is, *wast*, and we shall find the benefit of it amount to little more than nothing ... Tis labour then which puts the greatest part of Value upon Land ... Nature and the Earth furnished only the almost worthless Materials, as in themselves. (Locke, 1960 (transl.), pp. 315–16)

Rifkin (1980, p. 24) pointed out that, according to Locke's mechano-materialist theories on society and land, one must act as an individual competitor to amass as much personal wealth as possible so as to become 'effectively emancipated from the bonds of nature'. In the Lockean tradition the 'negation of nature is the way toward happiness'. Locke's theories accord then with the implied mechanistic value assumption that nature's disorderly 'waste land' 'ought' to be opposed, conquered and divided for the good or 'happiness' of civilized man.

Locke's characterization of nature serves as a salutary reminder of how the reductio-mechanistic power paradigm fosters a view of nature which, as if it were no more than a collection of worthless 'objects', legitimates its control and transformation. By 'objectifying' nature we inadvertently detach ourselves from it, giving the impression that our transformations of it are neutral. It is clear, however, that the Lockean theory of nature encapsulates an epistemology of power where methodological intrusions into nature are anything but neutral. Locke's social theory presupposes that power over and against nature is itself an intrinsic value to humankind by allowing the inveterate disposition of man to accumulate wealth to find its expression in the exploitation of nature. The unlimited progression and intervention of reductionist science and technology, industrial expansion and the consumer 'throw away' ethic, have all arisen from this very same reductio-mechanist methodology of power. Paradoxically, it is clear that the dominant institution for the transmission and propagation of the reductio-mechanistic epistemology of power is education. Let us consider the point more determinately.

Educational Ideology: The Transmission of the Reductio-mechanistic Power Paradigm

We have seen that if there is a defining characteristic of the modern age it is our unbridled commitment to an implicit form of knowledge which shapes and defines the way in which we interact with nature. Given that science has become the primary vehicle for the expression of this form of knowledge, the teaching of science may, at the level of covert value agenda, be tantamount to the promulgation of an ideology of environmental destruction. This being so, even the relatively new domain of what we call 'environmental education' will ultimately be self-defeating, in so far as it remains dependent upon the power-laden (anti-ecological) paradigm of interventionist, reductionist science.

If our thesis is correct, then the educative system to which we and our children are exposed presupposes a commitment to a power paradigm which covertly perpetuates and promotes a framework of anti-ecological and, ultimately, anti-humanistic values. Unabated reductionist science and its application through technology is a prime example of the utilization of knowledge for anti-ecological purposes. We have been educated in a 'macho-mechanistic' society for the future promise of consumer abundance and freedom from labour. Another radically different interpretation of the situation is that city dwellers now have to work longer hours to be able to afford the latest throw away commodities. Food and shelter are no longer considered the basic needs. In the west they are needs which are simply taken for granted. Instead, the new litany of needs include the latest style throw away camera, razors, video recorders, plates, utensils, clothes no longer fashionable and even cars and perennially obsolete computers. We have in essence been coaxed into tolerating cities, which are really over crowded cement jungles, pollution, crime and basic non-subsistence because we have become dominated and domesticated by the technological innovations and machines with which we now surround ourselves. As each new machine is invented it seemingly creates a new demand for its immediate use. As it does this, there is a sense in which, by virtue of what some people thus have and some do not, it changes the productive and social relations amongst individuals who are encouraged to compete for goods as a symbol of success and happiness. It is only recently that we have as a society become aware of the plight of western society, though we continue to rely on the same reductio-mechanistic framework that has brought us to this social chaos in the first place. As Rifkin aptly points out: 'Our entire learning process is little more than a twelve-to-sixteen-year training program for the Newtonian world view [i.e., the mechanistic world paradigm]' (Rifkin, 1980).

Just as science, technology and industry are subordinated to the reductio-mechanist knowledge as power paradigm and its anti-ecological value orientation, so too is education in its more general organization of the curriculum. Western education, that is to say, continues to function as a propagator and maintainer of industrial consumer values, underpinned by the preoccupation with power. Since the industrial revolution, our schools have functioned to prepare students for their role in the mindless reductionist expropriation of the earth's resources by trans-forming themselves into scaled down copies of specialized, industrial work places. As Toffler wrote:

> ... the whole idea of assembling masses of students (raw materials) to be pro-cessed by teachers (workers) in a centrally located school (factory) was a stroke of industrial genius. The whole administrative hierarchy of education, as it grew up (from the beginning of the mechanical age) followed the model of industrial bureaucracy. The very organization of knowledge into permanent disciplines was grounded on industrial assumptions. Children marched from place to place and sat in assigned stations. Bells rang to announce changes of time . . . The inner life of the school thus became an anticipatory mirror, a perfect introduction to industrial society . . . Young people passing through this educational machine merged into adult society whose structure of jobs, roles and institutions resembled that of the schools itself. (Toffler, 1971, p. 362)

The temptation of educational institutions to replicate by way of their own organizational structures the industrial contexts for which they prepare students has been overwhelming. Appreciation of this point makes it easier to discern the conceptual basis for Noam Chomsky's repudiation of what he calls the 'educational machine' in its service of the capitalist view of human nature. Chomsky (1975, pp. 206–7), opines that 'labour is a commodity to be sold on the market for maximal return, that it has no intrinsic value in itself; its only value and immediate purpose is to afford the possibility to consume'. In today's 'throw away' society consumerism is no longer a means to an end, but an end in itself. Along with the image of con-sumption as a form of social power comes competition as a measure of social inter-action. People are continually aiming for the better life — 'to keep up with', or to become better than, 'the Jones'. This in itself has resulted in massive social inequities i.e., the relentless vicissitudes of the 'haves' and the 'have nots'. By hypostatizing the presumption of knowledge as power, education serves inadvertently to instill not only competitive consumer values, but the associated 'throw away' ethic which conjures the mistaken belief that nature is both an infinite reservoir for commercial resources and a boundless sink for the disposal of the by-products of industry. The resultant philosophy is fundamentally anti-ecological and has fostered a false sense of security. Since few people actually produce anything themselves, their work becomes increasingly less creative and more tedious. It serves primarily as a means for pro-viding people with the opportunity to exercise freedom in the guise of unconsumption in a world of synthesized commodities from which they are systematically alienated.

Consistent with the exercise of power as a form of mindless consumerism, school children are constantly reminded of the importance of the linear process of specialization ('what will you be when you grow up Amy?'). This being so enormous, pressure is placed upon them to choose their occupations at ever earlier ages. The emphasis on acting the 'part' derives from a non-literal metaphor characteristic of 'social atomism'. One should let one's work define one's identity. The problem is that work which is conditioned by and designed for mindless consumerism is itself for the most part both mindless and meaningless. This being so, people find themselves living mindless and meaningless lives, full of things that are supposed to add value but do not.

The original view of science as a romantic pursuit for all, no longer exists. Modern science education aims to provide careers for the elite i.e., powerful knowledge for powerful people. As Ferguson explained:

> Long before science was a career, people tried to understand nature for their own amusement and excitement . . . Partly because the educational system has taught science only in a reductionist, left-brain style and partly because of society's demands for practical applications of technology, the romance of science fades quickly for most youngsters . . . In higher education science narrows further. The humanities-oriented sheep and the science oriented goats are herded into their respective pens; at many universities, the science and humanities centers are blocks apart. Most students sidestep any science beyond the minimum required hours; the science majors are funnelled into their specialties, subspecialties, and micro-specialties. By graduate school, they can scarcely communicate with each other. (Ferguson, 1988, pp. 157–8)

Those who choose to pursue science as a career must pass through a series of pedagogic filters that prepare them for the reductionist enterprise in which they are involved. The educational system thus progressively disenfranchizes them not only from the study of arts and humanities, but also from their own specialist colleagues in other scientific fields. Reductio-mechanistic attitudes will be moulded and reinforced, just as the reflective habit of mind will be stringently circumscribed and delimited. According to Ferguson (1988) these 'left-brain' occupations, the male or 'yang' oriented occupations of science and logic, are located at the top of the educational and professional pyramid. Students who are considered to be the brightest are almost invariably pushed towards these high-paying professions. If they 'don't make it', or decide to pursue academic excellence in the arts, they are contemptuously rebuked as academic 'drop outs'. Intuitive, aesthetic and spiritual development, emphasized as female or 'yen' attributes, are potential fields of mental developments almost fully repressed at the 'yang' professional levels.

Despite protestations to the contrary, reductio-mechanist education is concerned not so much with cultivating creative and questioning minds, as with the developmental mechanics of learning to 'fit in'. As Rifkin (1980) pointed out, the intellectual facets of this mechanical training have been neatly dissected into the 'classical' and the 'romantic', with the romantic being treated like an anarchistic tendency — only pursued by those who don't 'fit in'. Our classical mechanist training teaches us to 'think' causally and quantitatively, leaving out the qualitative domains of learning. Rifkin writes:

> At this very moment children all over America are taking tests or preparing for them. What they don't realize is that what they're really learning is not just facts but how to think in terms of causality and quantification. When our educators claim they are teaching our children how to think, this is the particular type of thinking they have in mind. Of course, few of them are conscious of the 'fact' that they are promulgating a particular ideology when they teach. They would probably protest that their only concern is to teach the child how to think 'objectively'. Need we say more? (Rifkin, 1980, p. 230)

Just as the reductio-mechanist epistemic orientation characterizes nature in such a way that its quantitative-objective dimensions become the subject matter of science, so it is that education is defined in such a way that a deep division arises between the quantitative-objective and the qualitative-subjective domain within the pedagogic context of science then projected as the paradigm for what we do in the context of the school curriculum. Simply put, the quantitative issues fall within the aegis of science, while the qualitative issues, become those of the arts.

From the vantage of pedagogic epistemology, it is clear that implicit in the very structure of the curriculum is a presumption that students working in the arts area are 'in fact' working with ideas which are subjective and thus not representative of 'real' or genuine knowledge. This recognition is especially important for the future of environmental education, since the question or whole constellations of questions on the intrinsic value of the things of nature, apart from their being transformed into commodities with market value, depends upon qualitative reflection which deepens our moral sensibilities. By reducing nature and the 'science' of its restoration to the quantitative domain, we unwittingly diminish the sense of moral conscience requisite for its qualitative reconstruction. This explains why there is little hope encouraging 'environmentalism' by implanting the epistemology of environmental concerns into the existing educative system which, as we have observed, continues implicitly to adopt and transmit the anti-ecological values enshrined in its reductio-mechanistic ideology of power. In this connection what we need to recognize in matters of environmental education is the not so obvious. As Gough puts it:

> ... [E]nvironmental education ... is part of a growing awareness of certain kinds of problems and critical issues in education. ... Many of these problems are not obvious (in the way that, say, fouling our own nest ... is obvious) but involve questions about the worldviews, paradigms and myths that are the subliminal foundations of our experience and practice in education. (Gough, 1989, pp. 1–2)

What we have argued in this chapter is that the 'subliminal foundations' to which Gough refers can best be seen to constitute the very reductio-mechanistic knowledge as power paradigm. This being so, the goals of environmental education are unlikely to be well-served by turning to the existing dominant paradigm of educational knowledge whose technological applications have proved by their very nature to be profoundly disruptive ecologically. We have in this chapter argued that beyond some of the quite obvious ways in which we exploit the earth are the more subtle ways in which technological subjugation in its reductionist mode converts living environments into dead ones. It has been observed also that dominant forms of technology, with which we interact with nature, are of such a kind that they degrade the earth by virtue of their very interaction itself. Far from being value-free, technology is 'epistemically biased' and thus every time it is used and in whatever way it is used, it will express that bias. What should by now also be clear is that the general philosophical presuppositions which underpin the present educational commitment to technological progress are themselves inimical to goals of environmental integrity. If we are ever to overcome the environmental crisis, we can no longer acquiesce in our obsession with unlimited growth and the continued invention of tools of menacing power consummate with this end. To do otherwise will be tantamount to continuing to encourage the expropriation of the earth's resources along with its deformation and ultimate toxic degradation through transformative subjugation.

In interpreting the origins of the environmental crisis it is tempting to blame science and technology, or even the off-shoot science of economics, as the main culprits. Such an interpretation would be more akin to 'ludite sensationalism' than reasoned argument, and it is not the one we would wish to proffer. Our argument is simply that educational knowledge is formulated, shaped and conditioned by the preoccupation with power and thus the technologies to which it gives rise will be technologies of power and control. To achieve the measure of control they seek, technologies of power will be transformative of the things of nature into the things of artefact. The more chemically inert and less alive a thing of transformation is, the more readily its behaviour can be predicated and its interactions controlled. This being so, the conversion of living things to dead things is an endogenous feature and part of the rationale of transformative subjugation. Since the methodology of transformative subjugation is reductio-mechanist, it is easier from the point of moral conscience to legitimate technological manipulations of the parts elementary constituents of systems such as DNA, than it is to legitimate the manipulation and exploitation of the integrity of things which are whole in themselves. The point here is that there can be no authentic pedagogic foray into environmental education which eschews the sense of moral responsibility of the earth which attends the concerns for its stewardship. At some point the relentless circle of anthropocentricity and human self-aggrandizement must be broken and this is the task to which we shall now turn in the remaining chapters.

References

BACON, F. (1960) *The New Organon and Related Writings*, ANDERSON, F.H. (transl.) New York: Bobbs-Merrill Co.

BARTELS, D. (1983) 'The uses of *in vitro* human embryos: Can the public participate in decision making?', *Search*, **14**, 9–10, October/November.

BIRCH, C. (1990) *On Purpose*, Sydney: NSW University Press.

CALILEO, G. (1957) *Discoveries and Opinions of Galileo*, DRAKE, S. (ed.) New York: Anchor.

CAPRA, F. (1982) *The Turning Point*, London: Fontana.

CHOMSKY, N. (1975) 'Toward a humanistic conception of education', in FEINBERG, W. and ROSEMONT, H. Jr. (eds) *Work, Technology, and Education: Dissenting Essays in the Intellectual Foundations of American Education*, Urbana: University of Illinois Press.

CRAIGE, B.J. (1988) *Reconnection*, Athens and London: University of Georgia Press.

DESCARTES, R. (1931) *Philosophical Works*, HALDANE, E.S. and ROSS, G.R.T. (eds) Cambridge: Cambridge University Press.

DESCARTES, R. (1966) *Philosophical Writings*, ANSCOMBE, E. and GEACH, P.T. (transl.) Sydney: Thomas Nelson.

EASTON, S. (1965) *The Heritage of the Past*, New York: Holt, Rinehart and Winston.

ELIADE, M. (1964) *Shamanism*, Princeton: Princeton University Press.

FERGUSON, M. (1988) *The Aquarian Conspiracy: Personal and Social Transformation in the 1980's*, London: Paladin Books.

FEUERBACH, L. (1964) 'God as a projection of the human mind', in HICK, J. (ed.) *Arguments for the Existence of God*, New York: Macmillan.

FLETCHER, J. (1981) 'Wild talk warnings galore, and cloning', in *Biomedical Ethics*.

GOUGH, N. (1989) 'Becoming ecopolitical: Some mythic links in curriculum renewal', Paper presented in a symposium, *Aspects of a Postmodern Pedagogy*, AERA (SIG: Critical issues in Curriculum), San Francisco, 30 March.

HALLEN, P. (1991) 'Genetic engineering: "Miracle of deliverance" or "destroyer of worlds"?', in HAYNES, R. (ed.) *High Tech: High Cost?: Technology, Society and the Environment*, Chippendale N.S.W., Australia: Pan Books.

HAYES, S.C. and HAYES, R. (1982) *Mental Retardation: Law, Policy and Administration*, Sydney: The Law Book Company.

HOWARD, T. and RIFKIN, J. (1980) *Who Should Play God?*, New York: Dell.

KASS, L.R. (1981) 'Implications of prenatal diagnosis for the human right to life', in *Biomedical Ethics*.

LAURA, R.S. (1981) 'Philosophical foundations of science education', *Educational Philosophy and Theory*, January.

LAURA, R.S. (1982) *The Impossible Takes a Little Longer*, Canberra: Commonwealth Press.

LAURA, R.S. and GAZZARD, A. (1980) *Problems of Handicap*, Melbourne: Macmillan.

LAURA, R.S. and HEANEY, S. (1990) *Philosophical Foundations of Health Education*, New York: Routledge.

LOCKE, J. (1960) *Two Treatises of Government*, LASLETT, P. (transl.) Cambridge: Cambridge University Press.

LYONS, A.S. and PETRUCELLI, (II) J.R. (1979) *Medicine*, Melbourne: Macmillan.

MERCHANT, C. (1990) *The Death of Nature*, New York: Harper and Row.

NEWTON, I. (1969) *Philosophiae Naturalis Principia Mathematica Mathematical Principles of Natural Philosophy*, CAJORI, F. (transl.) New York: Greenwood Press.

POULEDGE, T.M. (1981) 'You shall be as Gods — recombinant DNA: The immediate issue is safety; The ultimate issue is human destiny', *Biomedical Ethics*, MAPPES, T.A. and ZEMBATY, J.S. (eds) New York: Mcgraw-Hill.

RIFKIN, J. (1980) *Entropy: A New World View*, New York: Viking Press.

RIFKIN, J. (1985) *Declaration of a Heretic*, New York: Routledge and Kegan Paul.

RIFKIN, J. (1989) *Time Wars: The Primary Conflict in Human History*, New York: Simon and Schuster.

SIGERIST, H.E. (1955) *A History of Medicine*, Vol. 1, Oxford: Oxford University Press.

SINGER, C. and UNDERWOOD, E.A. (1962) *A Short History of Medicine*, Oxford: Oxford University Press.

STICH, S.P. (1981) 'The recombinant DNA debate', in COHEN, M., NAGEL, T. and SCANLON, T. (eds) *Medicine and Moral Philosophy*, Princeton: Princeton University Press.

SUTCLIFFE, F.E. (1968) *Descartes: Discourse on Method and the Meditations*, SUTCLIFFE, F.E. (transl.) London: Penguin Books.

TOFFLER, A. (1971) *Future Shock*, Pan Books Ltd., London.

VENZMER, G. (1972) *Five Thousand Years of Medicine*, KOEING, M. (transl.) London, Macdonald.

Chapter 5

Towards a Reconstruction of the Foundations of Environmental Education

We have thus far established that if there is a defining characteristic of the modern age, it is our resolute commitment to technological development as the primary way in which we interact which nature. We have also argued that our schools propagated a form of knowledge driven by a lust for power, which in turn leads to what we have called 'transformative subjugation', the process whereby technology converts living things into dead things. The next step in our argument was to show that the process of transformative subjugation is executed via the reductio-mechanistic methodology of breaking down wholes into their smallest and most fundamental parts, a method, which by virtue of its systemic mutilation of the integrity of living systems, sets us as a culture in opposition to nature. Inasmuch as this form of educational knowledge and its methodological predilections are enshrined in the institution of science, we have argued that the teaching of this kind of science is tantamount to the promulgation of an ideology of environmental expropriation and destruction, a pernicious form of anti-ecological indoctrination that has for too long escaped notice. Our schools may thus implicitly be conveying by what they teach explicitly a philosophy of nature inimical to the conditions of moral sensibility and responsibility required for environmental stewardship. In this regard, even the relatively new educational thrusts of environmental education will prove to be self-stultifying, as long as they remain dependent upon the power-driven reductio-mechanistic interventions of technology.

Unabated technological transformation as proliferated by reductionist science reveals the extent to which education can be covertly manipulated for anti-ecological purposes. Our schools also continue to educate children in the power-paradigm of an epistemology which expresses social control through consumer abundance and the promise of freedom from labour. Ironically, what has actually happened is that city dwellers now have to work longer hours to be able to afford the latest throw away commodities they have, for the most part, mistakenly come to think they need. To ensure the utopian dream of wealth and leisure we educate our children to tolerate over crowded, highly synthesized environments, cement jungles, urban sprawl, pollution, crime, basic non-subsistence and environmental degradation. The city is itself a symbolic manifestation of the way in which we have technologized and synthesized our social organization and form of living with nature. With each new technological innovation seems to come a rationale for its immediate use; thus creating illusory needs and market demands which, as intimated earlier, change the productive and social relations between individuals.

In this and the chapters that follow we turn to the task of educational reconstruction. We outline recent developments in the philosophy of science and quantum physics which reinforce a whole new picture of our relationship with nature and with each other. Given the seamless and indivisible unity which characterizes the quantum universe, a theory of knowledge which is driven by power and dominance will be seen to be hopelessly anachronistic.

The survival of the species depends unequivocally upon finding new ways in which we can connect with nature, rather than separate or detach ourselves from it in the name of objectivity. Participation in nature, not domination of nature, becomes a pivotal concept around which what we call '*epistemic-holism*' can be made to turn. Using a quantum-systemic approach, we show how holism in epistemology can serve as a new foundation for a more fruitful edifice of pedagogy and curriculum than is being provided by the current social critiques of education based on an outmoded perspective on educational knowledge. Given the difficulties which we have seen emerge from a reductio-mechanistic paradigm of education, it is clear that we need to seek an alternative philosophy of nature capable of underpinning a coherent and effective theory of environmental education.

Towards a New Paradigm of Ecological Empathy

Recent developments in the philosophy of science and quantum mechanics have lead us to a new and exciting understanding of the nature of the universe in which we live. It is clear from these explorations into quantum mechanics that the more we attempt to define the world in terms of its fundamental constituents and to isolate those fundamental constituents, the more we discover that they can only be explained by reference to each other. Paradoxically the culmination of the reductionist orientation forces the recognition that the world is one seamless indivisible unity. Out of the very science which was attempting to take the reductio-mechanistic paradigm to its zenith, the paradox which emerges is the recognition that there is no isolated fragment of fundamental integrity. There are only units which gain their integrity and identity by virtue of being related together.

We submit that reflection upon this new way of construing the world of nature may serve to provide an epistemic heuristic, a way, that is, of proposing hypotheses about the nature of knowledge which are much richer and more comprehensive than the traditional ones. In recognition that there may yet be better models for understanding nature, we can at least now see that the universe in which we live is one which depends upon its integrated unity for its cohesiveness and for its ontic integrity. This being so, we suggest that a more comprehensive interpretation of environmental education is one which reflects not so much an epistemology of power as an epistemology of participation, empathy and connectivity — an epistemology which reflects the degree of that seamless indivisible unity. It is our contention that by empathetically reconceptualizing the nature of the universe in which we live, it is possible to promote the aims of an environmental education which encourages an attitude of caring and participation towards the environment and indeed towards each other.

One of the most fundamental assumptions of classical science is that the world resembles a machine made up of separate parts, the interrelations of which are governed by specific laws which admit of precise mathematical formulation. On the classical view physical reality is in essence fragmented. Discovering the true character of reality depends upon its reduction to the material particles of which it is composed. The objective of classical physics is to show how the parts work together, thereby exhibiting patterns of organization in seemingly distinct tracts of experience which, when taken in conjunction, ultimately determine the character of experience as a whole.

With the advent of quantum physics has come the perception of a new and fundamentally different order in nature. According to this new perception nature does not yield its deepest secrets by being whittled down into smaller and smaller components in the reductionist hope of reaching absolutely simple building blocks of which everything else is made and can be understood. The paradox is that in the last analysis the purportedly primitive components in the reduction turn out to be so inextricably related that their coherent description depends upon the postulation of a world of seamless unity and indivisible wholeness (Bohr, 1958, 62ff; see also Bohr, 1934, 76ff; Heisenberg, 1963, 173ff; Heisenberg, 1971, 206ff). The ontology of primitive particles is expressed by way of their correlations with other particles. Subatomic particles exist relationally; the separateness and independence of their particulate reality are illusory and incompatible with the quantum theory by way of which they are defined.

Although there have been several developments in the history of quantum physics which attest to the fundamental indivisibility and systemic character of nature as a whole, none is perhaps more persuasive than Bell's theorem, first published in 1964 (Stapp, 1975, 29B 27ff; see also Aspect, Dalibard and Roger, 1982, pp. 180–4; Clauser and Shimony, 1978, 97ff). The force of Bell's theorem is best apprehended as a development in the tradition of the Einstein–Podolsky–Rosen thought experiment, often referred to as the EPR effect (Einstein, Podolsky and Rosen, 1935). The design of the experiment was motivated by Einstein's discomfort with Bohr's interpretation of quantum physics. The essence of the debate centred on Einstein's unwillingness to accept Bohr's contention that the behaviour of any specific quantum phenomenon depended upon the logic of its interconnections with the whole of quantum reality. To accept Bohr's view was tantamount to conceding a seemingly ineradicable indeterminacy at the quantum level, for how could a definitive causal account be given of events which are causally influenced by all other events? Without the possibility of identifying a specific casual sequence to explain say, the transitional jump of an electron from one orbit to another, only a probabilistic or statistical account of causality could be given to accommodate the peculiar nature of quantum phenomena. In short, Bohr's interpretation required the rejection of the very concept of local causality and determinancy upon which classical mechanics had been built.

Moreover, to admit that quantum events were determined by the dynamics of the whole system of quantum phenomena, and not by local connections which were themselves governed by precise laws legislating the behaviour of objects separated in space, was to challenge Einstein's view that the signal connections between such objects were proscribed by the speed of light. Rather than accept this conclusion, Einstein insisted that indeterminacy at the quantum level was merely a matter of not having all the facts, a matter of hidden variables still awaiting discovery. Bohr also accepted that the theory of hidden variables would feature prominently within the quantum domain; but the difference of view was that for Einstein the only hidden variable were those deriving from local causes. The EPR experiment can thus be reckoned as a bold attempt to demonstrate that Bohr's postulation of non-local causal explanations for quantum phenomena would require that superluminary communication was possible, a description which Einstein held to be a contradiction in terms. Using essentially the same experiment, it has taken the mathematical genius of Bell to show nearly three decades later than Einstein appears to have been mistaken on this point.

The original EPR experiment has been slightly revised by Bell, the principles underlying both experiments are the same. A simplified version of the experiment involves a two particle system in which each particle is spinning in opposite directions. Since the spin of the particles about the axis of rotation is equal but opposite they cancel each other, and their combined spin is said to be zero. Particle spin should not be construed as classical rotation about the axis, but at the quantum level the spin of a particle is bound mathematically by two conjoined variables 'spin up and down' and 'spin left and spin right', depending upon whether the axis of rotation is horizontal or vertical. By measuring the spin of one of a paired particle system, it is possible — since we know the spin of the other particle is opposite and the total spin is zero — to infer the spin of the twin particle without disruption. For example, if one of the particles had a spin right along its horizontal axis, it would follow that the other particle would have a spin left.

This classical picture of electron spin, however, is complicated by the fact that the classical concept of defining with certainty, say the spin of baseball about a definite axis, does not quite apply with quantum phenomena. At quantum level the electron cannot generally be said to have a definite axis; it simply displays a tendency or potentiality to spin one way rather than another. It is of course true that if a measurement is taken, the particle will exhibit a definite axis of rotation, but on the quantum view it is the act of measurement itself which influences or determines the definite axis of rotation. Prior to the performance of the measurement there is, so to say, a conversational impropriety in stating that the particle has a definite axis of spin. In the language of quantum physics it has only a potential axis of spin. This peculiar interface between the observer and the observed is at least partly explained by Bell's theorem, so we shall at this stage of the argument do no more than alert the reader to this interpretation. Since the spin of a subatomic particle can be oriented by magnetic fields, such as those generated by a Stern Gerlach device, the observer can convert the potential spin of a particle into an actual spin (Zukav, 1986, p. 282).

This brings us finally to the heart of the EPR experiment and Bell's theorem. Imagine that twin particles in a system of zero spin are separated by an enormously great distance. No matter how great the distance their combined spin remains at zero. Suppose then that on the horizontal axis of rotation the measurement performed on the first particle reveals a definite spin right. From this measurement it would seem that the spin of the second particle must be left. For Einstein, the contradiction in quantum theory arose from the fact that the observer could at the last minute choose the axis of measurement, though the twin particle were travelling light years away from each other. On Bohr's interpretation the performance of the measurement, and thus the assignment of a definite axis of rotation, to the first particle would instantly determine the axis of rotation for the second, independently of its distance from the first. Since it is impossible for a signal to travel faster than the speed of light, said Einstein, there would be insufficient time for a light signal to connect the two spatially separated particles in the sense required. On this ground Einstein thus deemed it impossible that the measurement performed on one of the paired particle could instantaneously determine the direction of spin of the second particle in the pair, despite the distance between them. The relevance of Bell's theorem can now be made explicit.

Although Bell's theorem is a highly technical mathematical construct, its implications for quantum physics can be distilled. What Bell's theorem provides is a coherent mathematical exemplification by way of which to define the instantaneous measurement effect between twin particles separated in space. Consistent with Bohr's interpretation of quantum reality, Bell's theorem demonstrates a fundamental connectivity among what have traditionally been regarded in classical mechanics as separate and logically autonomous parts of the universe. There is a wholeness to the universe, on this view, which defies reduction to independent and isolated material components. Appreciation of this wholeness requires that we reconceive the basic categories of scientific interpretation. On the classical view the scientific understanding of the world could best be advanced by reducing complex phenomena to their fundamental parts and then determining the relations among the parts. The properties of their parts and their interconnections were, so the argument goes, supposed to determine the logical character of the whole.

What Bell's theorem tells us mathematically is that it is the whole which determines the properties and behaviour of the parts. Bell's theorem thus signals a radical departure from the idea of an Einstenian universe made up of separate bits, the relations of which admit of precise mathematical formulation in accord with the principle of local causality. At the deepest level of structure we have instead a universe of fundamentally interconnected elements the specific character of which is itself a manifestation of the dynamics of interdependency which serves to express the unity of the entire system. The elements are not independent and isolated; they are in some almost mystical sense, undifferentiated facets of an indivisible whole. Bell's theorem shows that material objects signify not individual things or entities, but patterns of probabilities expressing interconnections among the various presentation of a unified and systemic whole. This is why non-local causal connections do not represent signal communications in the conventional Einsteinian sense.

Conventional signals such as the speed of light presuppose the very universe of independent, spatially separated objects which Bell's theorem impugns. By radically reconceiving the structure of matter itself, quantum physics provides a coherent conceptual scheme in which instantaneous communication is possible without reference to the speed of light.

Concerned to elaborate the quantum concept of the universe as a cosmic web of interconnections, David Bohm (Bohm, 1980, 42ff; see also Bohm and Hiley, 1974) has proposed an ingenious account of the nature of the interface between non-local connections and local connections. Underpinning the probability relations which define the subject matter of quantum physics is a deeper or 'non-manifest' substratum which he calls the 'implicate order'. At this deeper level the structural interdependencies to which Bell's theorem alludes are not spatio-temporally constrained. To put it differently, the whole of quantum reality is somehow 'enfolded' or in a special sense contained in each of its parts. The fundamental order of the universe is enfold into the process of its instantiation. Its instantiation is the world of ordinary consciousness, what we generally see, hear and experience, what Bohm calls the 'explicate order', the events of which have traditionally been explicated by reference to the principle of local causes.

The analogy employed by Bohm to depict the quality of enfoldment is the hologram, inasmuch as the whole is deemed to be encoded in each of its parts. It was Dennis Gabor who, in 1947, anticipated the principle of holography, a discovery which eventually brought him a Noble Prize. It was not until the invention of the laser, however, that the initial construction of a hologram took place. Holograms involve a process akin to that of lensless photography in which light waves of approximately the same frequency are passed through a half-silvered mirror. Light waves from a laser, being in general of the same frequency, are used for this purpose. The mirror directs some of the coherent light onto a photographic plate, reflecting other waves onto the object which is to be photographed. At the same time the object is situated in such a way that light will be deflected from the object onto the photographic plate, thereby colliding with the beam passing through the mirror. The resultant interference pattern is recorded as a hologram on the photograhic plate.

If a laser beam is now passed through the photographic plate, a distinct three-dimensional image or picture of the object is projected so that it hangs errily, suspended in space a short distance from the plate. This is itself quite remarkable, but even more remarkable is the fact that if light from a laser is used to illuminate any part of the resultant hologram, the pattern which emerges is simply a reconstruction of the whole hologram. Depending upon the size of both the photographic plate and the piece of the hologram illuminated, the resultant image will be more or less detailed and clear. The point is, however, that no matter how small the selected portion of the original hologram, it contains some of the original object. In principle, if the photographic plate could be infinitely extended in both directions, the holographic image could be as sharply defined as the original object. The whole of the object is thus somehow encoded in each of its parts.

It is in this sense that Bohm proposes that the structure of the universe embodies the same principles as the hologram. Although our ordinary consciousness of the world leads us to a reductionist description of independently existing parts of the whole, the deeper structure is a seamless, indivisible unity in respect of which the whole universe is enfolded in each of its parts. Bohm's emphasis, however, is not so much on the structure of objects as with the structure of the dynamical movement or rhythm of the universe, a movement out of which all 'objective' representations flow. Bohm introduces the term 'holomovement' to express the dynamics of the enfolded ground or implicate order which sustains the world of manifest entities as we in common sense terms know them.

Even space and time are enfolded in the holomovement, as is consciousness itself. Indeed, the world of mind and the world of matter are for Bohm interdependent, and though not correlated by local causes, they are intimately connected by non-local ones, being projections of a mutual enfolding of a implicate order of the universe which transcends consciousness and matter, as we know them. To relieve the obscurity of the concept of enfoldment and implicate order, Bohm uses the example of glycerin diffusion. The example is simple and effective. Imagine that we have two concentric cylinders, the smaller of which is placed inside the larger, while the space between them is filled with a clear viscous fluid such as glycerin. If we now deposit a droplet of insoluble ink onto the surface of the glycerin, a well-defined black spot will remain intact. Suppose now that the larger cylinder is rotated in a clockwise direction. With the motion of the cylinder the ink will be drawn out into a thread-like form which becomes thinner and thinner until it eventually disappears altogether. Although the ink droplet is no longer part of the 'explicate' or unfolded order of the system, it is still present in an implicate sense having been enfolded into the glycerin. If the cylinder is now rotated in counterclockwise fashion, the droplet will gradually reconstitute itself, becoming progressively visible as the previously invisible thread darkens.

According to Bohm, order and unity are enfolded in the universe in much the same way that the ink droplet is enfolded in the glycerin. Considering the ink droplets as subatomic particles, it is clear that they may be discontiguous, separated by vast spatial distances, and yet be connected and interdependent in the implicate order. Similarly, if the universe is like a hologram with order and unity manifest throughout its total dynamics, then each part of the universe contains within it the organizational patterns of unity sufficient to reconstitute the unity of the whole. The form and dynamics of the implicate order are thus encoded within every part of the explicate order. In what would seem the end-point or culmination in reductionist division, the elementary particle, whatever it may be, would seem also to enshrine the fundamental unity and interdependency of the entire cosmos.

The time has now come, however, to distil from this cauldron of seemingly arcane ideas, some principles of educational relevance. Although we believe that the emergent philosophy of 'holistic epistemology', which derives from the formentioned developments, has momentous implications for specific reforms within different areas of education such as health education, science education and environmental education. We want in what follows to adumbrate what we shall call a theory of *'Empathetic Ecology'*, as a key concept in the construction of a comprehensive framework within which reform in environmental education can occur.

We have observed that the power-based theory of knowledge assumes a distinction between the knower and the known, between subject and object, if you prefer. On this view, we have tried to objectify our observations of nature by detaching ourselves from it. The world exists, so we have been led to believe, independently of what we say and think about it or of even how we behave towards it. Realist epistemology rests firmly upon this presumption. We earlier expressed our scepticism of the way in which we have institutionalized distinctions between the subjective and objective domains of knowledge, and we submit that the traditional distinctions between subject and object, mind and matter are also spurious, though we make no pretense of being able to argue this latter point fully here. Consciousness is not an element which can be isolated and extracted from the external world. Consciousness is itself an essential feature of the underlying order and unity of the universe. The topology of nature cannot exclude the way in which consciousness is enfolded into it. This being so, nature cannot be objectified in the required epistemic sense because in essence, we become an element in the subject-matter we are trying to observe. We cannot separate ourselves from nature, because we are in the radically holistic sense of Bell's theorem, a part of it. In our attempts to measure and describe the world 'outside ourselves', we now find that we are at one and the same time measuring and describing ourselves.

The fundamental interdependency to which Bell's theorem alludes also inspires a profound paradigm shift in the covert value-orientation which underpins our traditional theory of knowledge. In our futile efforts to detach ourselves from nature to achieve a neutral perspective from which to view it, we inadvertently sever a relationship of basic bonding to nature which is integral to our viewing it holistically. Rather than sensing our oneness with nature, we see ourselves as distinct from it and we are thus disposed to use the faculty of consciousness to gain control over it. The more detached and removed we become from nature, the easier it is to assume a posture of exploitation towards it. By way of the reductionist analysis of wholes into parts, we effect a degradation of the integrity and identity of much of what we find in the natural world. Having reduced all living things to genetic compilations of DNA, for example, we feel less contrite of heart in using genetic engineering to manipulate the impersonal building blocks out of which all living things are made. There is less conscience and responsibility to be felt in manipulating the chemical substances of which human beings are composed than in manipulating human beings themselves. Western science has approached the earth with the same exploitive tendency. We rob the environment of its identity through the transformation of wholes into parts, of living things into dead things, thereby facilitating, in terms of moral responsibility, the manner in which we convert its resources into practical utilities for seemingly unlimited consumption.

It is easier to talk of uprooting trees than of uprooting forests or of disrupting ecosystems. Construing ourselves as separate from nature, we have been misled into thinking that nature is an adversary to be dominated, controlled and subdued. Consistent with this approach, western education has promoted, as we have seen, a theory of knowledge which is tantamount to a theory of power over nature. Knowledge is expressed and implemented as power and control. The desire for mastery over the environment has led to the evolution of a marriage between knowledge and technology which seeks to maximize our expropriation of the earth's resources while minimizing the time and effort devoted to the task (Rifkin, 1985, pp. 26–32). Implicit in Bell's theorem and the subsequent development in holistic epistemology which have followed from it are new principles of epistemic understanding, and we want now to conclude this chapter by making these explicit. We have observed that our traditional theory of knowledge presupposes a universe made up of independent and isolated entities which in various combinations constitute the whole. Human consciousness is independent of the things of which it is conscious.

On Bohm's interpretation of quantum physics, and according to Bell's ingenious defence of it, the universe is one seamless and indivisible unity, the dynamics of which entail an intricate web of interdependencies and interconnections among its elements. Nor is Bell's theorem intended simply as a characterization of the subatomic domain. It is the character of the dynamics of the whole cosmic order which determines the property and behaviour of its elementary constituents, as well as the complex events which take place within it. On this view, human consciousness is not something logically distinct from matter, as our thoughts themselves impact upon matter and thus shape the world through a constellation of synchronicities of which, in scientific terms, we are only just becoming aware. The universe is a vast and complex dynamical system of which we are ourselves an integral component. We are, on this view, not separate from nature, but in partnership with it. A theory of knowledge oriented towards domination and power over the environment is therefore ineluctably self-defeating. *Liberationist Epistemology*, as we shall call it, is concerned not to disempower nature, but to empower it through partnership rather than colonization. *Liberationist Epistemology* represents an approach to knowledge in which participation not domination is the key factor. In place of power and control are empathy and connection (Bateson, 1979, 120ff; see also Devall and Sessions, 1982; Jantsch, 1980; Jones, 1982; Lovelock, 1979; Sheldrake, 1981; Sperry, 1983; Tomlin, 1985). The aim is not to exploit human consciousness to achieve control but rather to achieve connection, relationship and balance through consciousness. Empathetic knowing involves seeing the fundamental interrelationships which express the character of the whole. We must learn to discern how our participation in the dynamical process of indivisible unity represents an investment in the future rather than an extractive lien on the past.

An example of this participatory concept of knowledge can be seen in the contrast between conventional and empathetic architecture. Traditionally, we have constructed our houses and buildings as though they were fortresses against the onslaught of nature. Imperializing their environment, they expropriate massive quantities of energy to sustain their separateness from the world outside them. It has been noted, for example, that the world's tallest building, the Sears Roebuck Tower in Chicago, requires more energy resources in one day than the neighbouring city of Rockford, Illinois, whose population is approximately 150,000 people (Rifkin, 1985, p. 84). Guided by different considerations and a liberationist epistemology, empathetic architects seek a better understanding of how a building cannot itself be an environment within an environment. Seeking through what is constructed to extend the environment rather than to disrupt it, empathetic architecture is cognizant of the manner in which a design can capture the integrity and rhythm of an environment, incorporating the dynamics of the surrounding ecosystem to minimize the extractive features of the technology employed.

Whether the power of pyrotechnology has genuinely advanced our mastery over the environment is we suggest, a moot point. What seems to me clear is that the power of pyrotechnology and the theory of knowledge which has generated it, have not in the end made us more secure. The logical extension of the quest for power and domination results in destruction and dissolution, a degradation not only of the environment but ultimately of ourselves. The traditional theory of knowledge, and the value orientation which undergirds it, has brought us to the brink of extinction. The only consolation is that we still have the power to choose how we define ourselves and our relationship to nature. The blinded giant of science has led us to a new consciousness of the limitations of conventional science. The time is long overdue to return the gift of sight to the blinded giant, so let us now turn to a consideration of *holistic epistemolgy* in the context of systems theory and other relevant developments in science, as they impinge on participatory consciousness in environmental education.

References

ASPECT, A., DALIBARD, J. and ROGER, G. (1982) 'Experimental test of Bell's inequalities using time-varying analyzers', *Physical Review Letters*, **49**, 25.

BATESON, G. (1979) *Mind and Nature*, New York: E.P. Dutton.

BOHM, D. (1980) *Wholeness and the Implicate Order*, London: Routledge and Kegan Paul.

BOHM, D. and HILEY, B. (1974) *On the Intuitive Understanding of Non-locality As Implied by Quantum Theory*, London: University of London.

BOHR, N. (1934) *Atomic Physics and the Description of Nature*, Cambridge: Cambridge University Press.

BOHR, N. (1958) *Atomic Physics and Human Knowledge*, New York: Wiley and Sons.

CAPRA, F. (1983) *The Turning Point*, London: Flamingo.

CLAUSER, J. and SHIMONY, A. (1978) 'Bell's theorem: Experimental tests and implications', *Reports on Progress Phys*, **41**.

DEVALL, B. and SESSIONS, G. (1982) *Deep Ecology*, Salt Lake City, UT: Peregrine Smith Books.

EINSTEIN, A., PODOLSKY, B. and ROSEN, N. (1935) 'Can Quantum-mechanical description of physical reality be considered complete?', *Physical Review*, **47**.

HEISENBERG, W. (1963) *Physics and Philosophy*, London: Allen and Unwin.

HEISENBERG, W. (1971) *Physics and Beyond*, New York: Harper and Row.

JANTSCH, E. (1980) *The Self-organizing Universe*, Oxford: Pergamon Press.

JONES, R. (1982) *Physics As Metaphor*, New York: New American Library.

LOVELOCK, J.E. (1979) *Gaia: A New Look at Life on Earth*, Oxford: Oxford University Press.

MUMFORD, L. (1966) *The Myth of the Machine: Technics and Human Development*, New York: Harcourt Brace Jovanovich.

RIFKIN, J. (1985) *Declaration of a Heretic*, London: Routledge and Kegan Paul.

SHELDRAKE, R. (1981) *A New Science of Life*, Los Angeles: J.P. Tarcher.

SPERRY, R. (1983) *Science and Moral Priority*, New York: Columbia University Press.

STAPP, H. (1975) 'Bell's theorem and world process', *Il Nuovo Cimento*.

TOMLIN, E.W.F. (1985) *Psyche, Culture and the New Science*, London: Routledge and Kegan Paul.

ZUKAV, G. (1986) *The Dancing Wu Li Masters*, London: Bantam.

Chapter 6

Extending the Boundaries of Educational Knowledge

In the previous chapter we were concerned to set the context for the transition from educational presuppositions based on knowledge as a form of power to a pedagogic conceptual system, the foundations of which are built on liberationist epistemology and participatory consciousness in environmental education. Our excursion into the subatomic, however, was not enough in itself sufficient to make transparent the process of distillation which links our philosophy of science to our philosophy of education. It is the burden of the present chapter to approach these matters more determinately.

The argument we have put thus far can be summarized as follows: However one defines education, it is clear that education is predominantly concerned with the transmission of knowledge. The central problem, however, is that the edifice of education has been built primarily on a concept of knowledge driven by western society's obsession with power. We observed that when a cultural consciousness driven by power defines the tools which express its knowledge, one social consequence is the advent of technologies of power mediated through education and manifested by the vested interests of industry. Knowledge as power is mediated educationally, we saw, via the institution of science as the core of curriculum development and as an all-pervasive world view. One sense of this pervasiveness of science was revealed by our earlier consideration of its ubiquitous intellectual imperialism. Not only do our educational institutions reserve a place — a huge place — for the school of science, but they stand by oblivious of the intellectual imperialization which lay behind the redefinition of non-scientific departments in terms of science. With few exceptions the renaming of departments, from their non-scientific descriptions to their scientific ones, has been greeted with acclamation, as the department of sociology has become the department of social science, while politics has become political science; engineering has become engineering science, computing is now computing science, medicine is medical science and health has been redefined as health science, to remind ourselves of our earlier discussion. To be dubbed 'scientific' or even better, *to be accepted as a science*, is tantamount to being 'educationally knighted'. It is the socially accepted accolade of being educationally legitimated.

The argument of this book has been to tease out the educational consequences of this quite remarkable socio-cultural phenomenon. In addition to the predilection towards academic conformity and the diminution of the intellectual imagination against which we have been inveighing, we have argued that the way in which science has been used to propagate an epistemology of power equates conceptually to an ideology of social and environmental destruction. When epistemologies of power give rise to scientific technologies of power, the outcome, we argued, is 'transformative subjugation', namely, the systemic conversion of living things into dead things and the reconstruction of the natural world into an increasingly artificial and synthesized one. In earlier chapters considerable attention was paid to the catastrophic and subtle environmental degradations and deformation which result from transformative subjugation.

In previous chapters special attention was also given to the extent to which the reductio-mechanistic framework provides the central methodological tool by way of which the process of transformative subjugation is realized. If the world is construed to resemble a machine, analysable into its fundamental parts the interrelations of which are governed by specific laws which admit of precise mathematical formulation, it follows that the goal of an epistemology of power and control through predictability of outcome is most assuredly guaranteed. On the reductio-mechanistic view physical reality is in essence fragmented, and thus discovering its true character depends upon reducing it to the material particles of which it is composed. The objective of classical physics is of course not limited solely to the analysis of the parts of the machine; its aim is to show also how the parts work together, thereby exhibiting patterns of organization in seemingly distinct tracts of experience which, when taken in conjunction, ultimately determine the character of experience as a whole.

In the previous chapters it was argued that with the advent of quantum physics has come a crystallized perception of a new structural order in nature which is fundamentally different from the machine-like ontic representation of classical physics. While it would be presumptuous to suggest that philosophy of science has reached a concensus on the insights capable of being drawn from quantum physics, we have urged that an heuristic can be distilled from the emerging picture of quantum reality which confirms that the commitment to an epistemology of power in the name of science is inimical to ecological sustainability. According to the quantum perception of nature we proffered in the previous chapter, nature does not yield its most important secrets by being whittled down into smaller and smaller components in the reductionist hope of reaching absolutely simple building blocks out of which everything else is made and can be constructed. The epistemological paradox to emerge from the reductionist approach to the quantum domain is that the purportedly primitive components in the reduction turn out to be so inextricably related that their coherent description depends upon the postulation of a world of seamless unity and indivisible wholeness. The ontology of primitive particles is expressed epistemologically, that is to say, by way of their correlations with other particles. If there are fundamental particles which constitute the substratum of nature, the insight we have taken from quantum mechanics is that they exist only relationally. This being so, the separateness and independence of their particulate reality are illusory and require a methodological rendering richer than that which the tool of reductio-mechanist methodology can provide.

To elaborate the relevance of these insights for liberationist epistemology of environmental education we need now to consider the roots of epistemic holism in what is now known as 'systems theory'.

Holism and Systems Theory

The 'holistic-systemic' conception of reality, in which 'everything is connected to everything', provided the main philosophical challenge to the reductio-mechanistic methodology by way of which transformative subjugation is carried out. Jan Christian Smuts, in his book titled *Holism and Evolution* (first published, 1926), coined the term 'holism' to represent the 'fundamental factor operative towards the creation of wholes in the universe'. The character of 'wholeness', Smuts declared, 'meets us everywhere and points to something fundamental in the universe' (Smuts, 1973, p. 86). Holism and the term 'holistic' is further explained by Smuts as the underlying 'dynamic', 'creative', 'tendency' of nature. As such, nature cannot be explained solely in reductio-mechanistic terms. '[T]he mechanistic concept of nature has its place and justification only in the wider setting of holism' (Smuts, 1973, p. 87).

Nature, Smuts argued, exhibits 'fluidity' and 'plasticity'. There exists in nature a universal 'trend' towards 'wholeness', or 'whole making', and interconnection or 'interpenetration' occurs between the various wholes through their 'fields' of influence (Smuts, 1973, p. 340). In contradiction to the reductionist approach, holism infers that any 'whole' of investigation — be it 'matter', 'life' or 'mind' — cannot be 'abstracted' or analysed to its 'composite' parts without loosing its integrity and identity, a point which is of crucial significance in the context of environmental education. Recognition of this point provides a force to the expression, 'the whole is more than the sum of its parts'. Leading onto this point and beyond, Smuts wrote:

> Wholes are not mere artificial constructions of thought; they point to something real in the universe, and Holism is a real operative factor, a *vera causa*. There is behind Evolution no mere vague creative impulse or *Elan vital*, but something quite definite and specific in its operation, and thus productive of the real concrete character of cosmic evolution. . . . The idea of wholes and wholeness should therefore not be confined to the biological; it covers both inorganic substances and the highest manifestations of the human spirit. Taking a plant or an animal as a type of a whole, we notice the fundamental holistic characters as a unity of parts which is so close and intense as to be more than the sum of its parts; which not only gives a particular conformation or structure to the parts, but so relates and determines them in their synthesis that their functions are altered; the synthesis affects and determines the parts, so that they function towards the 'whole'; and the whole and the parts therefore reciprocally influence and determine each other, and appear more or less to merge their individual characters: the whole is in the parts and the parts are in the whole, and this synthesis of whole and parts is reflected in the holistic character of the functions of the parts as well as of the whole. (Smuts, 1973, p. 86)

For example, one can say a great deal respectively about an oxygen and a hydrogen atom when they are considered in isolation but when they are combined new qualities may result from their interaction which could not be predicted by their respective reductionist explication. Such qualities have come to known as 'emergent properties' and in the combinatory case at hand it is the property of water that has emerged. In addition to the concept of emergent properties, Smut's work brings into bold relief the endogenous relationships of which 'cooperation' and 'coordination' exist amongst the various parts and between the various parts and the whole. A contemporary interpretation of this cooperative or 'harmonious' relationship between the parts and the whole is found in the notion of 'synergy'. As Russell explained:

> ... This harmonious interaction can be described by the word synergy, derived from the Greek *syn-ergous*, meaning 'to work together.' ... Synergy does not imply any coercion or restraint, nor is it brought about by deliberate effort. Each individual element of the system works toward its own goals, and the goals themselves may be quite varied. Yet the elements function in ways that are spontaneously mutually supportive. ... The word synergy has sometimes been used in the sense of the whole being greater than the parts. But this is not the word's root meaning; this interpretation is a consequence of synergy in its original sense. Because the elements in a synergistic system support each other, they also support the functioning of the system as a whole, and the performance of the whole is improved. (Russell, 1983, p. 110)

The principle of epistemic holism, particularly in its current relation to environmental education, presupposes a notion of synergy within all living systems. The parts are fundamentally independent and work together to maximize the functioning, health and creative development of the whole organism or community of such organisms.

By the mid 1940s, many of the elements of holism were incorporated into Ludwig von Bertalanffy's postulation of the *General Systems Theory*. 'General system theory', in von Bertalanffy's words, '... is a general science of "wholeness"':

> In one way or another, we are forced to deal with complexities, with 'wholes' or 'systems', in all fields of knowledge. This implies a basic re-orientation in scientific thinking. (von Bertalanffy, 1975, p. 5)

What von Bertalanffy found was that in the increasingly divergent fields of twentieth century knowledge, 'isomorphisms', i.e., simultaneous conceptual problems, were occurring, even in the absence of communication between the researchers in those various fields. The major problem lay in the reductio-mechanistic approach to knowledge itself. Simply put, scientists and researchers in all fields, including psychology, biology, sociology and philosophy were, at the end of the day, forced to deal with organized 'systems' or 'wholes', whose biological integrity was not comprehensible by reductionist investigations of constituent parts taken in isolation. Von Bertalanffy wrote:

These considerations lead to the postulate of a new scientific discipline which we call general system theory. Its subject matter is formulation of principles that are valid for 'systems' in general, whatever the nature of their component elements and the relation or 'forces' between them. . . . General system theory, therefore, is a general science of 'wholeness' which up till now was considered a vague, hazy, and semimetaphysical concept. (von Bertalanffy, 1975, p. 37)

Von Bertalanffy's general systems approach can also be understood as a reflection of the changing attitudes in his day in regard to classical science. As we have seen it also constituted a direct challenge to the epistemological inadequacy of the reductio-mechanistic world view. New concepts such as 'non-linear causality', 'feedback mechanisms' and 'teleology', were now entering the realm of systems theory to signal the need for a far more comprehensive epistemology than reductio-mechanistic science was capable of providing. As von Bertalanffy put it:

In the world view called mechanistic . . . the aimless play of atoms, governed by the inexorable laws of causality, produced all phenomena in the world, inanimate, living, and mental. . . . The world of the organisms appeared a product of chance, accumulated by the senseless play of random mutations and selection; the mental world as a curious and rather inconsequential epiphenomenon of material events. . . . [P]hysical reality was split up into mass points or atoms, the living organism into cells, behavior into reflexes, perception into punctual sensations, etc. Correspondingly, causality was essentially one-way: one sun attracts one planet in Newtonian mechanics, one gene in the fertilized ovum produces such and such inherited character, one sort of bacterium produces this or that disease, mental elements are lined up, like beads in a string of pearls, by law of association . . . .We may state as characteristic of modern science that this scheme of isolable units acting in one-way causality has proved to be insufficient. Hence the appearance, in all fields of science, of notions like wholeness, holistic, organismic, *Gestalt*, etc., which all signify that, in the last resort, we must think in terms of systems of elements in mutual interaction. . . . Similarly, notions of teleology and directiveness appeared to be . . . intrinsically alien to science. . . . Nevertheless, these aspects exist, and you cannot conceive of a living organism, not speak of behavior and human society, without taking into account what variously and rather loosely is called adaptiveness, purposiveness, goal-seeking and the like. (von Bertalanffy, 1975, p. 45)

According to von Bertalanffy, examples of purposive behaviour are contained in the notion of 'feedback' and cannot be accounted for reductionistically. Feedback is defined in terms of information being monitored chronologically backwards and in a dynamic process of overall 'circular causal fashion', from a system to its parts and *vice versa*. The purpose of feedback is to guarantee the homeostasis, or self-regulation, of the system in question (von Bertalanffy, 1975, p. 43). As Laura and Heaney elaborated, '[r]egulation of the system of feedback is thought to be of two kinds', 'negative' and 'positive':

Negative feedback is designed to keep the system in homeostatic balance. . . . To borrow an example . . . if the heart begins to function irregularly, say by pumping blood too slowly or too rapidly, it will jeopardize the level of blood flow needed by certain organs to perform their functions. This being so, other mechanisms such as neural and hormonal responses are triggered to speed up or to slow down the heart as required to return the overall system to homeostasis (basic equilibrium). 'Positive feedback' refers to the regulation of information flow often associated with growth and maturation. Deviation within the system is thus reinforced and enhanced to promote a change deemed to be beneficial to, or at least not incompatible with, the overall integrity of the integrated whole. (Laura and Heaney, 1990, p. 113)

It is important to point out, however, that the concept of 'feedback' does not in itself represent an impossible challenge to reductio-mechanistic epistemology. But when the concept of feedback is coupled with the idea of causal loops, the inter-connectedness of biological systems and their parts defies reductionist assessment. Apart from the addition of the casual loop, causality in the feedback system remains one-way and 'unidirectional', i.e., it is defined in terms of simple linear, 'stimulus–response', cause–effect mechanisms. Those who regard feedback as the sole principle of general systems theory are only serving to reinforce the very reductionist methodology which stands as antithetical to the unfolding of the integrative features of the general systems approach. Important as it is, the feedback concept should be viewed as just one of a number of interconnecting models integrated within the overall general systems approach. As von Bertalanffy has put it:

The concept appeals to a time when control engineering and automation are nourishing, computers, servomechanisms etc . . . Thus the feedback concept sometimes has assumed a monopoly suppressing other equally necessary and fruitful view points. (von Bertalanffy, 1975, p. 163)

Indeed, general systems theory also involves a non-mechanistic description of nature which far surpasses the simply 'closed' system of information 'feedback loops'. According to von Bertalanffy, the 'primary' systems are 'open', in the sense that matter and energy are constantly exchanged between the system and its environment. We ourselves can be construed as living 'open systems' dynamically interconnected with nature through the exchange of matter and energy. This is the basis of the systemic interdependence between ourselves and nature. Without this environmental interdependence we would rapidly reach a thermodynamic equilibrium in which there would be no flow through of energy, thus ensuring that we would cease to exist.

In the sections which follow, we shall see how the interconnectedness implied in holistic-systemic thinking aligns with the philosophy underpinning quantum theory and other recent theories which have challenged the reductio-mechanistic philosophy of nature. Based on the quantum theory perspective, which holds that the universe is a seamless indivisible unity, we shall explore the extent to which these new ideas can offer the necessary transition to a new paradigm in environmental education. This transition is of monumental importance in our time for it affirms the recognition not only that we do not exist apart from nature, but that we are intimately bonded to nature. By virtue of this, it also encourages the articulation of an alternative value orientation to educational epistemology. It is through the explication of this alternative value perspective that we can eliminate the 'macho-mechanistic' epistemology of power over nature and begin to foster the values of participation, empathy and connectivity in our world.

Further Reflections on the Paradox of Reductionist Physics

As the reductio-mechanistic world paradigm continues to dominate the 'hard nosed' twentieth century sciences, it is easy to forget that Newtonian mechanics itself was successfully challenged more than 60 years ago. That the Newtonian model should continue to be so prevalent is a commentary on the extent to which the reductio-mechanistic approach has been crystallized into a metaphysics of epistemological supremacy.

Albert Einstein initiated the conceptual challenge to the classical mechanistic view of reality. It was in 1905 that Einstein presented to the scientific world his three revolutionary theories. The first was his special theory of relativity, and the second was his unique interpretation of electromagnetic radiation. He formulated his general theory of relativity 10 years later, an extension of special theory which included non-uniform motion or gravitation, and at the same time his theory of electromagnetic radiation helped develop the initial framework for quantum theory and the consequent theory of atomic phenomena.

Einstein's relativity theory shattered one of the basic tenets of Newtonian mechanics, the notion of 'absolute space and time'. Time and space now depended on the point of view of the 'subjective' observer. Moreover, through the collective development of quantum theory, the remainder of the principal concepts of reductionist science would themselves also be shattered. Capra (1988b) provided an astonishing survey of this conceptual annihilation. He wrote:

> The notion of absolute space and time, the elementary solid particles, the fundamental material substance, the strictly causal nature of physical phenomena, and the objective description of nature — none of these concepts could be extended to the new domain into which physics was now penetrating. (Capra, 1988b, p. 62)

The underlying contention of relativity theory propounds that both space and time are 'intimately connected'. According to Einstein, space can no longer be regarded as a three-dimensional manifold. In the relativistic scheme he postulates both space and time are inextricably linked mathematically to a four-dimensional continuum. In frightenly simple terms relativity theory tells us that we cannot talk about time without talking about space, and *vice versa*.

Einstein's special and general theory of relativity has received considerable discussion, and even some high school students are now familiar, or have at least a nodding acquaintance with Einstein's theories. Among his basic principles which have been popularly espoused are: the interchangeability of gravity and acceleration; the curvature of space caused by the gravitational fields of massive bodies; the movement of matter and light through curved space in geodesic lines of 'best fit' and the idea that space warps time and time warps space etc.

As a consequence of Einstein's work, Newtonian physicists had to concede to a complete modification of their conceptual framework. One such modification came with the realization that matter and energy are one and the same. Einstein's famous equation $E = mc^2$ demonstrated that even the most stable, or rested, object has a mass of stored energy which is equal to that mass multiplied by the speed of light squared. This equation thus revealed the destructive power of the atom, though only a few people were distracted from their search for power. Despite this dimension of the conflict, students also continue to accept Euclidean geometry when they know that such a mathematical system, crucial to Newtonian science, is rendered invalid by the theories of relativity (Capra, 1988a, pp. 72–3).

As intimated in the last chapter, quantum theory arose out of a need to explain the scientific paradox of the dual nature of light (or electromagnetic radiation). As a mathematical theory, quantum mechanics successfully represented the statistical probability of, or potential for, subatomic existence. Yet unlike virtually every theory of physics that has ever preceded it, quantum theory derived its success from an epistemology of explicit uncertainty known as Heisenberg's Uncertainty Principle. The problem of classical measurement terminology was clearly outlined by Werner Heisenberg in his 1930 publication, *The Physical Principles of the Quantum Theory*. Heisenberg showed that whenever one attempts to apply classical mechanistic terminology, e.g. wave, particle, position, velocity etc., to subatomic events, they will invariably find that their definitions cannot be applied in a simultaneous and precise manner. Given that we have two pairs of classical concepts, the more emphasis we place on one, the less certain we become about the other (Heisenberg, 1930, pp. 10–20). The standard mathematical and philosophical interpretations of the Uncertainty Principle are somewhat bizarre. The philosophical advice it gave was that it is in principle impossible to measure simultaneously and with unlimited accuracy both the position and momentum of elementary particles. In this sense nothing that exists at the subatomic level can be located or measured with the determinate certainty claimed to be available at the macroscopic level. The difficulty is that in order to quantify the position and momentum of say, an electron, it will be necessary to illuminate it and this requires a light source. The problem is that the wavelength of light is reputed to be approximately one hundred billion time greater than the size of the electron. From this it follows that to illuminate an electron is literally to bombard it and to bombard it is to interfere with either its position or its momentum. This being so, the more accurate the scientist's measurement of the particle's position, the correspondingly less accurate will be the measurement of the particle's momentum or velocity.

Moreover, if we choose to measure the wave characteristics of light, the response to our choice is explicated as a wave pattern. If instead we choose to study the particle characteristics of light, then light will behave like a particle and so on. This suggests that the scientific observer is intimately connected to the outcome of his or her observations. In the quantum realm, the 'objectivity' of the principle of 'observer detachment' drawn from conventional science is an epistemic anachronism.

Searching for a more comprehensive and clearer understanding of the relation between pairs of classical concepts, Neils Bohr, Heisenberg's mentor, introduced the notion of 'complementarity' (Bohr, 1934). Bohr argued that both particles and waves are merely two aspects of the same reality. Both concepts are required to give a full account of atomic reality. For modern physicists the notion of complementarity is essential for the coherent explication of the nature of subatomic reality. Some philosophers go so far as to claim that complementarity may one day be an acceptable foundation for the study of all levels of reality (Heisenberg, 1930, pp. 62–65; Capra, 1988b, p. 68).

The word that was originally used to explain the nature of light was 'quanta', or package, and it provides another way of understanding the Uncertainty Principle. Quantum physicists generally used the word 'wave package' when studying all subatomic phenomena i.e., not just light, or photons, but the many hundreds of other subatomic particles. The wave package should not, however, be taken in the literal sense. It is best understood as a probability wave which can be used to determine the 'tendency' or 'potential' for a specific, particle, such as an electron, to exist in a specific region, such as an atom. If the package is experimentally compressed one is able to increase the potential for locating the particle, but when this occurs the individual wave amplitudes, or heights, are dramatically varied, thus making the wave frequency, velocity or momentum, even more indeterminate. Thus, by increasing the potential for locating a particle's position you automatically decrease the potential for determining its momentum. We can therefore look at an electron in two respects: as an electron cloud ('standing wave') or as a particle ('point mass'). Again, it is important to stress that both of these characteristics — either particle or wave — are dependent upon our choice of measurement. In the measurement of the quantum domain the experimenter is involved in an 'essential' way (Capra, 1988a, pp. 163–7; Capra, 1988b, p. 69; Hey and Walters, 1987, p. 17).

In 'bubble' and 'spark' chamber experiments, there is general agreement that electrons, apart from being both waves and particles, can also be viewed as positrons, or anti-electrons, flowing backwards in time. From this observation we cannot determine which came first, the electron or the positron, or which of the two was causally responsible for the existence of the other. The reductionist concept of strict linear causality simply has no clear application in this domain (Zukav, 1988, p. 236).

If one accepts the classical conception, as Einstein did, of a universe consisting of spatially disconnected phenomena, it is difficult to see how a coherent account of quantum mechanics can be given. If instead, however, one views objects and events as 'undifferentiated facets of an indivisible whole', one need no longer be logically committed to the idea of signalling, or communication, as a condition which is physically limited by the speed of light, or any other such law which governs determinate behaviour between two or more objects. This is the heuristic we wish to draw from the quantum debate and upon which the argument for epistemic holism admits of elaboration. On this view nature — our environment — is not to be regarded as something distinct from us. We and our environment form part of an interconnected whole, the integrity of which depends in part on our interactions with it.

Quantum Connectedness and Holism

'An essential feature of modern physics . . .', wrote Koestler:

> . . . is its increasingly *holistic* trend, based on the insight that the whole is as
> necessary for the understanding of its parts as the parts are necessary for under-
> standing the whole. An early expression of this trend, dating from the turn of the
> century, was 'Mach's Principle', endorsed by Einstein. It states that the inertial
> properties of terrestrial matter are determined by the total mass of the universe
> around us. There is no satisfactory causal explanation as to *how* this influence
> is exerted, yet Mach's Principle is an integral part of relativistic cosmology.
> The metaphysical implications are fundamental — for it follows from it not only
> that the universe as a whole influences local, terrestrial events, but also that local
> events have an influence, however small, on the universe as a whole. Philosoph-
> ically minded physicists are acutely aware of these implications — which remind
> one of the ancient Chinese proverb: 'If you cut a blade of grass, you shake the
> Universe.' (Koestler, 1978, p. 256)

Capra (1988a, Chapter 10) interpreted the holistic heuristic of quantum physics
as paralleling the spiritual descriptions of the cosmos given by eastern mystics for
centuries. Eastern spiritualism suggests that what appear on the surface to be separate objects and events, are in fact interconnected threads of a much greater 'cosmic
web'. Like eddies in a cosmic river, the events that participate in the 'cosmic dance'
cannot in themselves exist without the dance. The dance is not the sum of the dancers
(see also Zukav, 1988, pp. 30–43).

David Bohm (1990) expressed the quantum interconnectedness beautifully
with his notion of what we earlier described as the 'implicate' or 'enfolded order'.
The 'implicate order' he described as an 'unbroken wholeness' — a universal,
interconnected wholeness. Quoting Bohm elsewhere, in part, Zukav wrote:

> 'Matter is a form of the implicate order as a vortex is a form of the water — it is
> not reducible to smaller particles.' . . . Like 'matter' and everything else, particles
> are forms of the implicate order. If this is difficult to grasp it is because our minds
> demand to know. 'What is the implicate order the implicate order of?' . . .
> The 'implicate order' is the order of that-which-is. However, that-which-is *is* the
> implicate order. This world view is so different from the one that we are using that,
> as Bohm points out, 'Description is totally incompatible with what we want to
> say.' (Zukav, 1988, p. 325)

According to Bohm, we analyse the world into separate entities — including
mind and matter — primarily because we have come to view the world in total
'manifest' terms. In other words, we mechanistically define the things of the world
as invariably 'solid, tangible and visibly stable'. This general 'mechanistic' ordering of the world he referred to as the 'explicate' or 'unfolded order' (Bohm, 1990,
pp. 173, 185).

If we once again consider the complementary concepts of wave/particle dual-
ity, there is now reason for urging that the world we see in 'solid' particle form,

when measured or located, becomes temporarily unfolded from the implicate order into the explicate world. When we observe its wave characteristic it then begins to enfold itself back into the implicate order. This being so, it seems plausible to suggest that the experimenter is himself or herself connected with the implicate–explicate relationship, in such a way that that he or she unconsciously extracts explicate phenomena e.g., subatomic particles, from the fundamental, yet hidden, implicate order. Again, in this sense, there is no real scientific detachment from that which is observed or measured (see also Capra, 1988b, pp. 76–7, on the role of consciousness in observation).

If we are willing to reconsider our classically conditioned conceptions of reality, there is little doubt that our educational epistemology can be revised to accommodate a new vision of the environment. Instead of viewing, or perceiving, an object in the environment as a piece of a whole, it becomes plausible to view that piece and every other piece as containing the infinite pattern or 'code' of reality within itself — each piece contains the whole and interacts with the whole. Furthermore, instead of thinking in pieces, it becomes possible to substitute the concepts of 'relationships' and interconnecting 'forms' in place of linear causal sequences.

There is a significant relevance of these deliberations for the reconceptualization of educational knowledge. What quantum physics tells us is that on a subatomic level there are no truly separate events. There are instead relations, interconnections, and different expressions of reality within the underlying 'whole' that is reality, defined as an underlying flux, or field, of energy. Not only does quantum physics emphasize the interconnectedness of the whole, it also relates the human observer to the way in which expression of the reality of interconnections will make itself manifest.

We have already observed that holograms similar to photographs taken without the use of a camera lens, in which light waves of approximately equal frequencies — such as laser light — are beamed through a 'half-silvered mirror'. Half of the clean laser light is directed towards a photographic plate and the other half is redirected and reflected off a target object. Both beams are then recombined on the photographic plate. As both beams unite on the plate 'a fine pattern of interference fringes' result which contain all the information of the hologram. When another laser beam is directed through the developed photographic plate a 'suspended' three-dimensional image of the target object appears (Bohm, 1990, p. 145; Bohm and Peat, 1987, p. 175).

Apart from the fascinating image that is created by the hologram, it is clear when laser light is directed at any part of the holographic plate a complete, albeit, ghostly, image of the original object is reproduced. The concept of holographic reproductions provides an insight into the notion of implicate–explicate interrelatedness, in which each and every part contains sufficient information to replicate the whole. 'That is to say,' Bohm explained, 'the form and structure of the entire object may be said to be *enfolded* within each region of the photographic record' (Bohm, 1990, pp. 146, 177; Bohm and Peat, 1987, p. 175).

Empathetic ecology provides a way of seeing the world in which space, time, matter, and even consciousness, are enfolded into an implicate order, which by way of our interactions with it are manifested as environmental phenomena. Every environmental state of affairs is dynamically interconnected in a causal, but non-local, relationship with every other state of affairs. The dynamic process Bohm called the 'holomovement' i.e., an 'unending flux of enfoldment and unfoldment' (Bohm, 1990, p. 185; see also Capra, 1988b, p. 88) parallels the web of dynamic interdependencies which we claim characterize the world of nature.

The concept of the fundamental interconnectedness of every event in nature configures the notion of 'opposites', and more particularly, the parallel with the eastern mystical interpretations of 'yin' and 'yang'. As Capra put it:

> Throughout history, it has been recognized that the human mind is capable of two kinds of knowledge, or two modes of consciousness, which have often been termed the rational and the intuitive, and have been traditionally associated with science and religion, respectively. In the west, the intuitive, religious type of knowledge is often devalued in favour of rational, scientific knowledge, whereas the traditional Eastern attitude is in general just the opposite. Chinese philosophy, on the other hand, has always emphasized the complementary nature of the intuitive and the rational and has represented them by the archetypal pair yin and yang which form the basis of Chinese thought. (Capra, 1988a, p. 34)

We have already argued that educational knowledge relies heavily on reductio-mechanistic thought to describe the nature of reality and the reality of nature, in a supposedly objective fashion. If the things of nature exist as isolated environmental phenomena, the process of transformative subjugation will seem to be an appropriate way to interact with them. The more phenomena we control, the more secure we think we become. Because every event is interconnected with every other event, however, the victory of transformative subjugation is pyrrhic. The more synthetic our environment becomes, the more tenuous the survival of living things which remain. The problem is that we continue to interact with nature in a mechanistically interventionist fashion, though the world we interact with is essentially non-mechanistic. Our attempts to impose mechanistic order on a world, where the only straight lines are the ones we create ourselves, has led us into an abyss of environmental expropriation, exploitation and unwitting transformation of the world of nature into a world of artefact. In the process we have let ourselves and nature become victims of the very machines which were designed to save us.

The current awareness of having to deal with the dynamic complexity of a system of interconnected events has led to new offshoot theories of quantum science based, not on order, but on chaos. The new rules of chaos theory suggest that the deeper we probe, the more infinitely complex the world becomes. The more precision we attempt to apply, the more error we discover in our measurements. The tiniest variations in initial conditions lead to an infinite number of possible outcomes. Our attempts to measure and predict social phenomena, market trends and even weather patterns — using reductio-analytic techniques — seem to reveal even greater complexities with each decimal place of precision.

For example, the modern science of 'fractal geometry', itself based on chaos theory, provides persuasive examples of the impossibility of precise measurement.

It is tempting to think that the more refined our measurements become, the closer we must get to a precise answer to a precise question about the structure of nature, but fractal geometry reveals the fallacy in this way of thinking. Even the tiniest errors in measurement make accurate predictions impossible. Consider, for example, the measurement of a coastline from outer space. The coastline from this distance has a crinkly appearance. You could, for instance, measure the actual distance from one point to another but you would actually have to get much closer to refine this measurement. Once you begin to zoom in you are confronted once more with the same crinkly effect but within a smaller region. You may be able to add more decimal places to your original measurement but the closer you zoom in you will continue to meet the same crinkly effect — making precise measurement, or for that matter, a more refined measurement relevant to the chosen amplification of the region, totally illusory (Hey & Walters, 1987, pp. 24–26).

In the same way, the deeper we probe subatomic events, in our vain search for the fundamental structure of nature, the more we are met with what might be called a 'jiggly', fractal, landscape of chaotic complexity. This is not to say that we should deny the use of analysis and measurement in favour of intuition. But as the Zen Buddhists tell us, we need a finger to point at the moon, but once we have found the moon we should no longer concern ourselves with the finger (Capra, 1988a, p. 35). The Buddhists, the Hindus, and the Toaists were concerned with the balance and connection between apparent opposites, and the chaos that can result from even the smallest action considered apart from its place in the whole. As Capra puts it:

> . . . [It] is the awareness of the unity and mutual interrelation of all things and events, the experience of all phenomena in the world as manifestations of a basic oneness. All things are seen as interdependent and inseparable parts of this cosmic whole as different manifestations of the same ultimate reality. (Capra, 1988a, p. 141)

The conventional western educational concept of knowledge as power needs badly to be reconceptualized before genuine environmental contributions to the development of a more humane, balanced, and sustainable society can occur. It is the momentum of the western reductio-mechanistic world paradigm, however, through its vested interests and institutional expression, which resists change. We have, as a society, attended the grand school of classical mechanism and applied what we have learnt in an attempt to make us stronger and more secure. We have succeeded only in making ourselves more detached from nature and, as a consequence, less secure and more uncertain about our long-term survival. What our epistemology of power has done via its reductio-mechanistic methodology, is to alter our conscious relationship to the world through our commitment to transformative subjugation. In effect we have moved from a 'participating' to a 'non-participating' mode of conscious understanding (Berman, 1981) which has made it increasingly easier to despoil the world without moral conscience. At its most fundamental level we have taken the conscious framework of knowledge and designed it to enable us to interact with nature from a detached position — signifying a position of power and control over that which we seek to understand. The Cartesian distinction between mind and body reinforces this epistemic isolation. The body now represents the protective alienating shell in which the consciousness of nature resides. Berman reminds us that in more primitive cultures and in children from our culture we see the natural and seemingly magical, projection of mind and body into the world. The body was once seen to be infused with consciousness or at least unconscious or subconscious associations which were intimately connected with the external environment. The relation between mind, body and world on this view, gives rise to an empathetic and participatory interface with nature. According to Berman, it is these interconnected elements of human experience — empathetic participation and love — which have been filtered out of our epistemology in favour of the ratio-ego-centric model for human–nature interaction.

There is also, Berman suggests, another element of the 'participating consciousness' which has been shunted aside in favour of 'analysis'; and that is contained in the notion of 'mimesis'. The 'mimetic' element evolved from the Greek concept of learning by 'visceral/poetic/erotic identification'. Our insistence that knowledge can only be obtained by 'the act of distancing oneself from the experience', as opposed to identifying or immersing oneself with or within the experience, not only delimits the domain of possible knowledge to the 'objective' or 'impersonal', but is a contradiction in terms. As Berman interprets:

> [A]ll knowing takes place in terms of meaning, and thus the knower is implicated in the known. . . . [W]hat constitutes knowledge is therefore merely the findings of an agreed-upon methodology, and the facts that science finds are merely that — facts that science finds; they possess no meaning in and of themselves. (Berman, 1981, pp. 139–140)

In the light of these shortcomings we shall, in the final chapter, gesture towards a 'new paradigm' of knowledge better suited as a foundation for a holistic education indicative of renewed empathetic participation and stewardship with nature.

References

BERMAN, M. (1981) *The Reenchantment of the World*, New York: Cornell University Press.
BOHM, D. (1990) *Wholeness and the Implicate order*, London and New York: Cox and Wyman.
BOHM, D. and PEAT, F.D. (1987) *Science Order and Creativity*, New York: Bantam Books.
BOHR, N. (1934) *Atomic Physics and the Description of Nature*, Cambridge: Cambridge University Press.
CAPRA, F. (1988a) *The Toa of Physics: An Exploration of the Parallels between Modern Physics and Eastern Mysticism*, Glasgow: Collins Publishing Group.
CAPRA, F. (1988b) *The Turning Point: Science Society and the Rising Culture*, Glasgow: Collins Publishing Group.
HEISENBERG, W. (1930) *The Physical Principles of the Quantum Theory*, by ECKART, C. and HOYT, C., (transl.) Chicago: Dover Publications.

HEY, T. and WALTERS, P. (1987) *The Quantum Universe*, Cambridge: Cambridge University Press.

KOESTLER, A. (1978) *Janus: A Summing up*, London: Hutchinson and Co.

LAURA, R.S. and HEANEY, S. (1990) *Philosophical Foundation of Health Education*, New York: Routledge.

Russell, P. (1983) *The Global Brain*, New York: St. Martin's Press.

SMUTS, J.C. (1973) *Holism and Evolution*, Connecticut: Greenwood Press.

VON BERTALANFFY, L. (1975) *General System Theory*, New York: George Braziller.

ZUKAV, G. (1988) *The Dancing Wu Li Masters: An Overview of the New Physics*, London: Rider and Co./Hutchinson and Co.

Chapter 7

The Epistemic Resacrilization of Nature

In this final chapter we explore the implications of epistemic holism in education for a new theory of social interaction mediated through curriculum studies. The resacrilization of nature depends in large part, we submit, on the resacrilization of epistemology; in a recognition that the things of nature are not ours to expropriate and exploit as our preoccupation with power might otherwise demand. Consistent with the quantum and holistic visions canvassed in the previous two chapters, we argue here that the indivisible unity which binds all of nature together entails that a whole new sense of ecological responsibility must be embraced to explain the condition of environmental stewardship in which we find ourselves. What was previously seen as a 'right' in the epistemology of power is now seen as a 'privilege' in the epistemology of empathy. The attitude of connectivity with nature is thus sponsored on the assumption of gratitude for what is borrowed and a sense of moral obligation in regard to the stewardship of compensation and ecological balance.

Affirming the New Epistemological Paradigm for Environmental Education

In the previous chapters it was observed that education has relied primarily on an epistemology of power to provide, measure and form technological interaction with nature. Given the commitment to an educational epistemology driven by our culture's obsession with power and control, the resources of nature have been exploited mercilessly both in the name of progress and employment. Despite the dominance of the epistemology of power educational paradigm, it should by now be clear from the previous chapters that there exists the conceptual materials to reconstruct an epistemic framework which eschews reductionist methodologies of environmental degradation. The first step in the process is to recognize that the precious gift of human consciousness is not best used in the service of gaining knowledge to dominate, subjugate, suppress and subdue nature. The ruthless biography of humankind betrays that the same dimension of human psyche which lusts for power over nature expresses itself inhumanely within the human community as power over each other. Our willingness to treat animals cruelly betrays the same lack of moral consideration which prompts humans to treat each other as animals. Instead of allowing knowledge to be driven by our obsession with a form of power which is destructive and denigrating of everything it seeks to have power over, a conscious and concerted educational effort must be made to reconceptualize knowledge as connectivity, expressed empathetically.

In the case of animals, for example, it is clear that they constitute a far more important part of the ecological system than has been generally recognized. Consider for a moment the extent to which animals are responsible for the dissemination of the seed of flora, without which the balance of plant and forest renewal would be hopelessly disrupted. There are also subtle ways in which plants and animals have an instrumental value. It is no accident that North America has some 30 million bird watchers, making it the most rapidly growing 'sport' in that part of the world (Birch, 1993, pp. 87–8). There is little doubt that the health and wellbeing (especially the psychological and spiritual well-being) of the human species is highly dependent on the environmental presence of greenery, flowers, the sounds of birds etc. In his Book *Biophilia* (Wilson, 1984) E.O. Wilson argues that considerable evidence has accumulated to demonstrate that the love many people intuitively feel for nature can be explained by the fact that humans are programmed biologically, if you like, to find the world more conducive to healthful and happy living when they are in the presence of other living things. Studies have shown, for example, that patients recovering from surgery and serious illness recuperate far more quickly when they have access to gardens, flowers and even pets (Ashton and Laura, 1997, p. 128) Ruminations such as these help to explain why the transformative subjugations which follow from the educational epistemology of power is so threatening to those who live in a world progressively populated by the dead things of technology.

The foregoing discussion about the instrumental value of animals provides a rationale for why humans should value animals for human sakes, not for the sake of the animals, goes only part way towards replacing the value of connectivity for the value of power. The knowledge as power paradigm is challenged even more starkly, however, when the moral sensibilities in the search of human conscience are raised sufficiently to acknowledge the intrinsic value of the other species in nature. If animals were incapable of feeling pain and experiencing pleasure, it would be easier to pretend that the only value they have is in the use we can make of them. But animals do feel pain, and it is simply a failure of moral conscience and an act of specieism akin to racism to make them suffer major deprivations of interest on their part for the minor advancement of interests on our part. There is no comparison between the pain animals suffer in being separated from each other, isolated, confined, deprived of certain nutrients to give their flesh a preferred colour, and killed on the one hand and the socially accepted convention of meat eating on cultivated taste for meat as a means of titillating our palates on the other (see Singer, 1991).

To reconceptualize knowledge as the means to empathetic connectivity, rather than as the means to power, the role of education must be to educate the sensibilities of moral conscience to recognize *the value* and *the point* of moral responsibility. The human heart will be less enamoured of power when those who are disempowered by its exercise are seen to be unjustly harmed. The objective of the moral exercise is not 'in controlling' but 'in connecting' and it is upon this foundational principle that the edifice of environmental education can be built.

The second step towards the reconceptualization of educational knowledge involves recognizing that the conventional way of knowing encourages the learner to seek separation and detachment from the world of nature so that nature can, through transformative subjugations of technology, be manipulated without conscience, harnessed for commercial exploitation and mindlessly consumed. Transformative subjugation must be acknowledged as the menacing process whereby the things of nature, which have intrinsic value as they are found in nature, are technologically converted and reduced to forms in which their value and integrity is either diminished or destroyed.

The conventional concept of knowledge as power assumes, we saw earlier, a distinction between the knower and the known, or between subject and object, if you prefer the standard, though in many circles now outdated, terminology. Within the structure of the traditional school curriculum, however, knowledge is achieved by objectifying student observations of nature by detaching students from their observations. The world exists, so the realist presumption of the educational epistemology of power decrees, independently of what we say and think about it, or even how we behave towards it. We observed in Chapter 5 how the concept of knowledge as power rests firmly on this assumption, and we also saw that institutionalized distinctions between the subjective and the objective domains of knowledge are tenuous and misleading, as are the distinctions between subject and object, knower and known.

In the light of our earlier discussion of quantum interconnectivity, human consciousness can no longer be described unambiguously as an element which admits isolation and extraction from the external world. In the sense of Bohm's implicate order discussed earlier, consciousness is itself an essential feature of the underlying order and unity of nature. The topology of nature cannot exclude the way in which consciousness is enfolded into it. Nature cannot be objectified in the required epistemic sense because in essence we have ourselves become an element in the subject-matter we are trying to observe. We cannot separate ourselves from nature because we are, in the radically holistic interpretation of Bell's theorem, a part of it. In our attempts to measure and describe the world outside ourselves, we are at the same time describing ourselves.

If the concept of educational knowledge is driven by the desire to connect oneself with the rest of nature rather than master and molest it, the expression of the intention will be to find new ways of participating with the things of nature, not detaching ourselves from them in the name of objectivity. To achieve the goal of participatory interaction Rifkin reminds us that human consciousness must attune itself to the rhythms of the natural environment which define the participatory parameters of our interaction with it. Rifkin makes this point well:

> Architecture provides a convenient metaphor for describing these two very different approaches to the pursuit of knowledge. Many contemporary architects dream of building a skyscraper; a monument of invincibility that can stand self-contained and isolated, jutting above its surroundings in princely relief for the architects of skyscraper, the knowledge pursued is the knowledge of how to maximise power

and control the environment. Their works of art are designed to imperialise the environment, to expropriate and devour the surroundings . . . Then there are the new architects whose approach to knowledge is guided by very different considerations. They dream of building a passive solar home that is so elegant and unobtrusive, so meshed with its natural environment, that it is difficult to even distinguish where their work of art leaves off and the works of nature begin. They see their buildings not as a fortress, but as an environment within an environment; an extension of their surroundings that fully participates with the rhythms, beats and periodicities of its larger setting. (Rifkin, 1985, p. 84)

Rifkin's emphasis on a form of knowledge which helps us to rediscover how best to integrate the economic rhythms of commercial productivity with the biological rhythms that define the flow of renewal within the natural environment is, we submit, a concept of central importance for environmental education. When the concept of educational knowledge is motivated by our faith in the virtue of connectivity as the ultimate form of security within nature, our interactions with the environment will reflect a participatory mode of interaction with nature. The measure of security is shifted in epistemic terms from how well we know how to dominate and control nature to how well we know how to connect with and participate in it. This shift of epistemic vision encourages a transition of dispositional posture from doing battle against nature to being in partnership with it.

Rifkin (1989, Chapter 16) takes the concept of rhythm primarily in its metaphorical sense, but we shall in the section that follows endeavour to show that the rhythms of nature, upon which the holistic epistemology of empathetic ecology depend, enjoy a literal as well as a metaphorical sense which are difficult to separate. The process of transformative subjugation, as we have called it, reflects the way in which society's commitment to the technologization of nature converts living things into dead things to gain control of nature by enhancing human capacity to predict its behaviour. The deader or more synthesized a thing is, the easier it is to quantify it (i.e., make it 'equationally behave') and subsume it under scientific laws which allow us to control it by predicting its behaviour. One of the most significant socio-cultural representations of transformative subjugation reveals itself in the way in which our culture has synthesized time. The epistemology of power has encouraged us to technologize everything to be found in nature, so we have technologized even the rhythms of nature by virtue of which we might otherwise judge the appropriateness of the patterns of our interaction with it.

From the days long before written history was recorded, ancient civilizations, not unlike a few remaining primitive cultures today, patterned their lives in accord with the actual periodicities of nature. When the sun went down, it was pretty much time to rest and find renewal in sleep, a kind of daily hibernation. When the sun came up as it was light, it was *time* to get up. Time was thus demarcated by successions in nature such as the slight varying but repeating phases of the moon or the periodic flooding of the rivers. As the season approached which heralded the bloom of flowers, the time for seed planting had also come.

Discriminations of behaviours by appeal to the successions in nature fostered the idea of time as a cyclic phenomenon, and a rhythm of interplay between activity and renewal came into being. The more technological culture became, the more technological the devices for telling time became — for determining the rhythm appropriate to our interactions with nature. With the invention of fire, after all, and eventual artificial light, what reason is there to rest when we have turned night into day. Where there was once a natural rhythmic break in the pattern of expropriation of the earth's resources, there now is none. We work until we are finished, can work no more, or have extracted everything we can from the earth site at which we were kept busy.

As our ancestors felt more in control of nature, one can imagine that they began to feel less constrained to rely on its characteristic periodicities to define their relationship to it. Inasmuch as they believed it was technology that gave them power over nature, it was to technology that they turned to define the categories by virtue of which to understand it. Devices for measuring the periodicities of time thus roughly coincided with the state of technological subjugation of nature. By way of the technology of time telling, for example, we have as a society progressively abandoned our reliance upon nature's periodicities in favour of the periodicates of our own artefacts, for example from the time it takes the sun to change position on the face of the sundial to the time it takes a candle of a certain size to burn; from the time if takes the hands or digits on a battery clock to move and change, to the atomic interactions of the cesium clock which transcend our capacity to observe them directly. The shift of categorical interpretation and representation from the actual rhythms of nature to the technologized and highly synthetic measure of periodicity encouraged a radical reconception of the logical character of time and of our ability to keep it. The concept of time as cyclic, for example, gave way to its redefinition as a flowing, asymmetric and linear phenomenon not to be repeated. Rifkin's concern about the computer technic concept of time as recorded in 'nanoseconds' (one-billionth of a second) is not misplaced, since the time it takes computers to make decisions — many of which affect and shape our interrelations with nature — take place at a pace which completely and utterly transcends the realm of human consciousness.

Along with these technological changes in our concept of time came changes in our relationship with nature. The more we become dominated by the technology of chronometrics, for instance, the less attuned we become not only to the cycles and actual rhythms in nature but to the cycles and biorhythms in ourselves. For the most part we no longer eat when we are hungry or sleep when we are sleepy, but eat and sleep in accord with the technological devices we have invented to regiment our lives into temporal compartments. In a bizarre sense, through our attempts to dominate and domesticate nature, we have let ourselves become dominated and domesticated not by time *per se*, but by our technologized concepts of it. We have become subdued not by responding to the rhythms as manifest in the periodicities of nature, but as manifested in the patterns of our technology which reflect the way in which we see and treat nature. The technology we have used to dominate nature has come paradoxically to dominate us and our categories of self-understanding. In this sense the 'watch' is well-named, in that we use it to watch our lives pass by according to the time it keeps. One way of seeing it is that the watch is in essence a symbol of death, the goal of all transformational subjugations. Wedged in between birth and death, we coordinate our lives to the relentless flow of our watches and the clock. We literally watch our lives passing by, for we have unwittingly committed ourselves, through the technology of time, to a linear and reductionist view of nature in which time is running out and will never return.

At a fundamental level of the unconscious mind we have, structured our experience of nature in spatiotemporal terms which ensure that we are constantly bearing witness to our own demise. In a curious way we have, through our transformative subjugations, converted life itself into the medium for the experience of our own deaths. With every tick of the clock we are covertly reminded of our finitude and mortality; we watch our youthfulness escaping with every passing moment, and every passing second is a second closer to death. There are many reasons to challenge our mindless technologization of nature through the promulgation of educational knowledge and the temporal transformative subjugation of our own lives is most assuredly one of them.

The bright side is that you need to know what is oppressing you, if ever you are going to liberate yourself from oppression. Much work is being done to regain a sense of the rhythms of our own being and the rhythms of nature as Rifkin writes:

> In University biology departments, genetic engineers are asking the 'how' of nature so that they can design efficient, more commercially viable forms of life. On the other hand, there are those ecologists who are seeking to identify the subtle relationships and interactions between all living things so they can learn how to integrate the social and economic rhythms of society with the biological rhythms of the rest of the living kingdom. (Rifkin, 1989, p. 133)

Reintegration, or reconnection, with nature's rhythms and cycles is of critical importance to the empathetic ecological approach we espouse here.

'Empathy', as Koestler (1978, p. 143) put it, 'is [the] . . . term for a rather mysterious process of entering into a kind of mental symbiosis with other selves, of stepping out of one's skin, as it were, and putting oneself into the skin of the other. Empathy is the source of our intuitive understanding — more direct than language — of how the other thinks and feels . . .' It is the empathetic ecological approach, then, which seeks to put us back into the skin of nature and teach us how to be there responsibly. When knowledge is motivated by empathy, it generates connectivity and the associated mode of thinking we call 'participatory consciousness' which assists in helping to reconceptualize our epistemological-value orientation in a way that reconnects us with nature.

As a first step, it is of critical importance that the education curriculum be redefined to enable the explicit transmission of the new empathetic values of an epistemology of participatory consciousness. Without an awareness of the extent to which the reductio-mechanistic foundations delimit our interaction with nature, environmental education will inadvertently promote the very value of transformative subjugation which their ostensible environmental goals must overcome to be achieved. This problem is described by Gough as a tacit clinging 'to the "confident scientific materialism" of the past'. 'Holistic emphases', he wrote:

... are conspicuous by their absence in most schools — indeed, conventional schools reinforce the view of 'a world composed of separate entities' through every aspect of their design, construction and modes of operation . . . [For this reason,] . . . ecological subject matters can be regarded as only a superficial product of a holistic world view. (Gough, 1987, p. 52)

What is required is first the reconceptualization of the educational epistemo-logy of power; then a redefinition of the technologies of power which derive from it, along with the reductio-mechanistic methodologies which express it. This is a shift of epistemic world view. Consistent with our view Gough writes:

A shift towards an ecological paradigm does not simply mean more environmental education . . . on school timetables . . . A paradigm shift involves changes in our total world view, and it may be very difficult for most educators — even for environmental educators who are confident of the depth their own ecological understanding — to accept that the education system in which they practice, and of which they are themselves products, provides a structured misinterpretation of reality, nature and human nature. (Gough, 1987, pp. 52–3)

Robottom (1987) puts a slightly different slant to Gough's 'problematic' on environmental education. He refers to the 'technocratic' dependence of environ-mental education, pertaining to, as Drengson (1980, p. 240) has put it, 'the machine paradigm of the technocratic outlook'. Conventional educational reform in its rela-tion to the '*organization* of environmental education', according to Robottom, 'is predominantly managerial-hierarchical and technocratic in character':

Organisational responses to environmental education are based on a technocratic assumption: educational change is assumed to be independent of the beliefs and justifications of the social context in which the innovation is formulated and those of the social context in which the innovation is to be practiced. The teacher's role is perceived as that of a technician implementing educational values determined by others, and failure of an innovation is accounted for in teacher-deficit terms. (Robottom, 1987, pp. 98–9)

Robottom goes on to argue that:

[a] managerial-hierarchical form of organisation, informed by empiricist, objectivist epistemology, and adopting [a] . . . depoliticised, technocratic view of educational change, far from being . . . a *neutral* administrative process, is itself political. Its politics are the politics of preservation of the *status quo*, of reproduction, in this case, of non-critical education *about* the environment. (Robottom, 1987, p. 99)

What Robottom is referring to is that we, as teachers and learners, are the 'passive consumers' of knowledge *about* the environment which comes from the techno-cratic, i.e., the mechanistic, perspective. Until this changes, environmental education will be little more than an epistemic cosmetic, designed to deal with the indiscre-tions of technology by seeking new and better forms of technology reputed to generate fewer indiscretions. In this regard the conventional approach to environmental education, as a way towards the resolution of the crisis of transformative subjugation simply reinforces the same philosophical presuppositions which gave rise to transformative subjugation in the first place.

Elaborating on this general point, Robottom suggests that 'environmental education reproduces, rather than [reconceptualizes]' the conventional 'view of knowledge'. What is reproduced, according to Robottom, is the empirical rendering of scientific, truth claims 'reinforced by environmental education as education about the environment' i.e., 'facts' about the environment 'out there'. In the name of 'objectivity', he added, we see also the separation and 'primacy' of the 'rational'-analytic, i.e., reductionist, method of science, 'over such metaphysical matters as human values and interests' (Robottom, 1987, p. 102). Consistent with this theme he challenges the convention that science progressively moves us 'away from uncertainty' towards the 'truth': 'In the case of environmental education, the "one true answer" assumption is interpreted as "only one solution" exists for each environmental problem — an interpretation reinforced by the tendency in science education to stress technical . . . solutions to problems . . .' (Robottom, 1987, pp. 102–3). Here, it is salutary to reflect on what we earlier called 'the technological fallacy', whereby we persist in our faith that technological interventions can solve our problems without appreciating that technological intervention may itself be the problem.

In summarizing the technocratic approach, he wrote:

> [T]he dominant perspective of innovation in environmental education . . . assuming the trappings of neutrality by its objectivist epistemology . . . reproduces rather than transforms the social conditions which pose threats to both the environment and the forms of education which preserve rather than challenge critical consciousness about environmental problems. (Robottom, 1987, p. 104)

As implied by Robottom and others, success in the organization of innovative environmental education must involve some form of paradigmatic reconceptualization in conscious thought. In the final section of this work we shall consider the extent to which the concept of 'participatory consciousness' may serve to assist in the provision of a new mode of environmental education.

Empathetic Education in the Ecological Paradigm

Heshusius (1994) suggested that we need to foster a 'participatory mode of consciousness' if we are to leave the old paradigm of thinking. This will involve a 'somatic', 'non-verbal' reordering of 'our understanding of the relationship between the self and other' where the focus of attention is away from the self. There is, according to to Heshusius, a 'procedural' anxiety faced by educators which is a result of their trying either to be 'as objective as possible' in their methodologies, or as rigorous as possible in their management of subjectivity. This results, Heshusius suggests, in an 'alienated mode of consciousness' (Heshusius, 1994, p. 15).

'Before the scientific revolution', wrote Heshusius:

> ... the act of knowing had always been understood as a form of participation and
> enchantment. For most of human history . . . 'the world was enchanted and man
> [sic] saw himself as an integral part of it.' The very act of participation was
> knowing. Without direct somatic, psychic, and emotional participation . . . 'lack
> of identification was regarded as strange.' . . . For most of human history humans
> did not know objectively, and therefore did not know subjectively as we presently
> use the term. The belief that one can actually distance oneself, and then regulate
> that distance in order to come to know, has also been referred to as alienated
> consciousness, as the disenchantment of knowing, a mode of consciousness that
> has led to undreamed of technological advances, but has also left us alienated from
> each other, from nature, and from ourselves. (Heshusius, 1994, p. 16)

At the heart of a participatory mode of consciousness, Heshusius explained,
'is [an "holistic"] awareness of a deeper level of kinship between the knower and
the known'. (Heshusius, 1994, p.16). It is not a methodology as such, according to
Heshusius, but an act of consciousness which 'requires an attitude of profound
openness and sensitivity'. One suspends the egocentric 'self' and '. . . is turned
toward the other (human and non-human) "without being in need of it" or wanting
to appropriate it to achieve something' (Heshusius, 1994, p. 16). 'Participatory consciousness, then, involves identification or merging which . . . "bespeaks a psychic
wholeness" . . .' (Heshusius, 1994, p. 16). (For a full account on 'psychic wholeness' and the 'connection between participatory consciousness and wholeness', see
Berman, 1981; Harman, 1988; Schachtel, 1959; and Skolimowski, 1990.)

Referring to participatory consciousness and its parallel to the ecological crisis,
Heshusius reiterated Evernden's (1985) interpretation that the crisis:

> ... is not about throwing away: There is no away. The crisis . . . is about the nature
> of our consciousness, which has believed in a separation between internal and
> external reality. The crisis is the externalization of the distancing, alienated mode
> of consciousness we have chosen to live within. (Heshusius, 1994, p. 17)

Implicit in Heshusius' version of participatory consciousness is the notion that
the empathetic mind brings with it an 'ethic', or value, which sees intrinsic worth
in the 'other' i.e., other people and the natural environment. According to Blake
and Cock:

> Empathetic consciousness arises from the perception of some element of shared
> origin, experience, need or vulnerability — and hence identity — linking human
> subjectivity with external objects . . . Empathetic understanding entails a tacit recog-
> nition of the existential value and hence moral worth of the subject/object under
> examination. Reflection upon this recognition therefore leads to a perception of
> the moral obligations of the subjects towards . . . other people, creatures or natural
> objects. Repression of this empathetic moral understanding, for example, under
> the traditional methodological structures of 'objective science', leads directly to
> pathological, destructive consequences. (Blake and Cock, 1987, p. 7)

In relation to the moral and ethical dimensions of environmental education *per se*, Gough has pointed out that:

> ... environmental education (and, indeed, anything that is done in the name of education), is the product of human invention and purpose and, as such, owes its very existence to people holding certain moral principles and having made certain value judgments. This may seem to be stating the obvious, but many teachers ... are reluctant to admit that certain *moral* judgments and *value* positions are basic to their work. (Gough, 1982, p. 16)

In conclusion Gough wrote, '[e]nvironmental education cannot take place in a moral vacuum and, to the extent that environmental educators are committed to certain values, they will attempt to win issues. To obscure such values, which many scientific approaches to the study of environmental education encourage, is itself unethical' (Gough, 1982, p. 19).

So where do we go from here if environmental education is ever to serve the interest of the environment rather than an economic way of life dependent on the vicissitudes of transformative subjugation. It should by now be clear that unless the form of educational knowledge we select is motivated by empathetic connectivity with nature rather than power over nature, there is no place to go. Environmental education will simply reproduce, albeit in admirably cosmetic ways, the same contexts of technological invasiveness and intrusion that warrant extirpation from the school curriculum. Once the knowledge as power paradigm is shifted from its position of epistemic priority, however, and substituted by an empathetic knowledge of participatory consciousness, then the real work of environmental stewardship through education can begin. Appreciation of the need for empathetic connectivity with nature provides a new sense of the domain of our ecological responsibilities which emerge from our interactions with nature and this leads to an empathetic redefinition of the tools of technology. We have argued throughout this book that technologies which derive from the educational epistemology of power are never neutral. Motivated by power and the human desire that technology should enhance our well-being, technologies will by their very nature be tools of power and expropriation. The technologies we create are thus saturated with power. Given the fundamental interconnectivity of all of nature, for every increase in power brought to us by technology, will be a diminution of power and consequent disruption somewhere in nature which results. If technologies are motivated by the participatory mode of epistemic consciousness, however, it is possible — as we saw in the case of empathetic architecture — to develop technologies which connect rather than alienate us from nature.

Empathetic ecology also encourages moral reflection not just on the use of technology, but on whether certain types of technology should ever be invented. It is rare that education teaches us to question whether to accept or reject a certain type of technology. This being so, environmental education is possessed of concepts for doing little more than commenting on how a technology can be regulated and monitored. What the epistemology of connectivity requires is the recognition that some types of technology are so potentially disruptive of the established harmony of nature that they should *never be used* and thus *never invented*. Inasmuch as the mere act of using such technologies in any circumstances carries a risk that they threaten, as does nuclear technology, the source of life itself, there is a justification for refusing ever to use them if they exist and never to invent them, if they do not.

The issue for empathetic ecology then becomes a matter of developing tools of connectivity which maximize our participation in nature in ways that assist our stewardship of it. Questions of the level of technological interaction with nature as balanced against the capacity of nature to replenish itself in the face of expropriation will still be critical, but there will also be a difference. Underpinning our unbridled commitment to the technologization of nature is an attitude difficult to relinquish. The educational concept of knowledge as power carries with it the idea that through technology we can avoid having to confront the realization that it is the way we have chosen to live that needs changing even more than our technologies. We are obsessed with our technologies because they provide the promise that we can live lives of excess and indulgence without penalty as long as we have technologies around which compensate for our own shortcomings. In this regard our faith in technology is our faith in technology as salvation. If the foods we like to eat are bad for us, we simply turn to technology to excise, say the fat from cakes, so that we do not have to stop eating our cakes. The advent of low-fat foods betrays that our reliance on technology is a way of never having to deal with ourselves, with our unhealthy lifestyles, our unhealthy bodies, our unhealthy thoughts and our unhealthy behaviours. We are deeply committed to technology because we use it to allow ourselves to continue being as naughty as we want without ever having to pay the price of our naughtiness. But in the end there is always a price for our transformative subjugations. It turns out, for example, that the only way technology can produce low-fat foods is to make foods more processed, refined and artificial than they would otherwise be. Unsurprisingly, the human body finds it more difficult to metabolize lower levels of fat in highly processed foods than higher levels of fat in natural foods. It turns out that not all fats are equal. As long as we turn to technology to turn away from ourselves and the problems associated with selecting a lifestyle for which we were never intended, environmental education will be nothing more than a prophylactic to protect against authentic self-transformation and personal growth.

The final consideration for empathetic ecology is that it forces reflection on the idea of having a right to help ourselves to the resources of nature, an idea which is resolutely reinforced by a society committed to continued growth and expansion. Empathetic ecology, as we envisage it, recognizes that the resources of nature belong to nature and not to us. As Rifkin put it, 'the most important truth about ourselves, our artifacts and our civilization is that it is all borrowed' (Rifkin, 1985, p. 97). Once we introduce the concept of borrowing the resources of nature, the appropriate moral disposition of *gratitude* for that which is borrowed follows naturally. Rifkin points out that 'to acknowledge indebtedness is to accept the idea that we owe our being, our very survival, to the many living and non-living things that had to be sacrificed in order for us to perpetuate ourselves. It is, we believe, possible to reconstruct a theory of empathetic economy as a companion to the account of empathetic ecology we have enunciated here, but then at this late stage in the book, we must defer the challenge of doing so to the task of a different book.

References

ASHTON, J. and LAURA, R.S. (1997) *The Life Enhancement Handbook*, Sydney: Simon and Schuster.

BERMAN, M. (1981) *The Reenchantment of the World*, New York: Cornell University Press.

BIRCH, C. (1993) *Regaining Compassion*, Sydney: NSW University Press.

BLAKE, T. and COCK, P. (1987) 'Environmentalism and education', *Australian Journal of Environmental Education*, **3** (1).

DRENGSON, A.R. (1980) 'Shifting paradigms: From technocratic to person-planetary', *Environmental Ethics*, **2**, 221–240.

EVERNDEN, N. (1985) *The Natural Alien. Humankind and Environment*, Toronto: University of Toronto Press.

GOUGH, N. (1982) 'Environment and ethics: An educational perspective', Revised version of 'Environmental education and ethics', Paper presented to the Second National Conference of the Australian Association for Environmental Education, Brisbane 28 June–2 July.

GOUGH, N. (1987) 'Learning with environments: Towards an ecological paradigm for education', in ROBOTTOM, I. (ed.) *Environmental Education: Practice and Possibility*, Victoria: Deakin University Press.

HARMAN, W.W. (1988) 'The Need for Restructuring of Science', *Revision*, **11**(12), 13–21.

HESHUSIUS, L. (1994) 'Freeing ourselves from objectivity: Managing subjectivity or turning toward a participatory mode of consciousness', *Educational Researcher*, April.

KOESTLER, A. (1978) *Janus: A Summing Up*, London: Hutchinson and Co.

RIFKIN, J. (1985) *Declaration of a Heretic*, Boston: Routledge and Kegan Paul.

RIFKIN, J. (1989) *Time Wars: The Primary Conflict in Human History*, New York: Simon and Schuster.

ROBOTTOM, I. (1987) 'Towards inquiry-based professional development in environmental education', in ROBOTTOM, I. (ed.) *Environmental Education: Practice and Possibility*, Victoria: Deakin University Press.

SCHACHTEL, E.G. (1959) *Metamorphosis. On the Development of Affect, Perception, Attention and Memory*, New York: Basic Books.

SINGER, P. (1991) *Animal Liberation*, London: Jonathon Cape.

SKOLIMOWSKI, H. (1990) 'The world as sanctuary', *The Quest*, **3**(2), 27–33.

WILSON, E.O. (1984) *Biophilia: The Human Bond to Other Species*, Boston: Harvard University Press.

Index